Sermons On The Gospel Readings

Series

Cycle B

Paul E. Flesner

Robert A. Noblett

David G. Rogne

Stephen M. Crotts

Cathy A. Ammlung

CSS Publishing Company, Lima, Ohio

Copyright © 2002 by
CSS Publishing Company, Inc.
Lima, Ohio

Some scripture quotations are from the *New Revised Standard Version of the Bible*, copyright 1989 by the Division of Christian Education of the National Council of the Churches of Christ in the USA. Used by permission.

Library of Congress Cataloging-in-Publication Data

Sermons on the Gospel readings : Series I, Cycle B / Paul E. Flesner ... [et al.].
   p. cm.
Includes bibliographical references.
  ISBN 0-7880-1900-7 (pbk. : alk. paper)
  1. Bible. N.T. Gospels—Sermons. 2. Sermons, American—21st century. 3. Church year sermons. I. Flesner, Paul E., 1941-
  BS2555.54 .S47 2002
252'.6—dc21   2002004249

For more information about CSS Publishing Company resources, visit our website at www.csspub.com or e-mail us at custserv@csspub.com or call (800) 241-4056.

ISBN 0-7880-1900-7

Table Of Contents

**Sermons For Sundays
In Advent, Christmas, And Epiphany
by Paul E. Flesner**

Sermons For Sundays
After Pentecost (First Third)
by David G. Rogne

Sermons For Sundays
After Pentecost (Middle Third)
by Stephen M. Crotts

Sermons For Sundays
After Pentecost (Last Third)
by Cathy A. Ammlung

Sermons On The Gospel Readings

For Sundays In
Advent, Christmas,
And Epiphany

Paul E. Flesner

*These sermons are dedicated
to my father, Dr. Dorris A. Flesner,
and grandfather, Dr. Elmer E. Flack,
whose preaching touched my heart
and served as a model for me
to follow in my ministry.*

Preface

Faith or fantasy? A prominent theme in science fiction is about beings who come from outside our planet, as typified by the movie *Close Encounters of the Third Kind*. Does this mean we humans have an innate yearning for relationships which go "beyond" this earth? The fanciful technology needed to establish these relationships is what makes science fiction so intriguing. Yet, in spite of the best technology, it still seems to take a great deal of effort on our part to seek out these "extraterrestrial" beings.

I have experienced another innate characteristic of humanity. We have been created by the Holy God to have a relationship with our creator. However, unlike science fiction, God seeks us out and has come down to live with us as one of us. No technology needed. God took the step which makes it possible for us to have a close encounter with God, the Holy One, on our own turf.

The wonder of an encounter with the Holy One is that it happens in real life rather than in the realm of fantasy. During Advent, Christmas, and Epiphany the Bible takes us on the beginning of God's journey among us, as we travel from Bethlehem to Galilee. Each week we are given a new glimpse into God's power and glory in the person of Jesus. Each week we are privileged to have a close encounter with the Holy One. That is when the greatest wonder takes place — the miracle of faith.

Preparing For Something Big

How are you getting ready for Christmas? Have you gotten out your Christmas tapes or CDs yet? Have you started your gift shopping? Have you decided what Christmas cookies you are going to bake this year? Have you written your Christmas cards yet? Have you put up your Christmas tree?

Over the years it seems like Christmas preparations are starting earlier and earlier. Now some stores are starting to put up their Christmas displays as early as Halloween. While that may seem out of place, I suspect they are merely following that traditional advice, "One can never start too early to get ready for something big."

How are we getting ready for Christmas in the church? Let's allow the Gospel lesson from Mark 13 to set the stage for us.

> *"But in those days, after that suffering, the sun will be darkened, and the moon will not give its light, and the stars will be falling from heaven, and the powers in the heavens will be shaken. Then they will see 'the Son of Man coming in clouds' with great power and glory ... But about that day or hour no one knows, neither the angels in heaven, nor the Son, but only the Father. Beware, keep alert; for you do not know when the time will come ... And what I say to you I say to all: Keep awake."*

Are we talking about the same festival? Where is the spirit of peace and goodwill? Has the Church made a mistake? The answer is "No." The differences come from what we are preparing for. The secular world measures this time of preparation by the number of shopping days until December 25. The Church measures this time of preparation in terms of the number of days remaining until the time when Jesus will return to the earth in glory and power.

I don't know about you, but that completely reverses my personal expectations about celebrating Christmas, let alone getting ready for it. Don't get me wrong. I like to get caught up in the "Christmas spirit." I like to put up and decorate the tree. I like to get out our Christmas music. I like Christmas cookies and Christmas parties. I like shopping for Christmas gifts. But if the theme of this first Sunday in Advent is to focus our attention on the real meaning of Christmas, then we need to realize that celebrating the birth of Jesus was important to our ancestors in faith because he was coming back again!

I am not advocating a change in the customs used to celebrate Christmas. I am suggesting that we need to change the manner in which we *prepare* to celebrate Christmas. I believe we need to recapture the sense of eager anticipation about the second coming of Christ which was present in the early church. During this Advent season, we need to listen to God calling us to look beyond "today and tomorrow" to the time when Jesus will come back and usher in God's kingdom in all its fullness.

Unfortunately, throughout the church's history, some branches of Christianity have taken these apocalyptic words of Jesus and used them to paint a "horrifying picture" of the coming of this kingdom. Think for a moment. What feelings do you experience when you think about the so-called "end of time"? I would venture to say that far too many devoted Christians have "doom and gloom" images about this future. It's no wonder that we tend to ignore this dimension in our Christmas preparations.

Keep two things in mind: First, the early Christians looked forward *eagerly* to the return of Jesus. They were not frightened by it. In fact, they expected it to happen in their lifetime. If there were any problems, it was disappointment when Jesus' return did not happen when they thought it would. Secondly, those who claim that the return of Jesus will be "terrifying" are misinterpreting the words of Jesus! Jesus was saying that God's final kingdom will come with such power that the forces of evil will be toppled.

What does all this have to do with our daily living? While Jesus' second coming might not appear to have much to do with everyday life, it has a powerful effect on it. Why? Simply this: What we believe and feel about the future determines what we feel and do about the present.

It means, in the first place, that *life is not an endless succession of repetitive moments* in which we feel that we are caught on a treadmill that is seemingly going nowhere. That's all too common a feeling. It is easy to get caught up in the routine events of everyday life. The problem is that if we only look to the immediate future, there appears to be no end in sight. But when seen from the viewpoint of eternity, even what we sometimes feel to be monotony is moving us steadily forward toward God's kingdom. Remember — God measures time differently than we do. What seems to us like an "eternity" is to God but a "split second" and a "watch in the night." God's "eternity" is beyond our comprehension, but far more magnificent that we can ever imagine.

Secondly, it means that *adversity never has the last word in life.* Regardless of how terrifying or trying our present circumstances are, "they, too, will pass." In fact, that is the wonder of the apocalyptic language used in scripture. The supposed "gloom and doom" which it describes is really a picture of present adversity which the return of Christ will bring to a permanent end. There will be nothing more to be afraid of, for the "Lord God omnipotent will reign."

Those who use biblical imagery to instill fear about the end of time are not paying attention to the example which Jesus set. Eighteen times in the Gospels, Jesus said to the disciples when they were terrified, "Do not be afraid." My words to you this morning are, "Don't ever let someone, however well-intended, cause you to be afraid of the end of this age." It will be a glorious time when God returns all creation back to himself.

This morning we discover that we are preparing for much more than December 25. Because of the birth of Jesus, we also are preparing for that grand and wonderful day when there will be no more pain or sorrow or suffering or death. We are getting ready for an event which has no equal in human experience and for which we wait with eager anticipation.

As I tried to picture this sense of eager anticipation, I remembered what it was like for me to wait for Christmas morning when I was a child. That is when my family opened our gifts. The closer it got to Christmas, the more excited I became. On December 24, my enthusiasm reached its zenith. In the early evening was the Sunday School Christmas program. We children were allowed to stay up late so we could attend the midnight candlelight service. I still remember how difficult it was for me to fall asleep that night. Multiply that sense of anticipation by a thousand and you will have merely scratched the surface of the sense of anticipation surrounding Jesus' return to earth.

This Advent season I want you to expand your Christmas preparations to include Christ's coming back to earth in power and glory. No one knows when that will happen, but we do know that it will happen. Allow your eager anticipation of that event to spill over into your anticipation of this year's Christmas celebration. I promise you that such a vision will change the way you live from day to day. Remember — *"one can never start too early to get ready for something big!"*

Reverse Direction

It's human nature to be excited about meeting a celebrity in person. Whether it's a rock star or a sports legend or an actor or actress or a politician, it is not an everyday occurrence for most of us to come face-to-face with a well-known public figure. This may sound like a confusing introduction to a sermon that is supposed to be about preparing to celebrate Christmas, but it will make sense to you shortly.

I want to make one more observation about getting ready for Christmas. The way in which the church prepares for Christmas compared to the way the rest of the world prepares for Christmas is also confusing to many folks. Two examples: the "mood" of Advent is "penitential" and more somber (which surprises folks), and we don't sing Christmas carols, which baffles people.

These reactions to Advent aren't surprising, since we do bring our "secular" experience into church with us. If everyone else is singing Christmas carols, why can't we do it in church? After all, we're the ones who gave the world the Christmas holiday. However, the result of such expectations is that we frequently come to view Advent as "so many spiritual shopping days before Christmas," rather than seeing Advent as a time to *prepare ourselves for a face-to-face encounter* with the God of time and eternity.

The words of a Christmas song go something like this: "Oh, the real meaning of Christmas is the giving of love everyday." That sounds nice, but it is not the real meaning of Christmas! In the church we prepare for Christmas in a different way, because for the church, Christmas is a *holy day*, not a holiday. There is a profound difference between the two!

Christmas is a holy day because God became one of us! Christmas is a holy day because God began a journey toward a cross and an empty tomb to do for us what we cannot do for ourselves! Christmas is a holy day because the invisible God of the universe became visible in a way that we could see directly! If Christmas is merely a "holiday," then it is understandable to see Advent as a time when we try to get into the holiday spirit. However, since Christmas is a holy day, Advent is a time for us to prepare for *an encounter with the Holy One.*

You might not care too much right now about meeting the Holy One. Right now you might be more interested in singing Christmas carols, or buying Christmas gifts, or baking Christmas cookies — and generally getting into the Christmas spirit. However, before you "tune me out" as being out of step with everyone else, let me make a couple of observations: First, the day will come for every one of us when we *will* meet the Holy One, whether we want to or not. I am not saying that to scare you. It simply is. Secondly, if your life today is in any kind of disarray, an encounter with the Holy One will make a big difference.

Let me go back to the illustration I began with this morning. It is human nature to react to meeting people of importance. Meeting the Holy One face to face goes so far beyond such an experience that we cannot even begin to comprehend it. The prospect can even be frightening, for in the presence of God, you and I look shabby by comparison. Yet, that is what Christmas is about. God came to wrap us in the mantle of God's holiness so that our lives can take on a new look — a new luster — a new value — a new direction — a new hope.

How can we prepare ourselves for an encounter with the Holy One? Allow me to take you back to this morning's Gospel. The main character is none other than John the Baptist. I will grant you that his appearance is not in keeping with Christmas. A camel hair outfit is certainly not as festive as a Santa suit. Nor does his message ring with the "holiday spirit." However, he does address the matter of preparing to meet the Holy One, for that is what his message of repentance is all about.

In order to comprehend fully what this means, I think we need to examine our traditional notions of what repentance means. The Greek word for "repent" means "to change." But somewhere along the way we've picked up a different notion of repentance. I suspect our understanding of repentance is more associated with "hell fire and brimstone" and is characterized by cartoons with a long-bearded man and his sign which announces the end of the world and calls people to repent, lest they be damned eternally.

It's no wonder that people get turned off by this matter of "repentance." That's heavy stuff. If I had to live under that kind of a cloud, I wouldn't be too crazy about repentance. No, repentance simply means to change — *to turn around and walk in a new direction*. In short, to "reverse direction."

However, because Christmas is a time of tradition, it can be difficult for us to understand Advent as preparing to make changes. *But if Christmas is really about an encounter with the Holy One, then Christmas must also be about change* — changes in our values and priorities — changes in our attitudes — changes in the way we treat others.

What changes are we supposed to make to prepare ourselves? That is a fair question, but I will answer it with another question: "What are we currently doing in our lives that keeps us from being sensitive to God's presence in our life and the lives of other people around us?" Let me put it another way: "What are we doing that keeps us at arm's length from God and from someone else?"

For some of us, it is working too hard. For some of us, it is too much ambition. For some of us, it is too much greed. For some of us, it is a negative attitude and outlook. For some of us, it is inner hostility and resentment. For some of us, it is a chip on our shoulder. For some of us, it is a hatred that we won't let go of. For some of us, it is even too much religion in the form of false piety and arrogant self-righteousness.

The specifics of what God calls each of to change is different. But they do have something in common: we are called to drop the barriers that we erect in our lives which prevent us from being open and sensitive to the spirit of God! *As long as we have erected barriers in our lives against other people, the net result will be a barrier against God!*

My friends, if you're looking for the holiday spirit, you won't find it here. But if you are looking for an encounter with the Holy One — if you are looking for the presence of the living God who sent his Son to change the hearts and lives of people — then you've come to the right place! To paraphrase the message of John the Baptist, "Reverse direction, for the kingdom of God has arrived!"

Turn On The Lights

Many people don't realize the extent of the preparations involved when the President of the United States makes a visit to a local community. A raft of Secret Service personnel check out every building along the route he will travel and near the place he will be appearing. They go over each building with a fine tooth comb from roof to basement in their efforts to prepare for his safety. We often refer to them as "advance persons." They work invisibly behind the scenes to make sure that everything is ready for the big event that is about to take place.

In today's Gospel we encounter such an "advance man." However, he's not a member of the Secret Service. He's not preparing for a visit from a head of state. He's not checking out parade routes to assure their safety. He is telling us to get ready for a visit from the most important person in human history. His name is John the Baptist, who was introduced to us last week in Mark's Gospel, and we are told today that "he came as a witness to testify to the light."

That statement may not seem to mean as much 2,000 years later as it did back then. That's because we already know the ending to the story, which they didn't. Our world has already been visited by the Holy One from God. We don't need an "advance person" to prepare his way like they did. Or do we still need to listen to John the Baptist? Perhaps there is something in his message that we are taking for granted. That is a problem with the familiar — we fall into a sense of complacency. As a result, Christmas can become simply a "festival of the familiar" rather than an "encounter with the Holy One."

Two words in the passage stand out: "witness" and "light." Last week we heard John call for repentance and change. Today we hear him calling us to prepare for Christmas by building a straight road in the desert for God to travel on. You'd think John had been watching them rebuild Elmhurst Road rather than quoting the prophet Isaiah. "Fill up the low spots. Knock the tops off of the high spots. Level it out. Make it straight and smooth."

What does Isaiah say is the purpose of all this construction? "So that the glory of the Lord may be revealed for all the world to see!" Folks, John's message about Christmas is that God wants every person in the entire world to know the power and glory of God. In his oratorio, *Messiah*, George Frederic Handel majestically captures these words of Isaiah in music. "And the glory of the Lord shall be revealed, and all flesh shall see it together, for the mouth of the Lord hath spoken it."

Getting ready for Christmas is not about decorated trees — or office parties — or even family gatherings. It is *about a mission* that God has placed upon every one of us: to open up a path to God for others who are in need of God's love and grace. If we really "hear" that, it will have an effect on both our preparation for and celebration of Christmas. *John is telling us that God expects us to do something as a result of what God did at Christmas.*

While that may seem like a trite statement, I have observed that there are any number of folks in our pews who have what I call an "armchair faith." To be sure, they come to church. But they seem to want to be spoon fed, and after they leave this building, it's the end of it until the next time they come.

Our relationship to God is not a "consumer faith" in which everything is neatly packaged for us and all we have to do is pick it off the shelf when we need it. Nor is faith a "let George do it" affair in which we allow a dedicated few to burn themselves out doing the tasks which belong to all of us. John is saying that Christmas road building requires the active involvement of every one of us year around. He is saying we are to build these roads everywhere — into our jobs, our schools, our communities, our neighborhoods — anywhere and everywhere we go!

The second word that stands out is "light." A couple weeks ago I read about an experimental generator that runs on natural gas and that can be set up in a home to provide for almost all of its electrical needs. It made me realize that we have come a long way technologically in providing light to see by. However, as I read the same newspapers and hear about shootings in schools and messy divorces and people dying of drug overdoses, I also realized that technology cannot generate light for our hearts and souls.

If actions do speak louder than words (and they do), then at Christmas God has virtually *shouted* to the world that God cares enough to enter the place we live and bring light to the dark spots in our lives that we cannot seem to light on our own. Christmas light is about an end to isolation and despair that even our best efforts can't seem to fix. Christmas is about hope when the stage of life is the darkest. Christmas is about a future that God has provided for eternity when death appears to be the final word in life.

We need to hear this message again and again. Somehow the passage of time takes a subtle toll on our spirits. Because it happens little by little, even to the most dedicated people, we usually don't notice it. Then, one day it suddenly gets dark and we wonder what happened.

This morning we have heard from the "advance man." He reminds us that God has turned on the brightest light in the universe — brighter than any sun or star or gas powered electric generator. He also reminds us that we are the advance people of this generation. We are to tell everyone who will listen that the light has already come. Once again I want to paraphrase John's Advent message, "Prepare the way of the Lord," for our times: "Turn on the lights."

Promises, Promises, Promises

This morning's Gospel from Luke recounts God's announcement to Mary that she was to become the Mother of the Savior. It describes Mary's initial reaction of fear and confusion, and Joseph's reaction to the fact that his fiancee was about to have a child that wasn't his. Then Luke records Mary's song of praise (called the "Magnificat") which she sang in response to this announcement. You see, God's announcement to Mary was in reality a promise to her that she would become the mother of the Christ child.

That's what I want to talk about this morning — *promises*. How does that phrase go? "Promises, promises, promises!" Promises are an integral part of life. They are easy to make, even easier to break, and, once broken, bring untold pain and anguish. In fact, without promises it would be impossible to live together with other people. And yet, the "broken promise" is an all too common experience ... one that for many folks is most difficult to recover from.

I can't think of one human relationship that doesn't depend on the making and keeping of promises — whether it's the relationship between husband and wife, or between parents and children, or between business associates, or simply between friends. This morning, however, I want to talk about God's promises — for if we depend on human promises, we are far more dependant upon the promises of God ... even though we sometimes take God's promises for granted or twist God's promises into something God did not intend them to be.

I want to digress a moment. Have you ever noticed that when you and I read passages of scripture, we tend to put halos on the events we read about? Because we consider the Bible "holy," we somehow mentally conclude that the events had a "holy aura" about them — that they were somehow different than events which happen to us today.

The problem comes when you and I look for the presence of God in our lives today. I have a hunch that we secretly look for that "holy aura" in the things that happen to us, and when it doesn't appear, we mistakenly conclude that God is "avoiding us." What I'm trying to describe is actually the subject for an entire sermon in itself, but I mention it today because I suspect it is a factor in how we today expect God's promises to be fulfilled.

You see, it's easy to get God and "Santa Claus" confused when it comes to the matter of our expectations of God and God's promises. Why? Because when we in the twenty-first century think of having a promise fulfilled, I suspect we usually associate it with getting what we want. Or at least we associate it with a happy and uplifting atmosphere — or with what I call the "Hollywood ending."

Think carefully. What I am suggesting is that you and I look to the promises of God to transform our difficult situations into situations of complete joy and happiness. And, when such an expectation does not happen — when we do not "get what we want" — we conclude that God has not acted or has not been present in our lives.

Think about that. We generally teach our children (and that means we were taught that way, too) that Santa Claus will bring them the presents that they want ... perhaps not all, but at least one or two of the big ones. I am sure that we have all had the experience of what happens when some really "hoped for" present didn't appear under the Christmas tree — even when the other presents were nice ones.

Let me bring this all back to the story of God's promise to Mary that she was to be the mother of the savior. Folks, *there was no "halo" on this event!* Mary was pregnant out of wedlock, and back in those days that was a major catastrophe. The shame and humiliation was far more than we in the twenty-first century can comprehend.

That's what Mary was wrestling with when the angel announced to her that her baby was to be the Messiah. And Joseph ... well, not only was there an out-of-wedlock pregnancy, the baby wasn't his. And that compounded the *grim situation* in which he and Mary found themselves. If that had happened to us today, I'm positive that we would *not* see this as a situation in which the promise of God was unfolding. I think we'd try to get out of it. I think we'd get angry at God for allowing such a mess to take place.

My point is that the promises of God most often unfold in life as trials and problems, not as glowing halos and singing angels. You see, if we are expecting those "halos and angels" in our lives, we can easily become disappointed and bitter towards God for not fulfilling God's promises to us. But what is worse, if we are expecting those promises to come to us with "halos and angels," I suspect we will completely miss those situations in which God is fulfilling a promise to us!

I think Mary's reaction to her situation is worth noticing. Pregnant out of wedlock and facing the wrath of her friends in the community, she still responds to the grimness of her situation with a song of praise to God: "My soul proclaims the greatness of the Lord and my spirit rejoices in God, my savior...."

I often wonder if we could respond like Mary did when we find ourselves in the middle of life's seamier situations. I wonder if we can see that even the "messy side of life" can be the opportunity that God is using to fulfill a promise to us. I'll go out on a limb: If we can continue to praise and thank God, even in the face of adversity, life will be different. Problems will be different, and we will be more open to being able to see the promises of God unfold in our own lives!

Yes, even our Christmas expectations of God will be different! What about you this Christmas? When you will sing "the hopes and fears of all the years are met in thee tonight," what shape will you be expecting God's promise to take for you this year?

God Is Now Here

Theologian Reinhold Niebuhr once observed that the Christmas event can only be spoken about in poetry. He went on to comment that over the centuries preachers have analyzed it in their sermons and have turned Christmas into dogma. "Dogma," he said, "is rationally petrified poetry." I think I understand what he means. He means that Christmas speaks to the heart.

As I reread the Christmas story, images of Bethlehem and the shepherd's field flooded my mind. I kept "seeing" the darkened sky and the village not far off in the distance. The angel message was brief: "I bring good news" ... "the savior is born" ... "you will find him in a manger." Over the centuries that short message has prompted millions of sermons, and the worship of the shepherds has turned into elaborate rituals in ornate cathedrals as well as plain pageants in simple churches. That is an impressive result for such a simple action.

However, I found myself asking: "Is the meaning of Christmas found in our pageantry or is it found in the event?" In our efforts to make Christmas festive, have we obscured the mystery of the event itself? Was Niebuhr right — can only poetry communicate the wonder of Christmas?

Tonight I want you to talk with you in poetry. Not with words that rhyme, but with thoughts that create images in your mind. I want the Christmas *event* to touch your hearts. I realize that you cannot physically go to Bethlehem tonight, but I am convinced that the event itself has the power to give your celebration of Christmas a new sense of wonder and meaning.

Close your eyes. Imagine yourself on that dark Bethlehem hillside. Listen to the angel: "You will find a baby lying in a manger ..." Lying in a manger — not in the palace of king, but in a stone cave where sheep huddled to eat. Picture the town just off in the distance across the open fields. It is a rural village in out-of-the-way Palestine — hardly at the top of a vacation list of places to visit. It was only Caesar's decree for a census that brought Joseph and Mary there. I doubt they would have come otherwise.

It was a long trip (especially by donkey) from Nazareth — much too long for a woman who was almost nine months pregnant. I can picture the conversation between them: "But, Joseph, I am almost due. I can't go there." "Mary, Caesar has spoken. We have no choice." Because the town was crowded with other travelers, the bed and breakfast inns were filled. Picture a "no vacancy" sign on every window. It was only because a charitable innkeeper realized how pregnant Mary actually was that they were given a place to stay. That is why Mary's baby was born in a manger.

A child was born. It was that simple. Yet that birth was different. The angels' message was to the point: The baby was the Son of God! The mighty God of time and eternity was coming to live with us. In the past, God had spoken through prophets. But this time God was coming to earth in person! Therein lies the wonder of Christmas! *It is a face-to-face encounter with the Holy One.* Not with a president or a king or a great military commander. With God!

I want you to bring your mind back to the present so that we can allow the event to touch us now. The Christmas event suggests that we can look in three directions to encounter the Holy One today. First, notice that the shepherds looked up to the sky to hear the angels' message. That is a good place for us to start also, especially since "feeling down" is one of life's more common experiences. It happens to all of us to some degree or another, ranging from simple discouragement all the way to depression and despair. Christmas invites us to "look up" when life is "looking down."

When life seems to be closing in, look up to see God. Don't be afraid to pray. Don't be afraid to worship. God is in control of history. God is here for you. Jesus' words are dependable: "Ask, and it will be given to you! Seek and you will find."

I know we have discovered that our universe doesn't consist of three stories where heaven is up, earth is here, and hell is down. That doesn't make any difference. We simply need to know that God, the Holy One, is behind it all. God has lovingly created us, and God wants us to look to him for strength and support. Whether it is "up" or "out," God is here.

Christmas suggests a second direction in which to look to encounter the Holy One: look around at the everyday world in which you live! God came to earth in a smelly cattle shed — the last place one would expect to find God. But those are the kinds of places where we do find God.

I think it's hard to visualize meeting God in everyday life. What does God care about dirty dishes? What does God care about driving children from one school event to another? What does God care about commuting to and from the office? What does God care about all the homework the teachers assign? What does God care about homes full of dust and disarray?

Let the manger speak! Let it show you that God does come to us in the drudgery and routine events of life. God is at the kitchen sink. God rides the commuter train with you. And, yes, God is even in your home that you might not have cleaned up as much as you would have liked to. To meet the Christ of Christmas face to face, start by looking up. Then, look around!

Finally, look beyond the world immediately around you! Why? Because God wants the whole world to know that God is there for them, too. I guarantee that as you become a messenger for God, the reality of your encounter with the Holy One will become more vivid.

God is where people are starving and hungry — where people are powerless and homeless — where people are fighting or dying — where people struggle for freedom and justice and human dignity. It is when we look beyond our immediate world that we hear Jesus saying to us: "As you did it for one of the least of these my brothers or sisters, you have done it for me."

Christmas is a mystery which occurs over and over again each time we respond to Christ's command to reach out to the lowliest of society — and especially those whom society would ignore. In short, Christmas is an encounter with the Holy One that continues to happen to us as we look up, look around, and look beyond.

There is one more dimension to the poetry of Christmas that I want you to hear tonight. Christmas can only be experienced through eyes of faith! If you are in church tonight for the first time, or if you are here tonight looking for proof for your faith, even if you are here tonight as a "skeptic" because the rest of the family insisted that you come, I can think of nothing to say that will be able to "prove" Christmas for you.

However, there are a few things I can tell you about with certainty. I do believe that there were shepherds in those fields of Bethlehem that night. I do not need to see the records of the county clerk. I do believe that angels from God told the shepherds of the savior's birth. I do not need a psychological analysis of the phenomenon. God has spoken to people in so many different ways during the course of history. That he chose to use angels to speak to those shepherds is not a problem for me.

I do believe that the shepherds made a speedy trip into Bethlehem to see this wonder first-hand. I used to think it was a long trip. Not so! Bethlehem is barely more than a stone's throw from the fields where they were grazing their sheep.

I also believe that Mary was a virgin and that the child she gave birth to is God's very own Son, even though the medical discipline of obstetrics does not allow for such occurrences. I cannot defend my belief scientifically, but that does not make any difference to me.

Most of all, I believe that in the fullness of time, God fulfilled his promise and came to earth as an infant human person. And I believe that in becoming a person, God so completely identified with us — through the rest of eternity, we are now completely identified with God! "His name will be called Emmanuel." "God With Us."

God is now here! That says it all.

Waiting And Witnessing

My message this morning is about two biblical senior citizens and what we can learn from them about the nature of faith. The setting for today's Gospel jumps from the stable in Bethlehem to the temple in Jerusalem where Mary and Joseph had brought Jesus to be "presented to the Lord." It was there that they met Simeon and Anna.

Their reactions to Jesus suggest a question that I have for you this morning: "What are you going to do about Jesus now that Christmas is over?" These two biblical members of "Forever Young" suggest two responses which are the theme of my sermon: "Waiting ... and Witnessing."

Simeon had been waiting — waiting for a lifetime, in fact — for the coming of the promised Messiah. Waiting is a familiar experience which we talked about before Christmas as we waited for Christmas to arrive. However, this morning I am talking about a different kind of waiting. It's not like waiting in line at the supermarket. This kind of waiting is waiting to reach a goal or waiting for a "dream" to happen.

Children wait to be grown-up. Teenagers wait to meet the "right" boy or girl in their lives. Young adults wait to graduate from college. A husband and wife wait for their child to be born. Middle-agers wait for retirement. The longer we wait with nothing seeming to happen, the more impatient and discouraged we become.

Simeon had probably been to the temple hundreds of times without finding his hopes fulfilled. I can picture other people coming up to Simeon and saying to him, "Give it up, old man. You're never going to see any messiah in your lifetime. You are a hopeless fool. Forget your dream."

There probably were times when Simeon did feel like giving up on his hopes — when he felt that God's promise was nothing but the whistling of wind in the trees. However, Simeon clung to that hope. And therein he teaches us something about the nature of faith. At those times when he felt like throwing in the towel on his dream, when he felt like he was at the end of his rope, he tied a knot and hung on, even though the rest of the world called him a dreamer and a fool. Simeon kept his vision. And he did live to see its fulfillment! That's the part we read this morning. That's something I think we can learn from him. I would call it "trusting patience."

Too often we are tempted to "give up" when we don't see something happen immediately. The late Dr. E. E. Flack, Dean Emeritus of Hamma Divinity School (now Trinity Seminary in Columbus, Ohio), was often heard to say, "The mills of God grind slowly, but they grind exceedingly fine." I didn't understand it when I first heard it, but he was saying, "Be patient. God is keeping his promise, even though you can't see it now."

Simeon models for us how to wait with patience. His response to seeing Jesus that day in the temple has been preserved over the centuries by the church and is called the "Nunc Dimittis." "Lord, now let your servant depart in peace, according to your word. For my eyes have seen your salvation which you have for all people. A light to give light to the Gentiles and the glory of your people, Israel."

Anna models for us what to do after the dream or promise is fulfilled. Her response was one of enthusiastic witness. "At that moment she came, and began to praise God and to speak about the child to all who were looking for the redemption of Jerusalem." To put it in the words of one of our Christmas carols: "Go tell it on the mountain ... over the hills and everywhere ... that Jesus Christ is born." Her example is basic to the life and mission of the church. It is about evangelism ... an "enthusiastic sharing of a discovery that cannot be contained."

I hesitate to use the word "evangelism" in a sermon because it appears to turn off a good many people. For some reason, there are a lot of folks out there who think evangelism is telling others what they have to believe and how they have to live. Actually, evangelism is the business of the angels. The word "angel" really means messenger. Angels are not fluttering, white-winged beings. An angel is one who speaks for God — one who shares discovered joy. Someone pointed out to me that the word "angel" appears in the middle of the word "evANGELism." Evangelism simply means being God's messenger by sharing the good news of God's love in Christ with others.

The primary motive for evangelism is to bring others to a knowledge of God's love in Jesus Christ. However, an equally important motive relates to the life of the church. Unless evangelism stands at the center of a congregation's ministry, that congregation will begin to wither on the vine. Much has been said in our times about the decline of mainline denominations and the growth of fundamentalist denominations. In almost every case, the reason for the growth of any church can be traced to an enthusiastic witnessing to the gospel.

Lutherans are not comfortable with the "are you saved" approach to evangelism of some denominations. But that's not the only way to witness to one's faith. We don't have to be judgmental or pious to be enthusiastic about our faith. I can point to any number of people in congregations who are there because they were personally invited by another member. That's evangelism. That's enthusiastic witnessing. That is sharing our faith. And that is vital to the continued health and growth of the church's ministry.

The need for evangelism is greater now than ever before in our history. As long-time members retire to other communities, it is important that new people take their place. But these new families need to be invited! That is a task which belongs to every member of every congregation throughout the world. We can advertise about our congregation until the cows come home. But in the final analysis, it is through the personal witness of individual Christians that the church of Jesus Christ grows and fulfills its mission. It will take your active witness to make it happen.

Permit me to tell you a favorite story to illustrate what I am describing. Sandy MacTavish was one of the town drunks in a small village in Scotland. The local preacher had tried for years without success to get Sandy to go "on the wagon." In a last ditch effort, the parson called a meeting at the church of everyone in town who had trouble with alcohol. He was delighted when he saw Sandy MacTavish show up and sit in the back pew. He was so inspired that he delivered the most eloquent sermon of his entire career, telling about the evils of drink and the harmful effects it had on both body and soul.

At the end of the sermon, he announced that he was sending around a piece of paper that he wanted people to sign pledging that they would give up drinking. As he watched the list circulate, everyone signed it including Sandy MacTavish. After the service, he was so excited that he snatched up the list without looking at it and ran home to tell his wife about his victory. He unrolled the list before her eyes and sure enough, written across the bottom were the words, "witnessed by Sandy MacTavish."

I would repeat my challenge to you: It is through the personal witness of individuals that the church grows and fulfills its mission. It will take your active and enthusiastic witness to make it happen. This morning I hope that you will let Simeon and Anna shape your response to the good news of God's love shown to us in Bethlehem. It is what needs to happen once Christmas is over!

Our Hope For Years To Come

On January 1, 2001, our world marked the beginning of a new millennium in human history. In a way, it was no different than the beginning of any day. The universe continued to exist in the same way it was the day before. The sun still rose at its appointed time as night turned into day. The weather still reflected the conditions in the atmosphere above where we live.

What was different about that New Year's Eve and Day is the significance we attach to the arrival of a new millennium. It must be significant, for I have never before in my life celebrated New Year's Day every hour on the hour throughout the world. Through television, we were treated to a variety of celebrations from New Zealand to Paris to New York to Chicago to Honolulu.

Regardless of the different customs used to mark the new millennium, and regardless of the warnings or predictions associated with the day, they all have in common humanity's search for meaning, because it is inherent in our nature to seek meaning in the passage of time.

Time is the dimension that we use to organize, plan, and remember. We mark milestones in our history. We celebrate birthdays and anniversaries. We remember significant events. We keep track of the passage of time in order to preserve the past, make sense out of the present, and find direction and hope for the future.

Two Bible passages remind us that God does not measure time the same way we do. Psalm 90 (the basis for "O God Our Help in Ages Past") says: "For a thousand years in your sight are like yesterday when it is past, or like a watch in the night." And 2 Peter

3:18 (our second lesson) says: "But do not ignore this one fact, beloved, that with the Lord one day is like a thousand years, and a thousand years are like one day."

It is important to realize that God works in "patterns," not "moments." As we read the Genesis account of creation, we often think in terms of six 24-hour days rather than seeing creation as taking place from the beginning of time through the present moment in which we live. For God the past, present, and future are one single event.

The Bible uses two different words for time. God operates in *kairos*, a Greek word which means the "fullness of time." We operate in *chronos*, the Greek word which means the passage of minutes, days, years, centuries, and even millenniums.

For example: Mary did not give birth to Jesus on December 25 at 12:06 a.m. as we are prone to say in our society when a baby is born. Rather, the Bible says it happened when "the time came for her to be delivered" (i.e., the "fullness of time" for her pregnancy).

The opening words of today's Gospel couldn't be more appropriate for the first Sunday of a new year. If our New Year celebrations are about finding meaning in the passage of time, John starts his Gospel by taking us back to the beginning of time.

"In the beginning was the Word, and the Word was with God, and the Word was God. He was in the beginning with God. All things came into being through him, and without him not one thing came into being."

If John's Gospel were the only one we had, this is all that we would know about Jesus' birth: before his name was Jesus, his name was the Word, and he was with God from the very beginning of creation, bringing things into being, making things happen, shining light into the darkness.

He was God's self, God's soul, God's life force in the world. He was the breath inside all living things. He was the electric spark that charged peoples' hearts. He was the fire inside the sun. He was the space between the stars. He was the axis around which the galaxies spin.

John goes on to say that not everyone got that message. Many were blinded by this light and preferred the darkness they knew to the light which they did not know. The Word sidled up to them and hummed life into their ears, but they cleared their throats and walked away. So God decided to speak in a new way. God decided to speak body language. "And the Word became flesh and lived among us — full of grace and truth."

This is John's Christmas story in a nutshell. Like Luke, John is telling us about an encounter with the Holy One. God's Word was translated into a human being. God's self, soul, and life force were concentrated into one mortal life on earth, and as a result, nothing would ever be the same again. Not because everyone listened, because everyone does not, but because the eternal Word of God took human form.

Heaven married earth. The beginning of time merged into the present time. God's message was no longer ethereal. It had a face, a voice, and a pair of hands. This is the miracle of the Word made flesh: God delivered his message to us in person by becoming one of us.

The impact of this event has been earthshaking. Regardless of the number of world religions in existence, our present world marks time from the time of his birth. This Word of God is the pivotal person in our history. The meaning of all life — past, present, and future — is focused in this man!

If John takes us back to the beginning, the writer of 2 Peter 3:13 takes us to the future: "But, in accordance with his promise, we wait for new heavens and a new earth, where righteousness is at home." What God started from nothing in the beginning will reach its completion and full glory in the "fullness of time," whenever that might be.

This universe belongs to God, its creator. And we belong to God. That is why we begin and end the first worship service of a new year in confident trust: "O God, our help in ages past, Our hope for years to come, Still be our guard while troubles last And our eternal home."

Epiphany 1
(Baptism Of The Lord)
Mark 1:4-11

A Vision And A Voice

Today we remember the baptism of Jesus. Whether you are a long-time church member or you are seeking to discover more about Christianity, most folks have heard the word "baptism." Some people refer to the event as "christening." Regardless of the word used, it is associated with a special church ritual for babies soon after they are born.

There is much about baptism that is worth thinking about. Baptisms happen fairly often here. We follow certain procedures to prepare for a it. There are conversations with the pastor. A date is set when family and friends can be present at the service. Sponsors, sometimes called godparents, are selected. There is a class to attend about the meaning of baptism.

On the day of the baptism, there is an air of excitement. During the service, the children of the congregation are always eager to come forward and get a firsthand look at the new baby being baptized. The parents of the baby are frequently nervous that their child will be too noisy during the baptism. The godparents are proud to have been asked to be sponsors. The grandparents beam proudly from the second pew and take hundreds of pictures after the service. Of course, there is the baby who is the center of attention — whether asleep or awake — whether quiet or screaming.

Important words are said during the baptismal service. "Do you promise to fulfill these obligations?" *"We do!"* "Do you believe in God the Father?" *"I believe in God the Father Almighty, maker of heaven and earth."* "I baptize you in the name of the Father and of the Son and of the Holy Spirit." "We welcome you into the Lord's family...."

There are also significant actions that are part of a baptism: the splashing of water; the sign of the cross; the lighting of a candle. No matter how many baptisms we have, each one is a special occasion. Not even the most loudly crying baby can mar the event.

You would think that is how the Bible would have described Jesus' baptism. As important as baptism is and as important as Jesus is, you would think his baptism would have been rich with religious ceremony. However, Mark devotes only three short verses to it. No mention about the words said or the promises made. No mention about sponsors. No sign of the cross. No baptismal candle. Only a *vision* and a *voice*!

The vision was of opening heavens. But wait! There is no mention of golden shafts of light zeroing in on Jesus! There was only the appearance of a bird — a simple dove at that. And then, the voice: "You are my Son, the Beloved; with you I am well pleased."

Of course, John the Baptist did not have the Book of Worship to use at Jesus' baptism. Nor was Jesus dressed in a white robe that had been worn by his parents at their baptisms. But when all is said and done, that dove and voice tell the real story of what baptism is all about.

A vision and a voice! "Just as Jesus was coming up out of the water, he saw the heavens open up and God's Spirit descended like a dove on him." The only time in the entire Bible that God's Spirit is identified with a dove is at the baptism of Jesus. Yet, for 2,000 years the descending dove has been the church's most widely used symbol of God's Holy Spirit. That tells us something about the importance of its appearance at Jesus' baptism.

What was the vision? It was a vision of God's very own presence! It was a vision of the immediacy of God's Spirit. The dove's appearance said in no uncertain terms that God's Spirit was right there in the middle of that event!

The liturgy does not call for the use of live doves at a baptism (maybe it should). But what is important is that God's Spirit is equally present today as parents, sponsors, and child gather around the baptismal font. Baptism is far more than a nice religious ritual we conduct for children. It is an occasion when God's Spirit is right here among us! Baptism is called a "sacrament." Martin Luther described a sacrament as a "visible sign of God's invisible grace and love."

"A visible sign." Whether it is a baby who is presented by parents and sponsors, or whether it is adults who are presenting themselves to be baptized, the living God is in the middle of the people gathered here. How do I know? Because God has promised to be here just like God was present at Jesus' baptism.

Then there's the voice. The words of the voice echoed the Old Testament Servant Song of Isaiah 42 which told of the mission and purpose of the life of the one to whom they were spoken: "I have put my Spirit upon him; he will bring forth justice to the nations."

It is no easy task to bring forth justice in the world, or to work for an end to human suffering, or to bring peace where there is hatred and discord. And yet, that is the mission which is laid upon every person who is washed in the waters of baptism.

Justice does not happen naturally. Peace is elusive when the conflict of human wills are involved. Human suffering is easier to ignore because of its painfulness. But those are the arenas of life to which Jesus was sent. And because of our baptism, those are the arenas of life to which we are sent — to do something about them! We are to bring about healing, reconciliation, and change. We are to bring an end to injustice and oppression. We are to care for the hungry and homeless. We are to work to make peace a reality.

It takes a special power to face those kinds of issues. But the voice throws us back to the vision — for the power in the vision is the power of God's very own Spirit. We are not left to our own devices to do justice for God. We are given the power of God which comes from the Spirit of God!

Are we good enough for the task? Are we capable enough for the task? Has God given us a mission that is beyond us? Listen to the voice again: "You are my son ... you are my daughter. With you I am pleased!"

I find that astounding. God is saying that God accepts us just the way we are — at a time when we are small, helpless, and crying — at a time when we cannot even say God's name — at a time when we don't even know any theology about God. What's more, God tells us that once the waters of baptism have flowed over our head, *it's good for life!* What magnificent graciousness for God to make such a promise to us right at the start before we've even had the chance to botch things up!

Unfortunately, this is where Christians begin to quibble among themselves. Some say we've got to be old enough to understand what we're doing before the promise can be given to us. Others say that we can lose the promise if we don't stay on the straight and narrow.

Folks, such arguments put the focus in the wrong place. I am convinced that when we come face-to-face with a love that accepts us the way we are with no strings whatsoever attached, we cannot help but respond with the kind of gratitude which seeks to accomplish the mission which this gracious God wants us to do. "You are my son. You are my daughter. With you I am pleased."

Baptism is not some kind of "magic spell" or "death insurance" policy that we take out on little children. Baptism is about life, because baptism is an entrance into the life of Jesus Christ and into the life of Christ's Church. Whether we are baptized as an infant or as an adult, in baptism we are marked as belonging to God. We baptize young children, not because we are afraid a child will die. We baptize them because we want them to live in the company of God's people where they grow in faith, love, and obedience to the will of God.

This morning I have asked you to remember the *vision* and the *voice* at Jesus' baptism, because it is the same voice that was present at your baptism, or will be present on the day you will be baptized. Always remember the words and actions which are part of that day to remember:

"Pour out your Holy Spirit upon this person; the spirit of wisdom and understanding, the spirit of counsel and might, the spirit of knowledge and the fear of the Lord, the spirit of joy in your presence." Remember the sign of the cross made upon your forehead with the words: "Child of God, (today) you have been sealed with the Holy Spirit and marked with the cross of Christ forever!"

**Epiphany 2
Ordinary Time 2
John 1:43-51**

Making A Difference

How many of you know someone who is partially or completely color blind? Seeing colors is something we frequently take for granted until we try to imagine what the world looks like to someone who cannot. One such person described the task of getting dressed in the morning as one of the more difficult decisions that he faces during the day. He admitted that there have been many times when he went to work wearing some very strange color combinations.

He went on to say that he is fascinated by his wife's ability to pick colors that go well together. What is most fascinating is how she notices that the appearance of a particular color in a piece of fabric can be changed by the colors which are around it. She will hold up several different ties and say, "Oh — this shirt brings out the browns in this tie, but this shirt brings out the blues in it."

The same principle is true in all of life. The diverse hues of ethnic heritage, religious background, and cultural practices blend together in different ways to give the fabric of life its depth and richness. Of course, we are not always comfortable with such diversity, and so it frequently becomes a source of conflict rather than unity.

It is also how we are blended together as God's people in the church. Each of us has an impact on the other. Where you've been this week, what you've done, what you've said — all of it has had an effect on our life together as people of this congregation both within and outside of the communities in which we live.

I think we sometimes forget this dimension of the fabric known as our congregation. Through each one of you, the impact of our community of faith has reached beyond the four walls of this building into public schools, consulting firms, doctor's offices, hospitals, and company boardrooms. In fact, the list of places we have touched this week is too long to name each one.

It involves each of our unique perspectives and values that we share with others. It involves our concern for each other and for what is going on in the world around us. It involves both our common faith experiences and the faith experiences that are unique to us.

This "linking together" of humanity has been a characteristic of life since the beginning of time. But in our times it has taken on a new dimension. We now live in a global community. Through the medium of television and the Internet, we have almost instant access to each other, no matter where in the world we live. It means that what is happening in distant parts of the world can have an immediate effect on our lives right here, whether it is a millennium celebration in New Zealand or a military coup in West Africa. We are, indeed, like a multi-colored piece of cloth whose beauty and appearance is affected by who each one of us is!

This introduction is prompted by this morning's Gospel story about Nathaniel. He is mentioned only twice in the Bible, and then, only in the Gospel of John. Matthew, Mark, and Luke never talk about him. They do talk about Bartholomew in the places where John talks about Nathaniel. Since John never mentions Bartholomew, our best guess is that the two are the same person.

Nathaniel was the fourth disciple. According to John, Jesus called Peter and Andrew first. Then he called Philip. Then Philip went and brought Nathaniel. His only other mention is with the other disciples at one of the resurrection appearances. Beyond that, he simply blended in with the others.

What we do know about Nathaniel is that he was a person who was hoping and searching. We know it because of the fig tree. At a time when people lived in one-room houses, we know that they often planted fig trees in front of their homes as a place to "get away to."

A fig tree is about fifteen feet tall and its branches spread out about 25 feet in width like an umbrella, creating a space that is almost like a private room. If someone wanted to get away from the chaos of a one-room house, he or she would sit under the fig tree. They would sit there to read scripture or to reflect or to pray. Sitting under a fig tree was a sign of seeking and praying for God's living presence.

Now, I realize that this church looks nothing like a fig tree. But isn't that why we're here? We have come together here with the yearning to know the touch of the living God. We come to "retreat" from the chaos of the world around us so we can read scripture, reflect, and pray. I hope you will see that, despite his relative anonymity, we do have much in common with Nathaniel.

We also know about Nathaniel that he was a man "in whom there was no deceit." In modern English, that means he was a person who sought to be honorable and decent. He was not a prominent person, but he was a good person who tried to be a responsible participant in the community of which he was a part.

I think that describes you, too. I know you to be good people. I know that you are concerned about and care for the world in which we live. I know we are a diverse people with widely differing ideas about how things in life should be accomplished. I know that we often argue vigorously with each other about what courses of action should be taken in given situations. But that's part of the multi-colored fabric of human existence. My point is simply that regardless of your ideas and opinions, your motives are genuine. I could easily apply the description of Nathaniel to you: "persons in whom there is no deceit."

What does Jesus' calling of Nathaniel have to do with the multi-colored fabric of human existence? I must confess that our recent entry into a new era of history — a new millennium — had an effect on the way this passage spoke to me.

How is history made? There are two distinctly opposite schools of thought on the matter with shades and variations in between. One school holds that history is shaped by the "prominent" people of a given era who lead everyone according to their ideas and values. They are the Julius Caesars, the Alexander the Greats, and the

Franklin D. Roosevelts. The opposite school holds that history is shaped by movements arising from the "grass roots" — from people who hold their convictions so strongly that leaders simply appear to give leadership to a parade that is already underway.

I suspect that the truth is a combination of the two. Leaders do lead. Without the leadership of Martin Luther, there would have been no Protestant Reformation. But the momentum and direction of history also comes from very ordinary people. Without the response of the peasants and lower classes, there would also have been no Protestant Reformation.

I make a point of this because average people like you and me are often tempted to discount the ordinary. That is where I hear the story of Nathaniel speaking. God's will for history is not accomplished only by the elite or powerful. It is accomplished by the actions of ordinary disciples like Nathaniel — like you and me.

That's something we need to hear once in a while. We need to hear that our debates and disagreements about how to solve the injustices of life do have an effect on the course of human events. In a global community, it is easy to conclude we are such a small part of the picture that we can't possibly have an effect on the course of history in our time.

I've heard the comment many times. "I'm only one person. What good can I do?" Nothing could be further from reality. Church advocacy groups who work with legislators on public issues of justice have discovered a significant phenomena. Many legislators, both on a state and national level, have commented that if they receive as few as four letters about a given piece of legislation they take notice.

Ordinary disciples do make a difference. Remember, our concerns, hopes, and efforts are heard by God as God works them into the fabric of his Holy Will for humankind. Remember, too, the prayers of "ordinary people" — your prayers — are used by God to bring peace, justice, and healing to a world beset by turmoil and conflict, whether it is here or on the other side of the world. They may seem like ordinary prayers. But then, if we take the ordinary disciple, Nathaniel, seriously — we will know that it is through the ordinary that God's will is ultimately accomplished.

The Adventure Of Discipleship

Today's Gospel is about Jesus' calling of his first four disciples. It is about the first people who were called to hold the job which we hold today. Mark's story is not very elaborate. It is short and to the point. There is a certain note of adventure as the four men leave their fishing business to go with Jesus, but there is not much in the story that seems terribly upsetting.

What the story doesn't tell about is *what those men were getting in for* by becoming followers of Jesus. To find out what was really in store for them, we have to keep reading. And what we discover is that being a disciple was not glamorous. In fact, it was downright dangerous.

Later in Mark we hear Jesus say, "Whoever loses his life for my sake and the sake of the gospel will find it." Matthew includes another comment: "Do not think that I have come to bring peace on earth; I have not come to bring peace, but a sword." Those are disturbing statements, especially for those of us who are today's disciples.

He was saying that being his disciple is not an easy task. He was saying that the gospel is a disturbing force in the world which can upset individuals and nations alike. It brings change and new experiences to all who hear it. Being his disciple will not be easy because the task of the disciple is to be the bearer of this revolutionary gospel message.

We know what happened to Jesus. His message disturbed those in power and they tried to silence him. Of the four men in this gospel text, three were also executed for their witness. The powers that ruled the ancient world were upset by the gospel, and they tried to silence its voices. I'd like to be able to say that's all ancient history, but there are still governments today which oppose the gospel.

It is important for us to realize that the truth of the gospel is like a two-edged sword: it is both comforting and disturbing. The messengers of this gospel may find themselves similarly regarded by those who don't want to hear that message, even in countries where Christianity is protected by law.

Jesus' two-edged sword also strikes close to home. I wonder what Peter's mother-in-law and wife had to say about his chasing off with an itinerant preacher. I wonder how old man Zebedee felt when his two sons simply picked up and left their half-mended nets in the boat.

I suspect that the family relatives in this story were not too pleased. But that, too, is the nature of the gospel. It can upset individuals and disturb even family relationships. Jesus' call to service can be a call that provokes controversy and difficulty.

I think of a man named Hans Luther, Martin's father. He had dreams that his illustrious son's practice of law would be the means of pulling their family up from their humble origins. Hans probably had dreams of his son standing before kings. And Martin did stand before kings — but it was as an outlaw, not as a champion.

I think of a prospective member who told me: "I would like to join your church, but I have to live with my wife, and she'll have none of that. I guess I'll have to wait a while." Jesus points us to the reality that the gospel can be disturbing, both on a world-wide basis and as close as home and family.

Why? The answer lies in the power of the gospel to change people's lives. Once we meet Jesus Christ on the road of our own individual life, we will be changed! We will be different people! I don't know about you, but my nature is such that I tend to resist change.

I suspect that many folks see the gospel through rose-colored glasses — wanting to see only the joy, comfort, and light — and not wanting to see the difficult or disruptive. "Behold, I will make all things *new*," said Jesus. That's the other side of the two-edged sword.

There are two important words in this morning's gospel, one of which is the word *repent*! Too many folks think "repent" means to feel sorry for what you've done — and then, go do it again. That's not it at all. "Repent" means to *change direction*. It means a change in priorities. It means living with a whole new approach to life! While I do feel that the church can serve as an anchor in a world where everything else is changing so rapidly, that is only one side of the gospel. The other side calls us to embrace the newness and change which Jesus brings.

The second key word is *believe*. That doesn't mean listing your denomination as Lutheran on some application blank. It means trust and reliance and placing one's whole life in God's hands, regardless of what happens in life. It's called "the leap of faith." That's the kind of change which the gospel produces. That's what makes us different. There's no turning back, because it's a difference that won't go away.

To be sure, we will always experience the power of sin in our daily lives. We may even go as far as renouncing the Christ who brought us to faith. Peter knew about that, for he was the one who denied he ever knew Jesus. But later he went out and wept bitterly. The change was there. He couldn't turn back. He was changed by the power of a gospel that left an indelible mark upon his soul.

Being a disciple is a real blessing, despite the gospel's two edges. We know that God has promised to be with us always. That means that we are never alone in life, no matter how we may feel at a given moment, or how unsettling life's changes may seem to be.

Being a disciple means that God is not just a "Sunday friend," but a "daily companion" in our life. It means that all things "do indeed work together for good." Oh — it doesn't guarantee that we won't get the flu or have to face unpleasant experiences. It does mean that as God's person, God will take the events of our life and turn them toward the good, even though we may not be able to see that good at the moment.

Being a disciple also means that we will be part of the greatest change of all, the time when God will change this age into the age of eternity. The death and resurrection of Jesus Christ stands at the center of our faith, because we know that our mortal nature will be changed into an immortal nature. And we shall be changed — one final time.

The gospel is a great power. It does shake nations. It does disturb lives. It does change lives. But above all, it *gives new life* — both for today and for eternity. However, because the gospel does change people, we sometimes are tempted to hide in its words of comfort rather than embrace the new life to which it calls us.

I recently came across another pastor's sermon title which I found intriguing. I want to leave its thought with you. "If you were arrested for being a Christian, would you be convicted?" We are today's disciples, and it is not an easy task. Thankfully, our Lord gives us the strength to do the job which he has given us. The big question is: "What kind of disciple will we be?"

We Are Christ's — That Is Enough

In today's Gospel, Mark tells us more about Jesus by showing his power over unclean spirits. The ironic twist is that it was the demons who recognized Jesus as the Son of God, while the people who were "in the crowd" had no idea who he was. This reversal raises an interesting question: If we met Jesus "on the street" today, would we recognize him as the Holy One of God?

Being able to "recognize" him is related to what we expect from him. Do we need a leader with a charismatic personality to inspire us? Do we need a wonder-worker to set things straight that have run amok? Do we need a care-giver who will bring comfort to wounded spirits? Do we need a moral authority who will teach us how to make right decisions?

I want to make it clear from the start that this sermon is not directed to "seekers" but to people who are already part of the church. Would *you* recognize Jesus? What do you want from Jesus? What do you want Jesus to do for you?

I hesitate to take such an approach because I realize these are self-centered questions. They reflect the consumer mentality that permeates our society which begins with the question, "What's in it for me?" Christianity, by comparison, begins with the question, *"What does God want?"* Jesus came to earth to reveal God's will for us. Jesus came to show us what God has done for us. Jesus came to answer the question, "What does God want for us and from us?" So, that is the question I am exploring this morning.

Let's go back to Mark's story. It is the account of Jesus and a demon-possessed man. Mark makes it very clear that this poor man facing Jesus had somehow been invaded by a force from outside of him over which he apparently had no control. A great deal of speculation has taken place in modern times about what an unclean spirit really is. Some experts say it's what folks called "mental illness" back in those days. Other experts claim that people back then regarded all illness as being the result of some form of possession!

Oddly enough, things haven't changed much since biblical times. Granted, we live in an age of modern medicine. But we still are subject to maladies which defy scientific explanation. Oh, I know that medical research keeps trying to discover genetic causes. But it still remains that many of the ailments which come upon us lie beyond any kind of explanation.

Ask anyone who has a family member suffering from depression, for example. Depression plagues many people, despite the various drugs that are tried. Some experts claim it is due to a chemical imbalance. Others claim it is rooted in the emotions. No one has a clear cut answer. I find it intriguing that despite our science and technology, our age still describes the unexplainable in the same way. Haven't you ever heard another person's irrational actions described by saying, "I wonder what possessed them to do that?"

The Prayer of the Day which goes with this text begins with the words, "O God, you know that we cannot withstand the dangers which surround us." None of us have any guarantees. Any of us could be assaulted by a myriad of life's external dangers — whether it be an accident, an illness, or a drive-by shooting. I don't think I need to enumerate them all. My point is this: I wonder how frightening life must be to that individual who concludes that he or she must navigate through life's perils without any resources or guidance from without.

Today's Gospel suggests a way to approach facing the trials of daily living. As simplistic as it may sound, it suggests that while we acknowledge and recognize the perils of life, *our ultimate focus is not on them, but on Jesus!* Mark does not provide the answer to the phenomena which he describes. He gives no blueprint as to what demon-possession is, nor does he give a series of steps we can take to avoid it! What he does do is shift our focus from the malady to the messiah!

Notice how Jesus quickly silenced the demons at about the time they started to identify him as the Son of God! I find that rather curious to say the least! You'd think that Jesus would have welcomed such an identification of his power and authority! Yet, when seen in light of Mark's entire Gospel, we discover that Jesus did not want to become known as a "Mr. Fixit." He did not want people to find room in their hearts for him only because they thought he was a miracle-worker. He did not want people to follow him only because they thought he could be called upon simply to put bandages on the wounds of life.

That's important for us to see, because we often hold those same expectations of Jesus: miracle worker — Mr. Fixit — invisible protective shield. His immediate action to silence those demons could just as well be for our benefit, too, lest we cling to our own unrealistic expectations.

We need to be clear that Jesus' purpose was to free men, women, and children to enter into a new relationship with God! To persons whose lives were cluttered by everyday cares, he proclaimed that all people are fashioned in God's image and are the jewel of God's creation. To persons who were struggling with life's trials, he proclaimed that God's love is the anchor that will allow them to stand against the dangers both from within and without!

In short, Jesus proclaims a relationship with God that pushes back our darkness — that pushes back our secret fears — and that frees us to walk boldly, knowing that every single day of our pilgrimage through life is worth the effort, in spite of all its dangers. That's the good news for us this morning! It is not to argue whether or not there are really demons in this world. It is to proclaim the kind of trust which believes that God's love for us is so great that life's demons and dangers never have the last word.

Rather than talking about what we expect from God, Jesus is telling us about what God wants from us, and that is a relationship with God that is based solely on trust. I am sometimes afraid that such an expectation is too simple for our scientific mindset. We have been taught to challenge everything. Childlike trust is too simplistic for a complex world. But that is where Jesus is leading us.

How many of us have parents and grandparents who had that kind of trust in God? How many of us as young people used to think they were naive? However, over the years I have discovered *that is what faith is like.* To put it in the words of a modern phrase, to trust in God does mean to "let go and let God."

I want to tell you a story about a conversation between an African convert to Christianity and the missionary to his village. I think we have much to learn from Christians who live in places where native, animistic religions battle with Christianity for the hearts and minds of people.

One day as the two men were walking through the jungles outside the village, the African was reflecting on the change in his life that had been brought about by his faith in Christ. "These jungles," he said, "are very dark. Most of my life I have walked through them in fear of the demons that I was taught lived here." I no longer walk in fear on these paths. There may be demons or there may not be demons, but I am Christ's and that is enough!"

We who have been Christians all our lives often take faith for granted. I know that I need to hear that African man's simple expression of trust. The reality is that we all have our own jungles in life to walk through, whether they are covered with vines or paved with concrete. And there may or may not be demons on those paths. *But we are Christ's, and that is enough!*

Seeing Jesus Clearly

I'd like to begin with what might seem a rather strange question. "Do you *really* believe in Jesus?" Before you answer that with an indignant, "Of course I do," I want you to think for a moment about what your own mental image of Jesus is like.

Try to picture his face. Do you see it as hard, coarse, and set with wrinkles? Or do you see it as smooth, fine-featured, and more on the soft side? Try to picture his personality. Do you see Jesus as warm, congenial, and winsome? Or do you picture him as more stern, outspoken, direct, and forceful? Try to picture how he operated. Do you picture him as the kind of person who was up at the crack of dawn to catch the 6:56 express donkey into Jerusalem? Or do you see him as an easy-going itinerant who roamed about the countryside preaching, teaching, and healing?

Now I will grant that your image of Jesus may not be like what I just described. I was only trying to start you thinking. But my point is that each of us does need to have some kind of image of the person who stands at the center of our faith. You've heard the old saying, "Seeing is believing." I would suggest that the reverse is true: "Believing is seeing" — for how can we follow someone whom we do not know?

Let me give you an example that has been taking place in the world of politics. The biggest issue during the recent campaigns has been the extent to which a political figure's private life ought to remain private. I would suggest that the very fact that it has been an issue indicates people's need to know those individuals who would serve as their leaders. The very same thing is true of those who would follow Jesus. How can we follow someone whom we don't really know? Hence, I propose that my initial question to you was relevant: How clearly can *you* see Jesus?

From time to time in my life I have experienced what the "experts" call a "crisis of faith." I'm sure I'm not the only one these have happened to. Typically they have been times when doubts have crept in and when the teachings of the church have seemed to be only "words on a page" rather than "realities of life."

They're not the kinds of experiences one can plan for or even be prepared for. They just happen. And while they are unsettling experiences at the time they take place, they ultimately become the occasion for gaining new strength and understanding.

Looking back over these times of struggle in my own life, I've discovered that when they occur, I've not had a clear picture of Jesus. I've not had a clear image of him as a person to whom I can relate with confidence, and with whom I can be free and open. Strangely enough, it was as I began to "see" him again and began to be open to him again, my crisis of faith began to pass. It is important how clearly we can see Jesus!

Another illustration: a story about a small seacoast village in England that routinely would become covered by dense fog. The pride of that village was a lighthouse that had been built on the north end of town where the harbor was navigable and free from the huge rocks that dotted the rest of the coast. One night the villagers had gathered on the south end of town to celebrate a local holiday. Part of that celebration included the building of a large bonfire on the beach.

That same night, a ship in the vicinity developed engine trouble. The ship's captain, after checking his maps and charts, decided to locate on the beam from that village lighthouse and put in at that harbor for repairs. As he scanned the horizon through the fog, he caught sight of a faint glimmer of light. Thinking it to be the beam from the lighthouse, he set his course on it to go ashore.

As he came closer to land, he began to see the light more clearly and realized it was not the lighthouse but the bonfire. Quickly he changed course, later discovering that he had been only 100 yards away from one of the largest sunken boulders in that area and certain destruction of his ship. It made a difference how clearly he could see!

How clearly can *you* see Jesus? What do you see? I would like to turn your attention back to Mark's Gospel text for this morning. The season of the Church year is the Epiphany Season, and in a way, the theme of this season might be called: "Pictures of the Holy One." Today's Gospel is meant to be included in our "picture albums" of how we see Jesus.

This morning we see a picture of Jesus, the *friend*. The picture has a personal touch to it as Mark recounts Jesus' concern for a family member of one of his disciples. While all of Mark's Gospel is told with fewer words than the others, the fact of Jesus' concern for the families of his followers was significant enough for him to record the incident. If we did not know this side of Jesus, I am afraid that God would be more like a benevolent authority figure, rather than a trusted confidant with whom we can share our deepest feelings and concerns.

"What a friend we have in Jesus, All our sins and griefs to bear!" This cherished hymn captures beautifully a vital dimension of our relationship with the Holy One. Not only is God the ultimate power over the universe, God is personal. God is my friend. I can turn to God as one friend turns to another. Is this picture part of your image of the Master?

The second picture Mark shows us is of Jesus, the *healer*. "And the whole city was gathered — at his door — and he healed many who were sick with various diseases and cast out many demons." Again, note that Mark wants us to know Jesus as one who restores persons to health and wholeness. In an age dominated by medical science and high-tech health care, I need to be reminded of this dimension of who Jesus is.

Why? I must confess that I sometimes hesitate to pray for certain kinds of healing because modern medicine tells me that it is impossible. I suspect it is because I am afraid that the person I want to pray for will not be healed, suggesting that God really can't do anything about it. It is as if I am "testing" God, afraid that if what I pray for doesn't happen, God will have failed. Of course, that is the human side of my feelings. It is the side of me which forgets that God's healing comes in many forms and includes the spirit as well as the body. It is the "modern" side of me that needs to see this picture of Jesus again and again — showing me that I can dare to pray for healing, even when science tells me it is not possible. Is this picture included in your image of the Master?

The third picture of Jesus is as God's person for the entire world. "Let us go on to the next towns, that I may preach there also; for that is why I came out." Again, Mark wants us to see that Jesus does not confine himself to some "favored few," but his concern and compassion are extended to *everyone*. This is a picture that we often do not see, especially those of us who have invested time and energy in the church. Because of our humanness, we have a secret tendency to think that all our efforts have gained us a special place in the kingdom. It is offensive to think that someone who is different from us, or less dedicated than we are, would have a place of favor in God's eyes.

The Bible makes it crystal clear that God wants all humanity to be "saved." That's another way of saying that God wants to bring all people back into a relationship with God. The piety that we practice may be a wonderful way of expressing our faith, but when we use that piety as the criteria by which we expect God to include or exclude others, we have turned that piety into a pitfall. "Pious people" have a special need to be reminded of this dimension of who Jesus is! Is this picture included in your image of the Master?

I realize what I have described for you is not new. I also realize that Mark's "pictures of Jesus" may well already be part of your own images of the Master. So let's just say that today has been "picture album day." We do that in our family, occasionally getting out the family albums and remembering all the times we have shared together. I suspect that you do, too. Just as that experience renews our image of who we are as a family, looking at our "picture album of faith" can renew our images of who Jesus is and who we are in relationship to him. How clearly do you see Jesus?

The Wideness In God's Mercy

Many fundamentalist Christian groups would have us believe that the Bible has all the answers to the questions of life. For them, difficult situations are black and white when one consults scripture for the right choice to make or the wrong decision to avoid. In struggling with how to respond to a particular dilemma, the Bible tells us precisely what to do. What's more, such an approach to daily life also evaluates how acceptable we are to God in terms of how obedient we are to these biblical injunctions.

Given the complexity of life, that is a mighty appealing promise, as evidenced by the popularity of conservative fundamentalism in our country at this time in history. However, I have found such simplicity to be an illusion. Life is not all black and white. People are not either good or bad. Decisions are not always either all right or all wrong. I am reminded of a comment made by the theologian, Paul Tillich: "The character of human life, like the character of the human condition, like the character of all life, is 'ambiguity': the inseparable mixture of good and evil, the true and false, the creative and destructive forces — both individual and social."

As I read Mark's account of Jesus healing a leper, this ambiguity jumped out at me. A leper begged to be healed. Jesus was moved with pity. He sternly warned him. He sent the leper to fulfill Moses' commands. I realize it is a very short passage. But I found myself feeling puzzled about the widely varying feelings and reactions Mark described. I found myself asking if this was a story about God's compassionate concern or a message about so-called "tough love."

A favorite hymn for many has been "There's A Wideness In God's Mercy." One of my seminary professors insisted vehemently that we should stop singing the hymn because it contained "bad theology," referring to a line in the last verse: "Greater good because of evil, Larger mercy through the fall." He felt that phrase gave evil too much "importance" in our experience of God's goodness.

Although I could see his point at the time, I was not about to write off this wonderful hymn just because of one phrase. Over the years I have come to understand that these words poetically describe the ambiguity of life which I am lifting up before you this morning. Good and evil do exist side by side in each of us. Martin Luther describes us as both saint and sinner. Even the great Christian hero, Saint Paul, exclaimed, "The good I would I do not, and the evil that I would not, that I do. Oh, wretched person that I am. Who will deliver me from this body of death?" (Romans 7:19, 24).

As we look at the leper in today's Gospel, we discover that genuine Christianity is not a matter of "total" obedience, or correct decisions, or simple choices. Rather, it is a matter of faith in the goodness of God to whom we come without fear and to whom we can say without reservation, "If you will, you can make me clean," trusting that God's response to us will be, "I will; be clean."

I'm not sure that we realize the incredible amount of courage and faith it took for that leper to approach Jesus. Leprosy was one of the most dreaded diseases one could get. It resulted in the leper being exiled to a life without family and friends. A leper could not live within the city walls or eat with fellow Jews. A leper could never be touched by someone because the leper was considered "unclean," his illness the result of some grievous sin.

We now call leprosy Hansen's Disease, and we have learned how to treat it. We no longer exile people who have contracted it to communities far off the beaten path of society. We no longer attribute leprosy to the result of some prior sin. It occurs to me that our "modern leprosy" has become the disease of AIDS. When I see how society seeks to ostracize people with AIDS, I begin to wonder if they feel like that leper felt. I know that they are judged by many groups in society, Christians included. I see their situation as a striking example of life's ambiguity over good and bad in the same setting.

Notice what it took to change the leper's situation: the healing touch of Jesus. Throughout the Gospels, it is Jesus' touch which brings good from bad. It has nothing to do with the "moral fiber" of the person making the request. Remember the story of the adulterous woman? Did Jesus ask her to change her ways and then come back to him? Of course not. To be sure he did send her off with the command to "go and sin no more." However, that was a challenge to respond and not a condition! Jesus also sent the leper off with the command to fulfill Moses' cleanliness laws. But again, it was not a condition for being healed.

I hate to admit this, but I suspect that we Christians frequently turn our moral principles into conditions which must be met before others can receive the healing touch of the master. Unfortunately, we do it subtly and in the name of right and wrong. I hesitate to mention this because of its volatility, but the controversy in churches today over homosexuality is one example. Our public arguments over whether or not homosexuality is really a sin has obscured the need to extend the healing touch of Jesus to those in our congregations who are gay or lesbian. It is an issue filled with ambiguity. It is not a matter of black or white. But we must not lose sight of the fact that those on the receiving end of the church's judgments are persons who are valued by God and whose need for Jesus' healing touch is every bit the same as ours.

There is one other element in this story which is important to notice. After Jesus healed the leper and told him to fulfill the Mosaic conditions for cleanliness, he also warned him not to tell anyone about how this all happened. However, the leper could not keep quiet. The change in his life was so powerful that it prompted the response of personal witness about his experience. When Jesus touches your life, how do you respond? Do you tell others? Are you eager to share your experience of God's grace? Are you eager to share what you have with others who do not have?

I'll be blunt about this: personal witness and personal stewardship are not church membership requirements. They are a natural result of being touched by the grace of God. As a church member, are you required to do personal evangelism? Are you required to tithe of your time, talent, and treasure? The answer is, "No!" However, I will be equally direct and say that once you have experienced the healing touch of Jesus at the center of your soul, you will *want* to respond! You won't be able to contain yourself. It doesn't make any difference whether that touch has been physical or spiritual, the results are the same.

My prayer for all of us this morning is that God will help us stay open to the touch of Jesus. I pray that we will have the trust and courage of that leper to seek out that touch even when we don't feel worthy to receive it. I pray that we would have compassion for those whom others label as unacceptable and seek to accept them as already included in God's gracious embrace. I pray that the power of the Master's healing touch would produce the overwhelming response of wanting to tell others about the wideness in God's mercy.

Your Sins Are Forgiven

This morning Mark tells us about the healing of a paralyzed man. This episode goes to the heart of Jesus' approach to the needs of people. Throughout the Gospels we see his concern for the physical dimensions of life and for human suffering. "He had compassion on them" is a common phrase describing his response to the people with whom he came in contact.

However, this morning's event leaves no question that Jesus' primary concern was the spiritual needs of people. Not that their physical needs were unimportant. It was a matter of which came first. What good was it to heal this man's legs if he did not know where he should walk or why he should walk there?

Imagine that you were one of those who brought that man to Jesus. Picture the hope that you came with for the healing you wanted for your friend. Then imagine your reaction when the first words Jesus spoke were, "Your sins are forgiven." What would you have felt?

I am intrigued by Jesus' comment to the scribes who objected to his actions. Which is easier to say, "Your sins are forgiven," or "Get up and walk"? These two phrases are descriptive of the kinds of ministry done by the church today. But I found myself wondering if we have put them in the same order that Jesus put them.

In the past two generations we have worked hard to meet the physical needs of people. We have developed a network of places where the homeless can stay during the cold months of the year. We have set up food pantries in almost every community so that the hungry can be fed.

We have established advocacy networks to work with government and have fought for the civil rights of those in society who are disenfranchised. We have enhanced our response to natural disasters so that when a hurricane strikes, the resources of millions of church people are brought in to alleviate the suffering.

The church is involved in health care needs through its hospitals and social service agencies. Today it is only a matter of moments before a fully equipped ambulance with trained medical technicians arrives at a home or accident scene to save lives. Because of advances in medicine, people are now living longer, so there are more mornings that we will get up and walk than our grandparents had.

All this testifies to our concern that people will be able to get up and walk. On the level of material and physical need, the picture is bright and getting brighter. Yet, despite all our efforts, the eyes of people are still empty and fearful. Political demagogues find eager followers for their offers of security at the expense of freedom and justice. New age spirituality promises to fill the vacuum in peoples' souls with its brand of religion. Add to it a pinch of corruption in government, a dash of drive-by shootings, a cup of racism, and garnish with widespread traffic in drugs, and what we have is a bad recipe for the happiness of humanity.

It is not that we have ignored this emptiness. Society has developed a billion dollar entertainment industry whose prime function is to provide an escape — an opportunity to forget ourselves and the "soul sickness" of our age. And if that doesn't do the job, we throw ourselves into our work or our school activities or our household chores, only to discover at the end of a day we are jittery and tense, not merely physically tired.

Which is easier to say: "Get up and walk," or "Your sins are forgiven"? Perhaps we have been so focused on helping people get up and walk, that we have neglected addressing clearly the emptiness which is filled only by hearing, "Your sins are forgiven." It would appear that the word "sin" does not seem to be relevant in a society that has become the healthiest, longest-lived, most comfortable, and most technologically advanced that the world has ever known.

"Your sins are forgiven." We still need to hear those words. They are words of hope for those whose lives are disfigured by discontent and frustration. They are words of purpose for those who have become warped by the drive to carve out a place in the sun on their terms. They are words of direction for those who have strayed from living the way God intended humanity to live.

They are the words which, over the centuries, have drawn people to the cross of Jesus Christ. In the shadow of that cross there is a strange sense of peace. There we know that we are loved and accepted — not because of our brains or wit or good looks or career — not because we are better than someone else. At the foot of the cross we know that we are accepted simply for who we are — irreplaceable and infinitely worthwhile in the eyes of God!

The simplest analogy (and yet, the best I have heard) is the small child who is blessed with wise and loving parents. These parents love their child regardless of whether she is dull-witted or bright — regardless of whether he is homely or handsome — regardless of whether the child is devilish or well-behaved. With an assurance that he or she does not consciously recognize, it is this child who bounds out of the house to play because he or she knows that he or she is accepted, forgiven, and loved.

Call it "salvation." Call it whatever you like. It is what God has given to us. It is what we, God's people, have to share with our world today. The rest of it is merely commentary. "Your sins are forgiven!" This is what makes it possible for us to go out into the world with a sense of confidence that we are part of God's creative answer to the needs of our times.

> *"Which is easier to say, 'Your sins are forgiven,' or to say, 'Stand up and take your mat and walk'? But so that you may know that the Son of Man has authority on earth to forgive sins — he said to the paralytic — 'I say to you, stand up, take your mat and go to your home.' And the man stood up, and immediately took the mat and went out before all of them; so that they were all amazed and glorified God, saying, 'We have never seen anything like this!'"* — Mark 2:9-12

New Wine In New Wineskins

We humans are often schizophrenic when it comes to the old and the new. On one hand, we are creatures of tradition. We follow the same daily routine. We sit in the same pew at worship. We find comfort in things which are familiar. Change is something we'd rather avoid. On the other hand, we often seek those activities and items which have the potential to rescue us from the abyss of boredom — bigger houses — exotic vacations — fancier cars.

Actually, this is just the tip of the iceberg. All too often we find ourselves caught up in destructive behavior but are hesitant to confront it and make changes because we are afraid of the new and unknown. I also wonder how often we act out our boredom in ways that are unhealthy and hurtful. The writer of John's Gospel frankly acknowledges this phenomena in his opening chapter when he speaks about people preferring to live in darkness. Because this characteristic is ingrained in human nature, we need some outside help if we are to move out of our darkness and into the light of the new.

This morning we hear Jesus telling us that his mission and purpose are to do exactly that. He uses imagery that is unfamiliar to us in these days of bottled wine. Nevertheless, if we can get behind that imagery, we will discover a new dimension to life, which is so powerful that it cannot be contained by our old ways of doing things.

Let's talk about old wineskins first. I think about the shootings that have taken place in schools and that have been perpetrated by young people who are barely out of childhood. I think about the gang wars which are taking place in the neighborhoods of cities in which innocent bystanders get shot because they were simply in the wrong place at the wrong time.

I think about the fighting that is taking place in various parts of the world. Whether it goes by the name of ethnic cleansing or civil war makes no difference. People are still needlessly dying because the political powers that be are seeking to strengthen their control. What can possibly possess all these people to do the things they are doing? Can't they see the destructive nature of their actions?

I think about the racial and economic barriers that divide communities and neighborhoods. I see people who are trapped in poverty or in run-down housing projects or in jobs that pay less than a living wage. I think of people who have tried to improve their quality of life but found the doors closed because they were of the wrong ethnic background. The list is endless. Just pick up your morning newspaper or turn on a television newscast.

The discouraging part of all this is that it is not new. The methods of destroying life may have changed from spears to handguns, but the sin and evil in the hearts of those doing it have been the same since the beginning of time when Cain killed his brother Abel out of jealousy. Is there any hope for something new? The gospel proclaims the answer to be a resounding "Yes!" The power of God is like new wine in fresh wineskins, even when the "old" appears to be entrenched in the fabric of humanity.

This world still belongs to God, the creator of it all. Remember the words of a hymn we often sing: "This is my Father's world; Oh, let me not forget That though the wrong seems oft so strong, God is the ruler yet" (Maltbie D. Babcock). Nations may rattle their military weapons. Gangs may battle for turf control. But the one who is still in charge is God!

That brings me to the new wine that Jesus talks about. We often forget that God is still in control because we measure God's power in human terms. We wonder why God doesn't use the immeasurable power at God's command to step in and wipe out evil. We wonder why God doesn't assemble an army of angels to thwart injustice and oppression. That's where we miss God's message. The new wine of God's power is focused in a different kind of weapon. It is found on a *cross*! It is the crucified one, Jesus — God's power made known in weakness.

Rather than looking for new life in the pleasures that life offers, God calls us to find new life in Jesus. He was hardly a mighty warrior or a conquering hero. But his life, death, and resurrection on behalf of all humanity have restored creation back to its creator. That, my friends, is the ultimate in power!

Where do we find this new kind of life? Where do we meet this new kind of power? We meet it first in Holy Baptism in which God uses water and God's word to change us into new persons. In this event, God's powerful grace takes root in our life, even though it happens to most of us at a time when we do not realize what is going on around us. For those who are baptized at a later age, it is God's own Spirit who touches hearts and souls and calls repentant sinners who are tired of destructive living into a new way of living.

Much has been made in our generation of our renewable natural resources. The wonder of our baptism is that it is a daily renewable resource. Every day is a new day for us. Every day God wipes the slate of our sins blank and gives us a brand new opportunity to live for God. Every day is a new beginning to experience the richness and joy of our Creator's grace. Over the years I have discovered that a fair number of good folks still harbor secret guilt over some of their past sins. Forget them! Set them aside! God has forgiven them and God has forgotten them.

There is a second place where we meet this new kind of power — in the sacrament of Holy Communion. When I think that God has the power to make every person bow down at God's feet in worship, I am awestruck about the simple way in which God moves mountains through bread broken and wine poured. Here is what is truly new. "This is my body broken for you. This is my blood shed for your sins." It is this living presence of Christ that makes us new each time we share it alongside our sisters and brothers in faith. As Saint Paul puts it, "If any one is in Christ, he is a new creation; the old has passed away, behold the new has come" (2 Corinthians 5:17).

Notice that the setting for this sacramental power is communal. New life in Christ is never a "solo" experience. I think of people who have told me that they don't need to come to church because they have their own personal relationship with God. That's not what I read in the Bible. The new wineskin of God's new kind of power is the body of Christ, the Church. I realize that the Church has not been a perfect institution over the centuries. I realize that we still have debates over dogma. I realize that we still use humanly contrived notions to avoid sitting with each other at our Lord's table of grace. But the scriptural reality remains: God comes to us through the community of faith. Please remember Jesus' high priestly prayer that, indeed, the time will come when we will all be one in him.

New wine in new wineskins is a new kind of power for a new kind of living. May God grant us grace to let go of the old and embrace the new.

**Transfiguration Of The Lord
(Last Sunday After Epiphany)
Mark 9:2-9**

Missing The Point

Have you ever been in a group of people where someone told a joke and everyone else laughed except you? "I don't get it. I missed the point." Or have you ever been in the middle of a discussion where another person makes a persuasive point and everyone else nods their head in agreement — except you? "I don't get it. I missed the point."

That's sometimes how it is with life — sometimes we miss the point of it. Sometimes life doesn't make any sense. We experience disappointment, or our days seem filled with meaningless activity, or we are faced with crisis upon crisis. Sometimes we just can't figure it out. We miss the point. Like when we miss the point of a joke, we feel as if we have been missing out on the fun of it all. What's the sense of it all?

The same can happen to faith. We can sometimes feel like there is no joy in being a follower of Jesus because we can't make sense of what it's all about. We miss the point of what discipleship is all about. Today's Gospel story of the transfiguration of Jesus is about a similar experience. Jesus took Peter, James, and John on the top of a mountain, evidently to give them a special revelation of who he really was.

Perhaps it was to confirm the confession that Peter had made for the other disciples just a week earlier. Perhaps it was to prepare them for the events of his suffering and death which lay ahead. Whatever his reason, Peter and his friends completely missed the point of it! Which, by the way, is a theme that runs throughout Mark's entire Gospel. Jesus would teach or heal or tell parables, but his disciples would not understand the meaning or purpose of them. I find it strange that Jesus' messiahship was not understood by those closest to him.

Back to the top of that mountain. If we are not steeped in Jewish tradition, we really can't understand how dramatic that mountaintop experience was for those three men. Moses and Elijah were two of the great "heros" of the Jewish faith. It was like having a ring-side seat on heaven. To help you visualize the drama, imagine that your third grade school teacher took you to the top of a mountain where he or she was joined by George Washington and Abraham Lincoln. That's the kind of drama it was for those disciples.

But Peter missed the point. "Lord, this is really great stuff! This is quite a show. Let's build three tents — one for you, one for Moses and one for Elijah." Jesus was giving them a *once in a lifetime* revelation, but Peter wanted to make it *permanent*. He wanted to put up three tents so that he could keep the show going. But he missed the point that this was a special experience that was not intended to be repeated.

We're not much different 2,000 years later. We want to institutionalize the dramatic so that we can find a spiritual shot in the arm when we need to counteract the boredom of the routine. We build tents out of tradition so that we can contain Jesus and the heros of faith, and then sit back and "enjoy the show." Some Christians even insist that dramatic experiences are the normative ones and that one's faith is lacking if they don't happen regularly.

Jesus didn't respond to Peter's idea. And he doesn't respond to our attempts to build tents, either. That's because he knew that even greater things were going to happen that would reveal the magnificence of God's glory. Notice what I said: *reveal the magnificence of God's glory.*

That's where Moses and Elijah fit into the story. Each of these heroes had an experience of the magnificence of God's glory that became important to the whole community of faith. Moses' experience also took place on a mountaintop — on Mount Sinai where God gave him the Ten Commandments. On that mountain the lightning flashed and the thunder rolled and the whole mountain was covered with the fiery glory of God. And when Moses came down from the mountain, his face glowed brightly because he had been in the direct presence of the glory of God.

Elijah, the prophet, had been discouraged because he thought that he was the only one in Israel still worshiping the true God. And so, God sent him up on a mountaintop where God had arranged a contest between Elijah and the prophets of Baal. The prophets of Baal set up their altars and sacrifices and prayed to Baal to come down and burn up their offerings. But nothing happened. At day's end, Elijah set up his altar and even doused it with water. As he prayed, God revealed his glory by sending fire from heaven which burned up the offering, the stone altar, the water, and even the ground on which it stood.

Jesus was setting the stage for the greatest revelation of God's glory — a revelation that was not to human beings, but through a human being. "This is my beloved son ..." God had come directly into the midst of life — not through a law given to Moses or through words uttered by a prophet — but through a living human being! This is not a "God from a Distance" like Bette Middler's song goes, but God in the flesh! God among us! God right here!

When the disciples tried to contain it, the vision disappeared. And Jesus led them down from the mountain toward the greatest vision of God's glory yet to come: *a cross and an empty tomb!* A rugged cross and a rough-hewn grave. There's the true glory of God. But there must be a mistake somewhere. Glory is supposed to be "glorious." Glory is supposed to be "spectacular." Glory is supposed to be "magnificent." The cross and tomb are none of these. Rather, they are the marks of a suffering servant who gave his life as a ransom for humankind.

Let me make a long story short. It wasn't until Pentecost and the coming of the Holy Spirit that Peter and the disciples finally "got the point." But when they did, the purpose of their lives took on a new dimension. They started doing the things that Jesus did when he was with them — teaching, healing, forgiving. They even did some of the miracles that he had done. But most important, they became witnesses to this glory of God that had been with them in Jesus.

They began telling others about this glorious God whose forgiving love had been made real for them in Jesus Christ who died and then was raised from death. That's the purpose of Mark's Gospel: The followers of Jesus have been given the task of telling others the good news about this glory of God.

The purpose of faith is not to have "spectacular" and "dramatic" religious experiences for ourselves. The task of faith is to tell others! And it is the Holy Spirit that moves us to do that. The Spirit given in baptism and nourished through scripture and the sacraments. The Spirit who calls us to reflect God's glory in our lives.

I know what you're thinking: I don't always feel like that. I'm not always loving and forgiving and kind like Jesus. I sometimes have doubts and fears and questions. I have failings and shortcomings and sins. Don't be discouraged! We have the same answer for failure and guilt and doubt that the disciples had — Jesus Christ, God's answer to it all!

Jesus is not only our example, he is also the power that makes us able to follow him! He is the forgiveness and renewer when we fail to follow! That's the point of it all that we dare never miss! This cross — this empty tomb — has made it possible for "failing me" to be transfigured once again into one of God's beloved children who are so pleasing to him!

Sermons On The Gospel Readings

For Sundays In
Lent And Easter

Robert A. Noblett

For
Russell G. Edwards
and
The Reverend Dr. Donald B. Morris

and in memory of
Wilbur F. "Bill" Napier

Each of whom, by word and deed,
encouraged my ministry, blessed my life,
and showed me what it means to be a man.

Preface

These sermons, with one exception, were all preached at the First Congregational Church (UCC) of Kalamazoo, Michigan. They commence with Ash Wednesday and continue through the Ascension of Jesus Christ, and as such, deal with various themes of the Lenten/Easter period.

I am grateful to my congregation for its unswerving support and encouragement. In a time that is rife with religious changes, fads, and special challenges, I salute my congregation for its constancy and dedication. As one who came kicking and screaming into the computer age, my thanks as well to our office manager, Becky Ramsey, for her computer counsel as I developed this manuscript.

Most especially, my gratitude goes out to my loving wife Ruth for her sensitivity to the peculiarities of my calling, and her invaluable technical help in preparing this volume for publication.

It is my faith that in places small and large all over the globe, God continues to use the preaching event as an exciting time of self-disclosure.

Robert A. Noblett
Kalamazoo, Michigan

Heaven's Applause

Some words fall into the mud puddle, are never cleaned off, and become permanently tarnished by the mud that was never removed. Piety is such a word. Think about the way you have heard it used. Usually it has a pejorative taint to it.

Bishop Spong of the Episcopal Church has certainly caught religious people's attention. The bishop was interviewed recently and spoke of how he didn't much like religious people. He went on to say that he often finds them petty, small-minded, and prejudiced. Those are precisely the kind of people who come to mind when we think of folks who are pious. You have met them and so have I. Thomas Merton once referred to them as "plaster saints."

Happily, not all church people are like that, but enough of them are, enough of the time, to warrant attention. Obviously that has always been so because Matthew takes note of them.

Please note that Matthew is talking not about piety per se, but a particular kind of piety. So let's first get out the hose and clean off the caked mud that has gathered around this word.

The word comes from Latin roots that mean dutifulness and dutiful. Synonyms would include devoutness, devotion, godliness, reverence, and humility. So a person of piety, or a pious person, is one who is dedicated to the things of God. We get a flavor for the essence of piety, in contrast to a besmirched variety, in some lines from Wordsworth:

My heart leaps up when I behold
a rainbow in the sky;

85

So it was when my life began;
So it is now I am a man;
So be it when I shall grow old,
or let me die!
The Child is father of the Man;
And I could wish my days to be
Bound each to each by natural piety.[1]

A pious person, then, is a person who takes God seriously. Henry Ward Beecher said it like this: "The strength of a man consists in finding out which way God is going, and going that way too."[2] We could alter that just slightly and say the word *piety* is "finding out which way God is going, and going that way too."

What concerns Jesus, by contrast, is a piety that is misused and therefore becomes misshapen.

People occasionally use a tool for a purpose other than its stated one. For example, if one uses a screwdriver as a crowbar, it is highly likely that the screwdriver will become bent. When that happens, it cannot be used for its intended purpose unless it is first straightened out.

Likewise with piety. Matthew tells us about people who practice it "before others in order to be seen by them," and that's not piety, but misshapen piety that comes out as spiritual exhibitionism, a form of religious immaturity.

One of the dangers of wearing a cordless microphone is that you will forget to turn it off, with the unfortunate consequence that everything you think you are saying privately is being broadcast. People who suffer from a misshapen piety make a conscious decision to leave the mike on because they want other people to know what they are doing. You may remember that old line from Mark Twain to the effect that when some people discharge their responsibilities, you can hear the report for miles around. That's what misshapen piety is all about.

Jesus discusses this issue as it relates to three aspects of faith — giving, praying, and fasting — and in each instance the misshapen piety comes — like cereal boxes used to — with a little prize. In each context Jesus' comment is the same: "Truly, I tell you, they have received their reward." And what's the reward? Of course, it's the adulation of others. We all want to be appropriately saluted for doing a good job, but require that salute too much and the tail begins to wag the dog — good things being done for wrong reasons. After a time, our needfulness undermines and threatens the good we have set out to do.

Performers usually bow at the end their performances and the bowing, of course, is intended to be an acknowledgment of the audience's applause. It's the gracious thing to do. But I find myself wondering whether it is more than that. What if the performer stood there bolt upright and let the applause hit him squarely in the face, treating the applause as his due? Would not that be vainglory of the highest order? Therefore the bowing not only acknowledges the applause, but even more importantly, it physically and symbolically signals to ourselves and others that we are derived and indebted, recipients of far more than we can ever give back.

What John Flavel once said of ministers is true for every calling: "Ministers are like trumpets, which make no sound if breath be not breathed into them. Or like Ezekial's wheels, which move not unless the Spirit move them. Or like Elisha's servants whose presence does no good unless Elisha's spirit be there also."[3]

True piety acknowledges its indebtedness.

And finally, let it be said that such piety does have its just reward. Jesus says that those with a misshapen piety will "have no reward from your Father in heaven" (Matthew 6:1). The truly pious do.

What kind of reward do you suppose that is? Clearly it is not a reward after the fashion of a carrot enticingly dangled in the hope that we will do what we should be doing anyway. Rather, it is that sense of satisfaction and quiet delight that follows in the wake of doing something that we know, in our heart of hearts, to be in sync with what is ultimately in keeping with the wishes of God. What's more, it is a satisfaction and delight that is all the sweeter and purer because it is between us and God. The longer I live the surer I am that God sees the heart for what it holds and grants the heart that sense of well-being we awkwardly refer to as a reward.

Ultimately it does not matter whether what we do is acknowledged in a plaque, or written on a piece of paper, or covered in the press, or carried on the Internet, or announced on the evening news. The only applause that really matters — and really lasts — is the applause of heaven. When you feel that applause, you'll really know you did "good."

---

1. John Bartlett, *Familiar Quotations* (Boston: Little, Brown and Company, 1955), p. 406.

2. Margaret Pepper, *The Harper Religious & Inspirational Quotation Companion* (New York: Harper & Row, Publishers, 1989), p. 318.

3. John W. Doberstein, *The Minister's Prayer Book* (London: Collins, 1964), p. 196.

Up And Running

We all have a stake in making sure that our young people get up and running. This is a given for families, but it is also true for congregational families too, for the simple and obvious reason that today's young people represent tomorrow's church leaders. Our text is about the process whereby we get up and running.

It begins with a curious picture of Jesus being baptized. On a wall somewhere in a church building you have seen an artist's depiction of this. Jesus' experience is such that he sees the opening of the heavens and out of those heavens comes the Spirit "descending like a dove on him." Jesus' baptism even has an auditory dimension. "You are my Son, the Beloved; with you I am well pleased" (Mark 1:9-11).

If you juxtapose his baptism to yours, yours probably pales in comparison. It's unlikely that it packed the kind of drama his does. But don't be so quick to underplay your experience, nor assume that nothing like this has ever happened to you. What is initially happening here has to do with a sense of being called.

When you were growing up, you played all kinds of imaginary games and in those games there were roles you gleefully fulfilled. You were the teacher, the mom, the dad, the physician, the nurse, the musician, the figure skater, or the whatever. Assuming those imaginary identities brought you hours of delight, experiences like that are enriching and enable us to begin to imagine who we might become in the future.

We can't be all those things, but eventually a clearer picture of who we are begins to take shape and in time we feel called — or led — in a particular direction. Not medicine, but teaching; not a technical field, but one that more directly deals with others; not business, but the arts; not sales, but service. It can happen gradually, almost imperceptibly, or it can suddenly dawn upon us. There is about this process, though, a sense that we alone are not calling the shots; somehow we are in the grip of a force that both compels and attracts. There is a door and we feel both drawn to it from this side and called to walk through it from the other. Such is the nature of vocation.

Vocation, too, has more to do with meaning than happiness. There is a measure of rote and tedium in any calling, but we live with that knowing that we are participating in an endeavor whose significance transcends the sometimes irritating baggage it brings with it. Medicine, teaching, fathering, mothering, working in the institutional church — point to whatever calling you will — not one is insulated from the possibility of burnout.

But then what is burnout, if not the emergence of a kind of tunnel vision whereby we cannot see the forest for the trees? Some people wear two different contact lenses, but for different reasons. With one contact, they are able to see well close at hand; with the other, they are able to see well off in the distance. In burnout, we tend to see only through the lens that grants vision up close. We become absorbed in the minute and mundane. Translate that in terms of raising children, and we see parents so focused on the daily frustrations of raising children — scheduling, transporting, managing, and all the rest — that they forget what they are ultimately about, namely the shaping of character and the fulfillment of maturity.

C. S. Lewis said it well: "To follow the vocation does not mean happiness; but once it has been heard, there is no happiness for those who do not follow."[1]

We gather weekly for public worship and one important reason for doing that is this: Worship helps us become disentangled from the trees so we can see the forest. Worship reacquaints us with both the larger picture, and the One who holds before us — and draws us into — that larger picture.

Now our text flows from calling to chastening. "And the Spirit immediately drove him out into the wilderness. He was in the wilderness forty days, tempted by Satan; and he was with the wild beasts; and the angels waited on him" (Mark 1:12-13). I am thinking of chastening in the sense of being refined and made purer in style.

Again, please do not let the imagery be off-putting for you. We too have such moments, even though we might paint the experience using different colors and figures. We call these wilderness moments, these times of testing, by other names: student teaching, field work, internship, or on-the-job training.

Some of our theological schools sit high atop hills. One can leave the din around the base of such hilltops and ascend to a place of bucolic loveliness just a block from urban sprawl. The symbolism of it does not go unnoticed, issuing in a question like this: Is the place of the church above and beyond the world, or in the world? It is, I believe, both. There is a problem in both directions: Stay in the world too long and you can lose your way; but stay in the church too long and you can become, as the old expression puts it, "so heavenly-minded that you are no earthly good."

Theological educators, as well as educators in other disciplines, know that the academic must be tempered by the practical. The late Roy Pearson once put it like this to students graduating from Andover Newton Theological School:

> *The Lord our God said to us in Horeb, "You have stayed long enough at this mountain; turn and take your journey...." It is obvious that I have no way of knowing whether all members of this graduating glass have stayed long enough at the mountain of Andover Newton. One fact, however, is clear: you have stayed long enough to qualify for your diplomas, and unless you are remaining here for further study, you are about to "turn and take your journey."*[2]

The purpose of any educational program is to prepare students so they can eventually "turn and take their journeys." It's not to keep people in school. And to ease the transition from academia to

91

the work-a-day world, most educational programs involve hands-on experiences that go on shoulder to shoulder with the presentation of theory.

Of particular note in our text is the fact that Jesus was tempted by Satan, the personification of evil. In every calling, there is present the opportunity to exploit, misuse, and abuse. Sadly in every calling there are those who succumb to these temptations: teachers, ministers, business people, doctors, social workers, psychotherapists, mothers, fathers, grandparents; in the ranks of each there are those who abuse trust and behave in wantonly selfish ways. We fool ourselves if we think the seeds of such are absent from us; always they are there. Therefore the agenda? Admit they are present and then consign them to our internal jails and throw away the key. And there is help with that assignment: "... and the angels waited on him." On us, they also wait.

Calling, chastening, and now commissioning: "Now after John was arrested, Jesus came to Galilee, proclaiming the good news of God, and saying, 'The time is fulfilled, and the kingdom of God has come near; repent, and believe in the good news' " (Mark 1:14-15). To commission is to put into service.

Among those who collect toy trains, a distinction is drawn between the collector and the runner. The collectors amass their favorite trains, put them on shelves, and just look at them. Runners are those who take the trains off the shelves, turn on the electricity, and enjoy them. We are to be in the latter camp.

In the economy of the kingdom, everyone is to be moved in the direction of being a runner, someone on the move with and for God. The pithy preacher of Ecclesiastes said it like this: there is "a time to seek, and a time to lose...." Worship and church education are seeking times — times when we seek the closeness of God and the knowledge needful to fulfill our ministries. Then we walk through the portals of the sanctuary and out into the world, there to lose ourselves in the interests of others only to — given Gospel logic — find ourselves in a deeper way.

Up and running. God knows it beats the alternative: down and crippled. Not only, though, does it beat the alternative; it is, more to the point, how God has wired us for Kingdom service. Everyone up and running — with God, for God, through God, and to God.

---

1. Quoted by Gilbert Meilaender, "Divine Summons" (*The Christian Century,* Nov. 1, 2000), p. 1111.

2. Roy Pearson, "Long Enough at the Mountain" (*Andover Newton Quarterly,* January, 1976), p. 210.

Lent 2
Mark 8:31-38

Life — From The Inside Out

Eleven people, so goes the story, were dangling from a rope beneath a helicopter in a rescue scenario. Being rescued were ten men and one woman. Word came down from the pilot that one of the eleven would have to let go; if not, everyone would perish. The woman spoke right up and said her whole life had been one of sacrifice — for her children, husband, and parents — and now she would be willing to sacrifice one last time by letting go. With that, the ten men applauded! The story's point? Never underestimate the power of a woman!

Never underestimate the power of the gospel because it too is full of surprises, reversals, paradoxes, and strategies that on the surface don't seem to make sense. If someone wants your coat, give him your cloak as well; if someone strikes the right cheek, turn the left one too; both are representative of surprising strategies that initially make us pause and scratch our heads, but the longer we live with these strategies and learn about them, the more sense they begin to make.

Anticipating what was ahead, Jesus began to acquaint his inner circle with how difficult life would become for him; it was to be short on joy and long on pain. Peter took exception to this, and having just completed a Dale Carnegie course on winning friends and influencing people, began to take Jesus to task for his foreboding anticipation. Jesus had to be more upbeat, Peter implied. Jesus would have none of it though, and in effect said to Peter that if the latter were to persist in those sentiments, he would be clearly aligning himself with the forces of Satan, not the forces of God. "For

95

you are setting your mind not on divine things but on human things," (v. 33) is the way Jesus put it.

Then Jesus presses his case to a larger group nearby: "If any want to become my followers, let them deny themselves and take up their cross and follow me. For ... those who lose their life for my sake, and for the sake of the gospel, will save it" (Mark 8:35). There we have the paradox. If you try really hard to find your life, you are going to lose it in the process.

Remember the last time a simple tune began reverberating in your head and you couldn't seem to get rid of it? Every few minutes, it would return. Clearly there was no intentional way through which you could get rid of it. But then you got involved in some other undertaking and later suddenly realized the tune was no longer going off in your ear. Paradoxically, what you wanted to achieve came when you gave up your ardent effort to make it happen.

Jesus follows up then with this question: "For what will it profit them to gain the whole world and forfeit their life?" (v. 36). What Jesus is asking reminds us of that question that asks the whereabouts of the life we have lost in the living.

Jesus, you see, turns conventional wisdom inside out and bids us live life from the inside out.

Saving our lives and gaining the world are tantamount to losing and forfeiting those lives, and that happens, Jesus suggests, when we live life from the outside in. The pressure to live from the outside in is strong indeed.

This pressure is something advertisers have long known and is why, according to one estimate, the average adult encounters 3,000 advertisements each day. Advertisements cover the gamut, all the way from products that address personal hygiene to plans for covering the cost of your funeral so you won't be a burden to your children. Professor James Twitchell from the University of Florida in Gainsville contends that many of modern advertising's founders ironically had religious backgrounds. It was a Baptist minister's son, Bruce Barton, who co-founded the large ad agency Batten, Barton, Durstine & Osborne.

The professor points out that the founders of modern advertising modeled their messages after parables they heard. In selling a product like deodorant, a supplicant consults another person who gives witness: "If your deodorant doesn't hold up past 1:30 p.m., try this brand instead and suddenly your whole life — including its romantic dimension — will fall into place beautifully." One secular sin (halitosis or dandruff or whatever) after another will fall as it is confronted by this or that product.[1]

Powerful forces try to shape the decisions we make: the houses we live in and where they are located; the cars we drive (whose manufacturers are not above taking a word that belongs to the religious community like "soul" and using it to push their vehicles); the clothes we wear; the food we eat; the beverages we consume; the places we vacation; and all that is not even a tiny part of the iceberg's tip.

But it's much more than advertising. We can also subtly teach our children that what's most important in life is pleasing other people, setting out on a course whereby we introduce them to the dynamics of being excessively and fawningly nice, even when that course begins to undermine their own sense of integrity and rightness. The prize in all this? — The assumption that such maneuvers will mean we are accepted and respected by other people. The opposite, in fact, is what is going to happen.

Were I to create a short list of people who live from the outside in, it would include people who don't know what their political beliefs are until they've read their favorite political columnist; don't know what books they want to read until Oprah tells them; don't know how to decorate for Christmas until Martha Stewart directs them; don't know what to believe until their denomination tells them; don't know what to wear until they have consulted a fashion guru; don't know how to respond to the controversial issues of the day until they check their windsocks to see which way the breeze is blowing.

People with this pattern are like submarines cruising through life at periscope depth and they will not come to the surface until they have surveyed the surrounding territory, making sure that their emergence will occur within optimal conditions for safety from others they perceive to be potentially menacing critics.

Living life from the outside in — we have all been there at one point or another in our journeys. And when we are accurately so described, we are the same folks Jesus had in mind when he talked about people who have gained the whole world, but forfeited their lives.

We've gotten it backwards, Jesus says. Instead, turn matters inside out and live from the inside out.

I recently read a fascinating news story about a fifteen-year-old girl who was triumphantly strolling out of a Gap store with her new $150 black leather coat when her cell phone rang. Of all people, it was her mother. Said Mother, "A leather jacket? Are you sure this is what you need with your money?"

Now here's the kicker. Although Mother was more than 100 miles away, she still knew what her daughter was doing, thanks to an instant e-mail from Pocketcard Inc. Every time this daughter uses her mother's debit card, Pocketcard Inc. e-mails mom and alerts her. Soon it will be possible for parents to download live Web-cam videos from home on their cell phones and see precisely what's going on in their absence.

Technology is more and more awesome and impressive, but is there not a downside to all of this? What good is the technology if children are not being helped with the creation of an internal set of controls, making self-governance possible? We are talking here about the development of character, and parents do their children no good if they simply use technology as a further extension of discipline externally applied and not eventually internally cultivated. Self-control is absolutely necessary if one wants a life worth the living.

Or think of the value and joy of being soulful instead of reactive and shallow.

A friend had a rather large tree taken down recently. It looked basically healthy, but was very close to his driveway, and leaning in an ominous way. When the trunk was cut into fireplace lengths, he was surprised to discover that the tree was rotting from the inside out.

When we do not develop soulfulness, we run the risk of beginning to rot from the inside out.

By contrast, think of a body of water that is spring-fed or a tract of land that is loam. Both images convey richness, replenishment, creativity, receptivity, containment, and more.

Soulful people are not rotting from the inside out; they are living from the inside out. Whenever we are understanding, or forgiving, or accepting, or creative or wise, we are evidencing soulfulness. Tending to our interiority, whether it be through reflection, artistic exposure, wonderment, or pensiveness, indicates soulfulness.

Then, as well, soulfulness has to do with the making of meaning. It interprets and names. It takes the "sound and fury" of Shakespeare's *Macbeth* and says, unlike the bard, such has significance. It reads, and not reacts, to human behavior; it sees in the words of others disclosures that even they may not, in the short term, see. It understands how each human life is a mini-series, featuring the grand themes written about by philosophers and theologians, musically expressed by the great composers, and painted by the great artists.

Sam Miller was getting at this fifty years ago when, in a little volume titled *The Life of the Soul*, he wrote this about the grand stories of faith:

> *The stories of Eden, the Tower of Babel, the parables and the life of Christ all have truths that evade the literal nets of the historically wise. They are the ageless formulary in concrete terms of unending human experience. In all of them the eternal and historical meet and fulfill each other in such perfection that the truth is neither abstract nor merely local. It becomes rooted in life, but not limited by time or space. To be on the outside of such things, to be unable to use them, is indeed to be poor in spiritual health, for in them are the ample means of expression and communion for the soul.*[2]

Life — from the outside in or inside out? I believe that what we call eternal life is what's at issue. That's what hangs in the balance as we decide which way we will go.

1. Richard and Joyce Wolkomir, "You Are What You Buy" (*Smithsonian*, October, 2000), p. 102.

2. Samuel H. Miller, *The Life of the Soul* (New York and Evanston: Harper & Row, Publishers, 1951), p. 86.

Holy Vexation

We have all probably had the experience of being in the presence of someone who is normally composed and tranquil, and having that person suddenly erupt. A topic is introduced and immediately goes to the quick. It all seems so out of character.

I can imagine Christian folks having a similar reaction to this story (found, incidentally, in all of the Gospels) of Jesus cleansing the temple. If you are fifty years or older and remember singing the old gospel song that talks about Jesus calling us "softly and tenderly," this story gets your attention. If you are any age and have had contact with violence in your personal and/or family life, this story gets your attention. Or, if you are familiar with the many times in the ministry of Jesus when his behavior is marked by patience, compassion, and gentleness, again, this story gets your attention. It has that stinging quality we associate with anyone who is on a tare. Considering Jesus' usual deportment, this episode from Jesus' life seems more acute than chronic, more an unusual explosion than a lifestyle.

So what do we do with it? What is in this story you can take home and feast on this week?

It is popular, for openers, to see in this story evidence for the humanness of Jesus. Like all of us, Jesus got angry and received anger too. Raymond Council captured vexation in Jesus' life in a litany he wrote years back. The worship leader in this litany lists those times of vexation. They go as follows:

Lord, you who were angry at Simon Peter and called
  him Satan,
Lord, you who were angry at the super religious and
  compared them to whitewashed tombs full of death,
Lord, you who were angry at the moneylenders and
  overturned their tables,
Lord, you who were angry at those who gave a scor-
  pion calling it a fish and a stone calling it bread,
Lord, you who were angry at all that keeps people sepa-
  rated, walled in, cut off and locked up,
Lord, you at whom the world was angry and who took
  upon yourself that rage, endured and transformed
  it through the cross ...[1]

As members of the Christian community we might, by extension,
say to ourselves: "It's okay for me to be angry, as well."

But look at the difference between what triggers our anger and
what led Jesus to become vexed. We are apt to get vexed when the
supermarket fails to open that additional lane when all the others
are backed up; when we encounter a driver going fifty miles an
hour in a seventy mile an hour zone; when someone grabs the very
Beanie Baby we wanted and there are no more. A news story out of
Grand Rapids told of how a trucker became enraged because an
85-year-old man maneuvered his car in a way that rankled the
trucker. The trucker subsequently saw the man pull into a gas station. A quarter of a mile later, the trucker pulled over to the side of
the road, ran back the quarter of a mile to that gas station, and — as
the 85-year-old was filling his gas tank — pommeled him to the
ground. Such behavior is categorically inexcusable.

Jesus' anger was light years from the kind of vexation that often
grabs us. It was vexation directed at grave miscarriages of what was
just, civil, and pleasing to God. It is the counsel of the psalter that we
"be angry, but sin not" (Psalm 4:4). Jesus knew how to be angry
without sinning; we often find it difficult to do that.

But there is more here than just an example of Jesus' vexation,
and finding in his, justification for ours. There is something about
Jesus' vexation that transcends the immediate focus of his attention. Look with me for a moment at the people selling cattle, sheep,

and doves, and the money changers. All this was part of the temple machinery. Cattle, sheep, and doves were used as burnt offerings, and since Passover was a pilgrimage feast, people would have come from long distances and couldn't bring such animals with them. What's more, the temple tax could not be paid with Greek or Roman coinage because these coins carried a human image (the emperor's head) and foreign currency had to be changed into legal currency; hence the need for the money changers. Were there abuses in this system? Of course there were. But Jesus, as painted by John, is concerned about the entire system. As has always been the case, religious institutions can tragically lose focus, major on minors, and become stumbling blocks to the very ends for which they were created in the first place.

Certainly this can happen to the clergy who are a part of such institutions. It's not uncommon for clergy to be approached by people who want them to supplement their incomes by hawking this or that product within the life of a congregation. Imagine, for example, a minister taking communion to someone's home and then, following the communion service, awkwardly segueing to the point where he says: "By the way, did I tell you about this jim-dandy product I am now making available that will remove resistant grease stains, help your tomatoes grow, and cure your arthritis when topically applied?" Clearly this would constitute pastoral abuse.

But look as well at the institution itself. It is deceptively easy to lose sight of why we are here and, like an unmanned garden hose to which a powerful force of water is introduced, jerkingly squander our energies in any number of directions.

Any parish worth its salt has a governing body of some sort that oversees various boards and committees. When it comes to undertakings like securing ushers and greeters and church school teachers, or running out to buy grape juice for communion, it is absolutely essential that people see the deeper reasons for doing what they are doing, else they fall prey to a sense of roteness void of meaning. This is why Paul counseled the Corinthians to "... do everything for the glory of God" (1 Corinthians 10:31). Ultimately we are here not to do all that we do as ends in themselves; we do them because we understand them to be manifestions of our mission to share the love and purposes of God as we have come to know them in Jesus of Nazareth.

Primarily the cross is a symbolic reminder of what has been wrought in Jesus the Christ. But it is also a reminder of the need for both the horizontal and vertical dimensions in life. The board and committee work, the programs we make possible, the monies we give, the bulletins we run and all the rest has to do with the horizontal dimension. But the horizontal can only be placed in its proper context when it is seen against the vertical. The ubiquitous spire that sits atop so many worship centers is a visible reminder of this vertical dimension that gives meaning to all that we do, however mundane and routine it may seem at the time.

Only penultimately are we in the educational business, the emergency aid business, the space lending business, the publication business, the music business, the day care business, the building maintenance business or the grant business; ultimately we are in the salvific business and all that we do should be soaked to the core with, and radiate to the greatest extent possible, a passion for making available to folks the good news of what has come to pass in and through Jesus, who for the Christian community is the Christ. That is the one essence that makes us different from a school, or a social agency, or a business, or an employer, or a performance center.

So what we have in the end here is, yes, a story of vexation, but a story of vexation that focuses not on what is trivial and excusable, but on what is absolutely central and critical, and that kind of vexation can only rightly be modified by the adjective *holy*. John is writing this many decades after Jesus' death and resurrection, and he is writing to help the people of God see that their proper focus is not ultimately on matters institutional, but on the figure of Jesus and what Jesus would have us be about. How easy it is to focus on, and become split over, matters related to Jesus himself, when Jesus would have rather have us focused elsewhere. How deceptively easy it is to become caught up in dynamics related to the perpetuation of the institution and its own interests, having lost sight of matters related to fundamental mission.

Jesus says to the temple vendors: "Stop making my Father's house a marketplace!" (v. 16). And John has Jesus' disciples remembering a text from the Psalter that applies: "Zeal for your house will consume me" (Psalm 69:9) — a reference to the religious establishment and the role it would play in his death. In so many words, Jesus is saying to his and succeeding generations: Beware of becoming so caught up in perpetuating what is ancillary, derivative and secondary that you lose sight of what is primary, essential, and foremost.

This is not just a problem of religious institutions; it is a problem throughout the culture. It is lawyers spending inordinate amounts of time at the sidebar; it is public school teachers having to tend to matters that used to be the province of Mom and Dad; it is the medical doctor having to spend inordinate amounts of time on insurance issues; it is insurance companies making decisions that intrude significantly on the physician's prerogatives in providing medical care; it is even the automobile companies who no longer want to sell me a means of conveyance from one place to another, but have gone into the theological business by telling me that their product is going to meet the needs of my soul!

There is a time for holy vexation, a time to rise up and remind the church that its fundamental passion is its abiding love for God and the things of God.

Something that Harry Fosdick wrote in 1952 sounds amazingly applicable today:

> *The real God is Purpose, hard at work getting something done on earth to redeem our race from its sin and misery, calling every man to some task which, in the place where he is put, no one can do in his stead.*
>
> *Ah, Church of Christ, the proclamation of such faith is your task today. You fritter away your strength on trivial sectarianisms. You insult the intelligent and alienate the serious with petty dogmatisms that do not matter. You fiddle trifling tunes while the world burns. But back of all that, still the glory of the true church within the church, is a message without which mankind is doomed. If you really believe the Christian gospel —*

God behind us, his cause committed to us, his power available for us — then proclaim it, live it, implement it, for humanity's hope depends upon it.[2]

That's holy vexation, and holy vexation is very much a part of the reformed and reforming tradition in which we stand.

---

1. Raymond Council, "Lord, You Who Were Angry" (*Alive Now!*, Nashville: The Upper Room, May/June, 1983), p. 23.

2. Harry Emerson Fosdick, *A Faith For Tough Times* (New York: Harper & Brothers, Publishers, 1952), p. 124.

Placard Faith, Complex World

As you have sat in your easy chair munching on snack food during any NFL game, you have seen this sight innumerable times. The camera zeroes in on one of the end zones and just beyond the uprights, you see a person carrying a huge placard sporting the name John, followed by the numbers, 3:16. This text is one of the most famous in the Bible and it is the darling of those Christians given to cutesy evangelism. I suspect that in their view it is not cutesy — but gutsy — evangelism they are about. Be all that as it may, they are trying to lift up the winsome figure of Jesus and draw people to his message. While we may fault their methodology, they are to be applauded for their commitment and exertion.

Some of you learned this text when you were little people. A church school teacher asked you to recite it from memory and when you did so correctly, you were given a gold star. It simply and beautifully expresses the essence of our faith; and when we hear Stainer's musical setting for its truth, the beauty and richness of that truth are utterly moving. On the other hand, if you are new to — or inquiring about — the faith, this is a good place to begin. It is a text that Luther deemed "the gospel in miniature."

While people who utilize the Gospel of John for preaching and evangelistic purposes often see its focus on Jesus, the action of this Gospel is really on God. Whatever Jesus says and does through this Gospel is to be seen as an expression of who God is.

When we ask John questions about God's disposition, his enthusiastic and unequivocal answer is that God, who is alpha and omega, loves the world. Regardless of the variant feelings God may have about what goes on in this world, God's love for this world is unswerving and constant. Are there consequences for human behavior? Yes, of course there are. But those consequences are self-imposed. Drink too much and you will destroy your liver; exercise too little and eat too much, and you may have high blood pressure. We assign ourselves to such unpleasantness; it is not God doing the assigning. "For God so loved ..." says John. God still does and always will. Nothing will change that.

John goes on by relating the extent of that love. So much does God love that "he gave his only Son...." This is John reflecting on God's activity in the life of Jesus. So active through Jesus was God, says John, that to see the Son is to see the Father.

The kind of relationship being described by John can be illustrated by the relationship that exists between a composer and a symphony orchestra. When a group of musicians, under talented podium leadership, play a Mahler symphony for example, we know they have done their job well when we feel transported to the essence of what Mahler, through that particular symphony, is trying to say. The symphony becomes the vessel through which Mahler expresses his musical message.

Similarly, in the imagery of John, Jesus becomes the vessel through which God expresses love for the whole created order. To hear Jesus is to hear God, John is telling us. What Jesus did amplified, mirrored, and windowed God. Or (do I dare say it?) Jesus — in today's parlance — is an e-mail from God, beaming God's loving and inviting ways onto the screens of human hearts.

So far, so good. Loving God and reflectively expressive son. But then John launches into a condemnation conversation with the reader. There is an edge to his words. God's purpose is "so that everyone who believes in him may not perish but may have eternal life." Those who believe in God's work in Jesus are not condemned, but those who do not believe are condemned already. Here, says John, is the core of the issue: Are we going to turn to the light that is Jesus, or are we going to rummage around in the darkness of life beyond Jesus and perish, cast forever from the grace of God?

What do we, residents of the religious mainline, do with this text and its imagery, particularly when we are sensitive to the pluralistic world in which we live and want to be respectful of other religious traditions?

First, we can note that there is an understandable appeal to reductionism, to the desire to make matters simple. When people live in a culture where chocolate is in one day and out the next, where a presidential contest ends in unsettling uncertainty and where technological change occurs at a stupefyingly accelerating rate, people hunger for that which is clearly stated and easily digestible. John's statements about Jesus appeal to those who have a reductionistic bent. In effect these people say: "Look, we live in a world where there is enough uncertainty and confusion and so when it comes to my faith, I want it straight and simple." John, in these verses, obliges. Sometimes we yearn for a placard faith, given our complex world.

Two, we can give credit to John for being enthusiastic, even if enthusiasm can lead to excess. Each Gospel writer has his own slant on Jesus and what he was about, and John exhibits the passion of one who is utterly convinced of Jesus' specialness in leading us to God. Certainly part of the appeal of churches where worship involves praise music and utilizes high-tech resources can be found in their level of ardor. When gospel and glitz are wed, it is often some show! We might not be in theological agreement with such congregations, but that is no justification, on our part, for conducting ourselves with such sterility that worship takes on a level of anticipation one reaches when she is balancing her checkbook! "Let the redeemed of the Lord say so," admonishes the psalmist (Psalm 107:2), and that includes us also.

Three, we can be reminded that biblical truth is not to be found in just one location. If there are places that seem to lift up exclusiveness, there are other places where we find inconclusiveness. When Saint Paul says that nothing "can separate us from the love of God in Christ Jesus our Lord," presumably nothing means just that — nothing, including the inability to accept reducing Jesus to the creedal equivalent of a common theological pin number which, if accurately entered, will grant us access to the love and forgiveness of God.

Four, we can commend a humility befitting the children of an awesome God. Walter Lippmann once made this observation: "A man who has humility will have acquired in the last reaches of his beliefs the saving doubt of his own certainty."[1]

There is a certainty that quiets and centers us, but there is also a certainty from which we need to be saved, hence Lippmann's "saving doubt." Can we not remember times when we were certain in our assertions about another person, positively or negatively? We were sure she was as we thought she was, but then something happened in our experience of that person to make us alter our previous certainty.

To use John 3:16 and what follows as a yardstick, by which we presume to make evaluations regarding who is and who is not in God's camp, is to bestow upon ourselves an omniscience and inflation that are unfounded, dangerous, and haughty. Maybe we can somewhat accurately evaluate reading and math skills or aspects of physical prowess, but to set out to say who is, and who is not, in the folds of God's care is a mean and dicey business.

Then five, we can appeal to the largeness of God's heart. Who can say where, and in what form, the Spirit of God is at work in the hearts of people everywhere?

In Bruce Bawer's book *Stealing Jesus*, he tells of a comment made by the conservative columnist William F. Buckley at the funeral of Richard M. Clurman, a former *Time* magazine editor. "It came to me last Thursday," he said, "when the news (of Clurman's death) reached me just after midnight, that I have always subconsciously looked out for the total Christian, and when I found him he turned out to be a nonpracticing Jew."[2]

Ultimately the Bible is the story of God's love affair with the world God created. It involves countless men and women, who lived over hundreds of years, and culminates with the story of Jesus. But first and foremost it is God's story, and Jesus' story only inasmuch as Jesus brings God to us. That's what we mean by an incarnate faith.

Many people like to decorate their yards with accent lights. Those who use them and live in areas of the country with high annual snowfalls often find those lights buried under so much snow that no light is visible at all. But if one were to go out on a cold snowy night and dig through the snow at a point where she knows a light is located, she would eventually find not only the light beaming, but she would also discover the warmth of that bulb had melted away a sizeable portion of snow around that light. The work of the light had been going on all along, but looking out over the carpet of snow, one would never have known that.

I believe that on a spiritual plane, something like that is going on all the time — even when we can't see it happening. In the Christian community we talk about the light of Christ, but John tells us in the beginning of his Gospel that God is that light. So ironically this rich text, the location of which people like to put on placards at sporting events, is not about a limiting and particular approach to a parochial God, but instead it is about the magnificence of a loving God, whose overtures to men and women the world over continue to this very moment.

---

1. Margaret Pepper, *The Harper Religious & Inspirational Quotation Companion* (New York: Harper & Row, Publishers, 1989), p. 243.

2. Bruce Bawer, *Stealing Jesus* (New York: Crown Publishers, Inc., 1997), p. 322.

Lent 5
John 12:20-33

The Ministry Of Fading

We could spend our sermon time talking with you about John's Christology and how our text indicates Jesus' understanding of his impending death, but after a brief period, I would begin to see in some of your eyes that glazed look that would tell me you had gone off to a faraway place. It's true; this text is about Christology, but a Christology that comes with our names on it too. Says Jesus, "Whoever serves me must follow me, and where I am, there will my servant be also" (v. 26). Read this to mean: "What I am saying about myself applies to you also, even you living in the infancy of a new millennium."

Here's what Jesus says: "Very truly, I tell you, unless a grain of wheat falls into the earth and dies, it remains just a single grain; but if it dies, it bears much fruit" (v. 24).

One doesn't have to be a farmer to understand this. Always, and every day, we are planting seeds. Parents, teachers, advertisers, ministers, funeral directors, writers — you name the people — all are planters of seeds.

Congregational families are the matrix that births persons interested in the pastoral ministry. Congregations cry out for capable leadership and it may be that some young person being shaped in one of our families right now would make a fine pastoral minister. This doesn't happen automatically. Is there someone you know right now in our congregational family to whom you could say, "Would you consider a career in pastoral ministry?"

I have just planted a seed. Obviously there is no way of knowing whether it will produce fruit or not, but one thing is certain: no seed, no fruit.

Planted seeds are also buried seeds. Hence Jesus talks about a grain of wheat falling into the earth and dying. The seed is no good unless it does go into the ground and die. There is an intriguing line attributed to a writer named W. St. Hill Bourne: "The sower went forth sowing, The seed in secret slept."

Then too buried seeds lead to waiting planters. It's hard to wait while the seed "in secret" sleeps. All we can do is tend the seed, making sure it has the necessary moisture and nutrients. Every now and again we can fertilize, too. But primarily we wait. When it comes to people, we often speak of "waiting them out." There's a wonderful line from an old Ed Asner, Jean Stapleton movie titled *The Gathering*. Asner plays an aging business man who learns he is going to die and Stapleton plays his estranged wife. An eleventh hour rapprochement takes place. At one point the character played by Asner is reflecting on what his estranged wife has been doing all through the separation years and he remarks: "She has been sitting up in that house waiting for me to grow up."

For nine months a mom and dad wait for an embryo to grow into a person; for the next year or so they wait for the child to speak and walk; then they wait for the child to master the skills necessary to begin a program of formal education that might last up through graduate school; during the years of adolescence they simply "wait out" the youngster; and then they wait for the young adult to get up and running economically, so they can recall the credit card.

Then in time, the planted seed that became the buried seed becomes the fruitful seed. "... it bears much fruit," (v. 24) says Jesus. The child becomes a contributing adult; the visionary idea becomes a full-fledged program; the trainee becomes trained; the tune becomes a symphony. And so the process goes.

But there is a further twist to this. Jesus, as we implied when we began, sees himself as the planted and buried seed that will eventually bear much fruit. He models what we can call the ministry of fading. In a culture of shakers and movers, fading may seem to some a form of wimping out. But there is more to it than at first we might realize.

114

At the very least, fading is a form of courtesy. We have all been in groups where one person tends to do all the talking; it's as though that person has no ears and only a mouth. As we like to put it, it's hard to get a word in edgeways. If the person's loquaciousness goes on long enough, others begin to simmer, and still others will drop out of the group. Interestingly, when the preacher in Ecclesiastes is going through his litany of opposites and how each has intrinsic value, he mentions silence before speech. Everything in its season, he says, "A time to keep silence, and a time to speak ..." (3:7a). Minimally, the ministry of fading has to do with good manners and allowing others their mike time.

The ministry of fading also means that our ebbing can occasion another's flowing. If one part of the ocean didn't recede, another part couldn't flow.

A simple example of this can be seen in a recently popular television ad featuring a father and daughter at a time of transition. It is clear in the ad that the father is turning the reins of a business over to his daughter. They have worked together for some time, but Dad finally vacates his office. There is a poignant moment when the daughter is standing in her new office, looking at an earlier photograph of dad and daughter; then, as she looks out the open doorway, her father is graciously making his way out of the building.

Another common example of ebbing so that another can flow is the instructor pilot. After what the instructor takes to be a sufficient number of training hours, she gets out of the passenger's seat and signals her student that she can commence with her first solo flight. Fading instructor, flowering student. Good parents are about this maneuver in an age-appropriate manner all the time. At least those who don't want emotionally and spiritually crippled children are.

The ministry of fading can also be seen as a form of intentional depletion in the service of others. We need to save, but we can reach a point where our saving means others are losing. If four people are carrying a heavy couch and one decides to hold back and not exert himself as he could, that means the other three are being asked to carry a heavier burden. When one teacher coasts, it means that other teachers have to work harder. When a church committee of five in effect has two working members, that means three have asked two to do the work of five.

But the issue here is not just fairness, but also meaning. Jesus puts it like this: "Those who love their life lose it, and those who hate their life in this world will keep it for eternal life" (v. 25). Somehow, Jesus is saying, it's in the spending of our lives that we find them. And it's in our excessive guarding and holding of those lives that we lose them. No investment, no return. No overture, no symphony. No risk, no gain.

Then, ultimately, may it not be the truth of this teaching that our fading can become the avenue of God's coming? Isn't that what worship is all about — our stepping aside so that God can step forward?

Back in the early 1970s, a concert was given on the Boston Common by the late organ virtuoso, Virgil Fox. At that point Fox was into capes, and he cut quite a figure. He was a bit flamboyant, but one suspects he did that for a very good reason. The capes and color and pizazz certainly got people's attention, but once he got that attention, Fox ushered them into a musical kingdom where they were treated to the musical gold of someone like Bach. And when Fox did that, there came a moment when Fox faded, and Bach came into view.

Ultimately all that matters in this congregation — or any congregation — is that we fade and God comes into view.

Extravagant Gestures
In A Cost-Effective World

Families of faith that dwell in older buildings eventually have to struggle with the issue of restoring stained glass windows. Such restorations can be exceedingly costly. Those same families of faith often struggle to meet their normal operating budget responsibilities. What's more, within a short distance of most church families are community people who struggle to provide the basics for the people whom they love. Can one not therefore argue that spending thousands and thousands of dollars on stained glass repair is a form of poor and reckless stewardship?

Or perhaps there was a time when you went to an art event and you quickly spied an absolutely gorgeous vase. To your eye, it was singularly beautiful and you had to have it, and to this day you enjoy it. However it cost you $450 and every time you pass by it, you still feel a twinge of guilt. Should you have spent that much?

Our text is about such seeming extravagance. Jesus is in Bethany at the home of Simon the leper and while he is at table, an unnamed woman comes up with an alabaster jar in hand and pours over his head an extremely expensive ointment called nard. Nard was a fragrant ointment prepared from the roots and hairy stems of an aromatic Indian herb. How expensive was it? Plenty expensive. A worker in Jesus' time would have labored a full day for a denarius. In order to pay for this amount of ointment, a worker would have had to labor for three hundred days. Talk about pricey!

Her action evokes, on the part of some, a heated response. "Why was this ointment wasted in this way? For this ointment could have been sold for more than 300 denarii, and the money given to the poor" (Mark 14:4). The practical-minded folks then commence to scold her, but Jesus comes to her defense. She has honored Jesus, and his anointing is in anticipation of the dark hours that soon will befall him. Were all this happening in our day, the rebuke might take this form: "How dare you engage in such an extravagant gesture in our cost-effective world?"

Often there are strong reactions to extravagance. The minimalist school of architecture — a movement strongly associated with Mies van der Roe — was a reaction to the perceived excesses of other forms of architecture. The same has happened in music and art. Such reactions have also occurred in the history of the Christian church. We might call the Puritans theological minimalists, who reacted to ecclesiastical excesses.

Today, reactions to perceived extravagance occur in a cost-effective world. The prevailing mind set goes like this: If it doesn't pay for itself and more, it needs to go.

From the standpoint of the Christian faith, do extravagant gestures have a place in a cost conscious world? Jesus seems, in our text, to say they do. Let's look a bit more closely at this account.

Note first that this extravagant gesture is not an act that occurs in a vacuum. The extravagant expression is directed to a person and the extravagance itself is seen as a manifestation of the value of that person, in this case Jesus. There is a world of difference between sharing a bottle of vintage wine with a spouse or good friend, and dumping the wine down the kitchen sink. The former is extravagance with purpose; the latter is utter waste.

In our families and friendship circles, we gather at various times for a special, or extravagant, meal. We spend more money on that meal than we normally spend to eat, but it is a special meal because it is shared with people we love. The food we prepare is a reflection of the affection we have for these people.

Note, too, that this extravagant gesture is not in competition with other expressions of generosity. When Jesus reminds this lady's critics that they will always have the poor with them, he is not for a moment suggesting they be put off to one side and forgotten. Tending to their needs is a given, but what this lady has done to Jesus is in a special class all by itself.

Then third, something that is extravagant is, by definition, beyond what is usual. It's not done all the time, else it would not be special and extravagant. "... but you will not always have me," says Jesus. This seeming extravagance was a one-time event.

But let's get even more specific. This woman's act can be seen as an affirmation and celebration of the arts. Funding is usually a problem for the arts. When the numbers crunch is on, what first gets cut in a public school curriculum are programs related to the arts. If it's a choice between chemistry and music, chemistry is probably going to win out.

It was David H. C. Read who first established the link for me between the alabaster jar and art. Said Read:

> *Suppose we take this box and its perfume as a symbol of the beautiful. The response of the disciples to the incident is then typical of what many Christian people feel about the arts. They are an extravagance. They are not something on which a religious man will spend his money. The good, the moral, the correct thing to do with the alabaster box is to cash it in and use the proceeds for social work among the poor.*[1]

Read went on to say, though, that both the scriptures and the arts are concerned with the ultimate mystery of life and should, as he put it, "join hands in the service of the soul."

It is not happenstance that church buildings, mosques, and synagogues are often repositories for beautiful art. Certainly every sanctuary has its share of that which reflects beauty. What's more, that which reflects beauty occasionally needs to be restored and protected. We do that because beauty is its own form of ministry. Beauty also participates in, and reflects, the mystery of God's gracious countenance. Therefore we invest in that beauty, even if at times the cost seems extravagant. How much is beauty worth?

The late Henri Nouwen put it well:

> *The dominant question in work has become: "How practical is it and what does it cost?" Whole cities have*

been built so exclusively useful that their sheer ugliness did visible harm to the physical and mental health of those who live there. The irony of usefulness is, that, when beauty is no longer part of it, it quickly becomes useless. In the days when houses, churches, and cities were built which now attract tourists from all over the world, beauty was not perceived as an added decoration of useful things, but as the quality to which all work was directed.[2]

But appropriate extravagance is not alone connected to that which is inanimate. Not only was the essence the woman used costly; her act was an expression of extravagance, too. To be extravagant literally means to "stray beyond." We need parents who "stray beyond" an average commitment to their children; pastors who "stray beyond" a minimal level of pastoral care; doctors who "stray beyond" ho-hum medical care; teachers who "stray beyond" lick and promise pedagogy. The list is endless.

Jesus is saying, I believe, that there are those times when we should feel free to let go and be extravagant, in the service and praise of God.

1. David H. C. Read, *The Arts and the Scriptures* (From a series titled *The Bible and the Daily Paper*, aired on the National Radio Pulpit during February, 1972).

2. Henri J. M. Nouwen, *Care and the Elderly* (An address to the biennial luncheon of The Ministers and Missionaries Benefit Board of the American Baptist Churches USA, delivered on June 25, 1975, in Atlantic City, New Jersey).

Cross Connections

Good Friday is not an easy day on which to preach, nor is what happened on Good Friday easy to explain. Many thoughtful Christians have a difficult time understanding how this very bad day in the life of Christ has become for Christians a good day. What's more, many find it perplexing to say that Jesus died for their sins because he died some 2,000 years before they were born. Then perhaps most perplexing of all are those theories of atonement that come to us in the New Testament, theories steeped in a popular culture light-years removed from ours.

So at the outset, it is well for us to confess that there is a profound mystery about this Friday called good, a mystery that has, at least in part, been generated and fostered by those very thought-forms that were intended to make clear what happened. We have been aware of this for some years. P. T. Forsyth, many years back, said it like this: "What the cross is for the soul and the race can be put into no theology, adjusted in no philosophy. No thought or form can contain the greatness of the personality which it took the eternal act of cross and resurrection fully to express."[1] Leslie Weatherhead noted it too: "Few matters so muddle the thoughtful layman ... than the attempt to link the death of Christ in A.D. 29 with the sins of men today."[2]

But even more recently, there is the voice of John Macquarrie:

We can first of all clear the ground by setting to one side some theologies of atonement which, though they have been very influential, appear to me to presuppose

121

> *ideas of God which, from a Christian point of view, are*
> *very questionable. I mean theologies which represent*
> *God as angry and offended, or as a punishing God in-*
> *tent on exacting the penalty for sin.*[3]

Consequently, many of us don't know how to connect to the cross; or, if you will, feel disconnected from the cross. When Paul writes to the Corinthians about "Christ crucified" being a "stumbling block" to some and "foolishness" to others, many of us will understand those perceptions; but when Paul writes of the "crucified Christ" as "the power of God and the wisdom of God," we are apt to draw a blank. What good is this Friday in reconnecting us to God? Or, to use the imagery of a text from Hebrews, how do we make the leap from the suffering Son to the Son who is "the source of eternal salvation" or the "high priest" who bids us approach "the throne of grace" (Hebrews 4:14-16; 5:7-9)?

I suggest we begin by calling to mind the rather remarkable, but by no means uncommon, human pattern of experiencing intense difficulty or defeat and now, in retrospect, finding in that difficulty or defeat new lease and not dead end. With varying intensity, this happens every day.

A woman once went downhill skiing out west and took a fairly significant tumble. In the process of being x-rayed for possible internal injuries, it was discovered that she had a completely encapsulated malignant tumor in need of surgical removal. She was in great discomfort because of the fall, but in even greater discomfort now because of the discovery of cancer. But looking back on those very dark days now, she sees that as fortune, not misfortune. Ironically, had it not been for the skiing accident, she might never have discovered that malignancy and its potential to metastasize.

Christians look back on the cross in just that same way. What began in fact as a kangaroo court and ended as murder becomes, through hindsight, the very crucible of redemption. Perhaps imagery that helps me more fully understand that will help you also.

There is the image of *absorption*. This image is not flawless. Most of us probably associate the word "sponge" with absorption, but sponge can be a pejorative term. We sometimes refer to someone

122

who takes advantage of us as being "a sponge." But there is a different side to this matter of absorption, and it comes from the field of physics. In physics, absorption refers to taking in, and not reflecting, and in that sense absorption nicely describes part of the activity of the cross. There God in Christ absorbs — absorbs abuse, scorn, pain, rejection, sin — all that is sinister, morbific, and nocuous.

By contrast, we tend to be more reactive. If someone pummels us, by nature we want to pummel in return. The eye-for-an-eye and tooth-for-a-tooth mentality is deeply ingrained, both in the child and in the highest counsels of any government on the earth.

Please note that absorbency is not to be equated with being a doormat. To absorb can be a conscious and calculated decision.

Let me illustrate this way. In every human grouping we encounter people who are rough around the edges. Their touch is the touch of coarse sandpaper; their behavior is chafing. When they irritate us, it is natural for us to consider responding in kind. But there are occasions when maturity bids us think twice about doing that. Very likely, responses in kind will simply perpetuate more of the same. So we make a conscious decision to absorb the vexation. Sometimes we absorb and forget; perhaps other times we absorb and respond appropriately later. Absorption — not reflection; there is one image that can help us understand the cross today.

There follows the image of *neutralization.* Absorption can lead to neutralization. During the Second World War, a Lutheran bishop was imprisoned in a Nazi concentration camp and tortured by an S.S. officer. The officer wanted to extract a confession from the bishop, and since the Lutheran bishop wouldn't willingly give it, the S.S. officer was sure that torture would bring it forth. In a small room, the two faced each other and as it took its course, the severity of the torture was continually increased. The bishop, who had a high tolerance for pain, did not respond to the torture. His silence enraged the S.S. officer to such a degree that the Nazi hit his victim harder and harder until, exploding and hollering at this bishop, he exclaimed: "But don't you know that I can kill you?" The bishop looked in the eyes of the S.S. officer and slowly said: "Yes, I know — do what you want — but I have already died." At that moment, the Nazi lost any power over his victim. The grounds for violence had gone and torture was now a futile effort. Such is the power of neutralization.[4]

We also see this power at work in the three strategies (found in Matthew 5) Jesus suggests for interrupting the pattern of retaliation, the pattern of eye for eye and tooth for tooth. We are indebted to Walter Wink for a very insightful treatment of these maneuvers.

Particularly insightful is his treatment of this strategy: "... if any one strikes you on the right cheek, turn the other also" (Matthew 5:39). Wink asks why the right cheek and how one would go about striking someone in that location. A blow, he notes, by the right fist in that right-handed world would land on the left cheek of the opponent. What's more, to strike the right cheek would require the use of the left-hand, but in that culture the left hand was only to be used for unclean tasks. So the only way to strike the right cheek with the right hand would be to use the back of the hand. Hence, we are talking here about backhanding someone as a form of insult. The purpose is to humiliate and put someone in his place. In that culture, one did not strike a peer and if that happened, the fine was significant. But backhanding was the normal way of admonishing inferiors, and in the context of this teaching, Jesus is addressing people whom the culture deems inferior — slaves, wives, children, women, and Jews.

Why, then, does Jesus counsel these folks, already humiliated, to turn the other cheek? Wink indicates this action would say in effect:

> *Try again. Your first blow failed to achieve its intended effect. I deny you the power to humiliate me. I am a human being just like you. Your money, gender, race, age, or status does not alter that fact. You cannot demean me.*[5]

What's more, such a response places the striker in enormous difficulties. One can only backhand another's left cheek by using the left hand — and that's forbidden. And if you take your left hand and land a blow on the other's right cheek, you are declaring that other person a peer. Again, remember, that peers do not backhand each other; the back of the hand is reserved for reinforcing the caste system and institutionalized inequality.

In effect then, to "turn to them the other also" was a way of neutralizing their power. This wasn't cowardice; it was a strategy designed to place one's adversary in a no-win situation in a non-violent way. It stripped him of his ability to dehumanize you.

Absorption. Neutralization. But the cross also invokes the image of *transformation*.

What else can explain the seemingly inexplicable shifts that occur in the wake of Jesus' death? What is heinous becomes hopeful; what is deadly becomes salvific; what is seemingly an ending becomes instead a beginning; what is raised in hate issues in health; what is designed to be ignominious becomes something in which the community of faith glories; humankind's worst is met with God's best. We remember this gruesome, ugly event and it so dramatizes God's deadly determination to get our attention and win our hearts that we can do naught else than stand and sing, in the words of Isaac Watts:

> *Were the whole realm of nature mine,*
> *That were a present far too small;*
> *Love so amazing, so divine,*
> *Demands my soul, my life, my all.*

Such is the transforming power of love.

You may remember Edwin Markham's memorable lines:

> *He drew a circle that shut me out —*
> *Heretic, rebel, a thing to flout.*
> *But Love and I had the wit to win:*
> *We drew a circle that took him in.*[6]

The cross is God drawing a circle around the whole of creation and taking us in.

A man was walking down the gangplank from the *USS Massachusetts*, moored in Fall River, Massachussetts, and looking back over his shoulder, saw its massive guns against the backdrop of the sky. But he saw something else as well. Off in the distance, beyond that formidable armament, was a church steeple and atop the steeple was a cross. There, in juxtaposition, the fundamental options we always have: the cross and the cannon. Nations make that choice in the context of international politics; you and I make that choice when it comes to the bearing we assume with family, friends, and fellow believers.

What makes this bad Friday a good one is God showing the world a better way — this way of absorption and neutralization, leading to transformation. Easter is its vindication. Little wonder the author of Hebrews calls Jesus "the source of eternal salvation" and bids us "approach the throne of grace with boldness, so that we may receive mercy and find grace to help in time of need." Amazingly, the throne of grace is the cross.

Charles Allen Dinsmore had it right: "There was a cross in the heart of God before there was one planted on the green hill outside Jerusalem."[7] Cruciform disciples, likewise, continue to be the best hope for the world God continues to love.

---

1. P. T. Forsyth, *The Person and Place of Jesus Christ* (London: Independent Press, LTD, 1951), p. 74.

2. Leslie D. Weatherhead, *The Christian Agnostic* (New York: Abingdon Press, 1965), p. 113.

3. John Macquarrie, *Jesus Christ in Modern Thought* (Philadelphia: Trinity Press International, 1990), p. 401.

4. Henri J. M. Nouwen, *Reaching Out* (Garden City, New York: Doubleday & Company, 1975), p. 84.

5. Walter Wink, "We Have Met the Enemy ..." (*Sojourners*, December 30, 1986), p. 30.

6. Edwin Markham, "Outwitted" (*Masterpieces of Religious Verse,* James Dalton Morrison, ed., New York: Harper and Brothers Publishers, 1948), p. 402.

7. D. M. Baillie, *God Was in Christ* (New York: Charles Scribner's Sons, 1948), p. 194.

Easter
John 20:1-18

Easter Transportation

The eyes of our nation have, in recent time, twice been riveted on Antarctica and the need to rescue medical personnel from a weather station there. Happily both rescues were successful, but they were conducted in weather conditions that were exceptionally hazardous for flight. Aircrews had to wait for precisely the right time to make each rescue attempt. The rescuers knew they wanted and needed to get to the weather station, but it was all but impossible.

I am wondering whether a similar predicament obtains with regard to Easter. We see it off in the distance and desperately want to get there, but often we can't seem to quite make it. We are like Mary, as described by John, and on this text we focus this Easter sermon: "When she had said this, she turned around and saw Jesus standing there, *but she did not know that it was Jesus*" (John 20:14). So caught up was Mary in an assumed loss, that she could see nothing more. She hadn't yet gotten to Easter. Is that you? Is that me?

Maybe the transportation we have selected isn't equal to the task.

Some actually don't sense the need for any transportation to Easter. For them, Easter isn't an event that connects with them personally in any way; a trip isn't called for. It is an event that is saluted and acknowledged, but from a distance. It's rather like President's Day; we know it has to do with Washington and Lincoln, but more than anything else it's a day when our favorite department store has a whopping sale. There is a disconnect between the day as announced and the day as lived. We have nothing against old George or Abe; it's just that they were then, and we are now, and there is no wedding of then and now.

A young seminarian once received back his paper on systematic theology, and his professor had written this stinging comment: "I would call this 'notes for a paper in systematic theology'; you have all kinds of material, but you don't do anything with it." Sometimes Easter is just "out there" — we don't do anything with it, or let it do anything with us.

Of course, there are other times when we wish to ride the vehicle of reason to Easter. We do our best to become theological engineers, asking "how questions"; we endeavor to analyze our way to the resurrection. But if we could analyze and dissect Easter until it fit nicely into the contours of our minds, what would we in fact have?

Imagine going to a world-class art museum and finding a particular painting that captures your attention. If you wished, you could spend considerable time researching that painting — its history, purpose, the nature of the paints the artist used, its many characters, the culture that gave rise to it, the artist as a person and more. You could then write all of this up in formal fashion and present it to others for their consumption. But with all that done, what would we have? We would have some insights, but certainly not all that the painting encompasses. We would have facts and figures, but facts and figures are not exhaustive. Every set of eyes encountering that painting brings to it, and takes from it, something unique to those eyes and not shared by other eyes. There is what can be known by the mind, but there is also what is known only to the heart; there is the rational, but also the non-rational. As Pascal put it, "The heart has its reasons of which reason knows not, as we feel in a thousand instances."[1]

Similarly, if we knew all about the mechanics of Jesus' resurrection and could reconcile the varying accounts of where and to whom Jesus revealed himself, what would we really have? We would have the outsides, but not the insides; the shell but not the core; what is ephemeral, not what is essential. Halford Luccock said it well: "No doctrine can live in the intellect which does not renew itself in experience."[2]

Then again, we sometimes head toward Easter on the shoulders of other people's faith. We want to get there, but believe we can't on our own steam. And that's okay. In matters of faith, we sometimes carry each other.

It reminds me of the two characters in John Steinbeck's *Of Mice and Men*. George and Lenny are rootless men who till the soil, and George takes special care of Lennie, whom we would describe today as being significantly challenged. George is the keeper of Lennie's hope.

Early in the novel George says to Lennie: "Guys like us, that work on ranches, are the loneliest guys in the world. They got no family. They don't belong no place."

Lennie is delighted with what George says and responds: "That's it — that's it. Now tell how it is with us."

So George continues: "With us it ain't like that. We got a future. We got somebody to talk to that gives a damn about us."

Lennie breaks in: "But not us! An' why? Because — because I got you to look after me, and you got me to look after you, and that's why." Lennie then asks George to go on and George responds: "You got it by heart. You can do it yourself."

But Lennie, wanting to ride on the shoulders of George's hope, says, "No, you. I forget some a' the things. Tell about how it's gonna be."

Back and forth it goes, with George telling Lennie he knows the full story, too. But Lennie always saying, "No ... you tell it. It ain't the same if I tell it. Go on ... George. How I get to tend the rabbits."[3]

This is something we do for each other all the time. The young teacher gets discouraged, and the seasoned teacher paints the larger picture; the young medical student gets lost in the maelstrom of unending deadlines and exams, and the seasoned physician points to the ultimate destination. We regularly give blood transfusions to the hopes of others.

Transportation to Easter. We all want it. But there is a further angle on this and the news is good indeed. Here it is: We don't need any transportation to Easter; we don't have to get to Easter. Why? Because Easter finds its way to us.

Go back to Mary, standing by the tomb weeping. "They have taken away my Lord, and I do not know where they have laid him." Mary is clueless. Transportation doesn't even enter the picture, because she has no idea where she would even go to find Jesus' body. At this point, Jesus enters the picture, but she doesn't even know that. "When she had said this, she turned around and saw Jesus standing there, but she did not know it was Jesus." She takes him to be the gardener.

Transportation to Easter. We all want it. But do you suppose we are on the right track in doing that? I'm not sure we are; in fact, I've come to the conclusion that we are way off track in talking about ways to get to Easter. Here in John's account of the primal Easter is Easter — the risen Jesus — coming to Mary. She didn't have to seek; instead she was found! Jesus utters an emphatic "Mary" — and then Mary knows.

So here we all sit, doing our level best to find our way to Easter, when Easter is going to — maybe already has — find us.

The eyeglass wearers in the house will identify with this. You can't find your glasses; you had them just a bit ago, but now you have them not. So you race from room to room in search of them. You're sure they are lost, until that ridiculous moment when you discover that they have been on your face all along — it's just that you weren't aware of it.

I'm as sure as I can be that Easter has, or soon will, come to you. If it doesn't seem so, it may be that you, like Mary, are seeing, yet not seeing. "Supposing him to be the gardener," our text says of Mary.

Remember that time when you were in deep despair and it felt all the time like it was three o'clock in the morning? Then the despair lifted — and it was more than the St. John's Wort that did it. Help came, and to speak figuratively, you thought it was the gardener. It wasn't the gardener!

Do you recall that time when your vocation degenerated into a job and you could hardly stand to get up and do what you do any longer? But one day several things came together and again you were caught up in the rhythm of a vocation that speaks to your soul. Help came and you thought it was the gardener. It wasn't the gardener!

And how about that occasion when you all but gave up on that son or daughter of yours, so impudent and recalcitrant had that son or daughter become. Your parental agony wasn't a matter of months, but several years. Then one day that would-be adult became an adult and walked across that stage, or wrote you that letter of rapprochement, or simply stopped fighting. Help came and you thought it was the gardener. It wasn't the gardener!

In these and a trillion other circumstances, it was the spirit of God in the risen Christ creating those resurrections. Marilyn Oden put it beautifully:

> As we stumble though the cobwebs in the midnight mist, filled with loneliness and despair and bent double by our burdens, the whisper of God's love can penetrate the mist — even from the underside of the soul. We know the outcome of the Story. We do not have to remain entombed in the dark night. We do not have to wrap ourselves in the graveclothes of self-pity, blame, bitterness, cynicism, suspicion, vengeance. We do not have to become like the sea creatures of the deep who make bizarre adaptions to survive severe cold, pressure, and lightlessness. We are the Easter people, called "out of darkness into his marvelous light" (1 Peter 2:9).[4]

There are times when we rightly strain to achieve what we want. Easter is not one of those times. God, in and through Christ, is the achiever. We are the beneficiaries. There is no transportation to Easter because it isn't required. God, at this very moment, is rolling away stones and calling into tombs: Come out! Come out! Alleluia and alleluia!

---

1. Margaret Pepper, ed., *The Harper Religious & Inspirational Quotation Companion* (New York: Harper & Row, Publishers, 1989), p. 228.

2. Halford Luccock, *Marching Off The Map* (New York: Harper & Brothers, Publishers, 1952), p. 88.

3. John Steinbeck, *Of Mice and Men* (New York: Bantam Books, 1963), pp. 15, 16.

4. Marilyn Brown Oden, *Wilderness Wanderings* (Nashville: The Upper Room, 1995), pp. 105-106.

Easter For Thomas, Too

The urge to be a part of what is going on is very powerful. Or to say it differently, to be on the outside looking in can be unsettling at best. Just remember the last time you came into a room and found a group of people talking excitedly about a news event or something that happened to someone else in the office. You probably went right up to those assembled and in some way signaled your interest in their conversation.

Or think of it this way. Whenever you have been part of a group of three — perhaps at work — there have probably been moments when you have felt like the odd person out. Maybe you have been ill and while you have been absent, business has gone on and now upon your return to this group, you feel like an outsider. It's no fun being out of the loop.

If you can identify with anything I have said so far, you know something of how Thomas felt. All the other disciples were privy to the news of Easter and had experienced it firsthand, but for some reason Thomas was not there when that happened. Maybe he had the flu, or was out of town, or had a doctor's appointment. The point is, the other disciples experienced something he hadn't. "We have seen the Lord," they tell him and Thomas finds that absolutely incredulous. It's bad enough to be out of the loop, but it's even worse when — having been given the inside scoop — you find it impossible to believe!

I suspect that there are Thomases here today; or, if you will, I suspect that Thomas lives with varying intensity within us all. Well, I have good news: Easter is for Thomas, too. Thomas is our friend.

In fact, Gerrit Scott Dawson has called Thomas "a forerunner for all of us who were not there."[1]

So if you came here today with a certain reserve or skepticism — wanting to celebrate, but not sure if you should — you have a very good friend in Thomas.

Let's not be too hard on Thomas about his low threshold of disbelief; we are often just like him. Think of how frequently we say, in response to something we are told or hear about, "I can't believe it." News that comes to us can either be so good, or so bad, that for a time our powers of credulity are strained. Time is needed to process and integrate. "How Great Thou Art" is a hymn that celebrates the salvific work of Jesus and it contains a line that runs, "I scarce can take it in ..." Events can be so powerful and moving, that for a time we are in disbelief and "scarce can take it in."

I commend what we can call the "elevator theory" of doubt. I deem it a mode of transportation that can either take us downward to a level of deeper truth, or upward to a level of higher awareness. Doubt is faith's employee, not faith's nemesis.

What's more, just because we are historically removed from an event does not mean we cannot believe in it. Most of us don't remember the moment of birth, but the very fact that we are here is living proof that the birth occurred.

There are many things we believe that are historically distant from us and we know they are true because we have the testimony of those who witnessed what happened firsthand and their experience is undeniable.

In not that many years, there will be no one living who was at Dachau or Auschwitz. While regrettably we have people like David Irving and a handful of others who are Holocaust deniers, there are legions of people whose recorded testimonies will be the truth on this matter forever.

There are still people living who could show us photographs they took of liberated concentration camps at the end of World War II. We could hold those photographs in our hands and be transported back to a heinous reality that took place a half-century ago. We believe that such camps existed because there is evidence they did. So too we celebrate the resurrection of Christ Jesus because we see the evidence that it is so! "Blessed are those who have not seen and yet have come to believe," says Jesus. And Thomas says, "Amen!"

Strange it is that we have no problem seeing evidence of destruction. A spring tornado rips through a community and completely destroys homes and buildings. The evening news carries graphic video; the morning paper has gruesome pictures. By the same token, the signs of resurrection are slower to be seen. It takes months, and sometimes years, to see the work of resurrection become increasingly visible.

So much of the time, the signs of resurrection are so slight as to be imperceptible. But God's resurrecting activity is ongoing. It's timetable may vary, but God's intent does not.

While people naturally experience God in a wide variety of ways, there is an Old Testament notion that it is life-threatening to behold God face-to-face. You may remember the story of Jacob's nocturnal wrestle with an unknown man. The battle continues, but the dawn is coming and the man with whom Jacob is wrestling later becomes identified as God. As dawn approaches, Jacob's adversary says: "Let me go, for the day is breaking" (Genesis 32:26). For Jacob, that kind of daytime seeing would have been more than he could bear. In the wake of the struggle, Jacob says: "For I have seen God face to face, and yet my life is preserved" (v. 30).

How could we stand face to face with God at high noon and survive the intensity of the moment? Would not God's light blind us, God's intensity consume us, God's holiness shrink us, or God's "mysterium tremendum" send us packing? That doesn't mean we can't hear and see God, but it does mean that God's presence is always a mediated one. It comes to us "in" and "through." Through the bread and through the cup; in Christ; through this set of circumstances; in this musical composition or in that verse or thought; in this dream or through that hunch.

So it is with resurrection. It is God raising us in this or through that. But let there be no equivocating about who it is that is doing the resurrecting.

Show me a repaired relationship, and I'll show you resurrection. Show me a person with an attitude baptized in the fount of humility, and I'll show you resurrection. Show me a son or daughter who defiantly went off to the far country to waste and wander and is now on the way back, and I'll show you resurrection. Show me a community where people from distinctively different camps have found a common ground of promise, and I'll show you resurrection. Show me a self-righteous person who suddenly discovers her own shadow and weeps copiously, and I'll show you resurrection. Show me someone who has wrestled with the black dog of depression and has lived to tell about it, and I will show you resurrection. Every congregation is full of resurrection stories, if we will but take time to note them. And just because your story seems to be a modest one, don't be fooled: Modest stories are mighty in their own right.

We weren't there for the first Easter — only a handful were. But like Thomas, we don't have to be. Easter is for Thomas — the Thomas who lives in me and you, too. We have had, and will continue to have, moments when the presence of the risen Christ is made known to us; and like Thomas, we will only be able to say: "My Lord and my God!"

"Blessed are those who have not seen and yet have comed to believe." Blessed indeed!

---

1. Gerrit Scott Dawson, *Writing on the Heart* (Nashville: Upper Room Books, 1995), p. 132.

Too Good To Be True?

Here's the scene. The disciples are huddled together and they have just heard Simon's account of experiencing the risen Christ when Cleopas and his companion enter and add word of their encounter with the risen Christ. Luke describes the scene like this: "While they were talking about this, Jesus himself stood among them and said to them, 'Peace be with you.' They were startled and terrified, and thought they were seeing a ghost" (v. 36).

This account picks us up at a point where — were we to be present at Easter's ground zero — we also would have been — "talking," "startled," and "terrified."

Those words sum up how we behave in the face of unexpected news, good or bad. Yes, I said both bad and good. When the news is bad, such responses are understandable. But we also experience them when the news is good.

People sometimes feel their lives are unfolding in too good a way. They may even say that the goodness scares them a bit. The implication is clear: They are not sure life has the right to be that good. Consequently, they wait for the other shoe to drop.

The *Peanuts* cartoon I have in mind finds Lucy saying her prayers. When she is finished, she walks into the kitchen where Linus is eating and comments: "I was praying for greater patience and understanding, but I quit ..." In the last frame, she continues: "I was afraid I might get it."

James Evans McReynolds was onto something when he wrote:

> *Whatever else the resurrection of Jesus means,*
> *it means that God is getting close to us.*

We fear that.
Easter, we say, is a day of joy
and it really is.
We say it is a day of hope and it really is.
We say it is a day of promise and it really is.
But we are not as fond of it as we think.
We are afraid of it.
We are more afraid of it than we will ever say.[1]

Good news, here, but frankly, it makes us quake in our clogs. So little wonder that Jesus says to these shaking, quaking disciples: "Peace be with you." Or to put it colloquially, "Chill! It's going to be fine. I know you don't understand how all this has come to pass, but it's going to be all right. In fact, very all right."

What now follows is a time when Jesus invites these people to touch him and feed him, and in that way they come to know that they are a *companioned* people.

There is a world of difference between loneliness and solitude. When we feel lonely, it is as though we are in this big world all by ourselves, and no one else knows or cares about what we are experiencing. Solitude, by contrast, is the desire of the soul to commune with itself, knowing all the time that we are never utterly alone. We are companioned by the risen Christ, or as another once put it, "A solitude is the audience chamber of God."

There was a Scotsman who found it difficult to pray. He consulted his minister and the minister made a very simple suggestion. "Just sit down and put a chair opposite you, imagine that Jesus is in it and talk to him as you would to a friend." To the Scotsman, the chair made all the difference in the world. Companioned — that's what it means to be an Easter people.

Still, a part of us wishes we could have it as those primal disciples did; we too wish we could avail ourselves of Jesus' invitation: "Touch me and see." We also want to feel the touch of Jesus. The Easter point is, we do feel that touch, and probably most of the time we are not even aware of it.

Charles Wesley, whose hymn "Jesus Christ Is Risen Today" is sung on Easter morn in virtually every Christian congregation in America, died in 1788. But he continues to be present when we sing his hymn. Beethoven died in 1827, but every time we sing "Joyful, Joyful," Beethoven affects us in a very personal way. Similarly, every exertion of ours that can be called Christ-like happens because we are in the presence of Christ's risenness, whether we happen to feel it or not. At some level, conscious or not, there has been a knock on the soul's door and a voice has said: "Listen! I am standing at the door, knocking; if you hear my voice and open the door, I will come in to you and eat with you, and you with me" (Revelation 3:20). To do the Christ-like thing means that on some level we have heard that knock that is God-in-Christ and have opened the door.

Companioned — there's one Easter word.

Then a second one: *led*. We are a companioned people, and we are a led people. After breaking bread together, Luke tell us Jesus led them out: "Then he led them out as far as Bethany, and, lifting up his hands, he blessed them." John describes Jesus as the shepherd who "calls his own sheep by name and leads them out" (John 10:3b).

We all have had those times in travel when we have become utterly lost. With the route to our destination in dispute, we had to seek counsel.

Sometimes the church behaves as though it is lost. We know that's the case when it looks to the culture and begins to follow its lead. Take the business model. There is a sense in which the church must behave like a business. There is no questioning the need for accurate bookkeeping, effective equipment, and accountability. On the other hand, we can be sure that something is suspect when ministers see themselves as CEOs, or — as one minister identified himself — an entrepreneur. The richness and breadth of Jesus is compromised when the Lord of the church is marketed like any other product. A church can become so slick that it behaves more like a well-oiled machine, than a company of believers linked by faith, identified by loving ways, and united in a common mission to be a healing presence in places of suffering, loss, and discouragement. In fact, the church, unlike the world of business, sees loss as opportunity, links value not to productivity but essence, and finds in spiritual bankruptcy, God's opportunity. The church's bottom line is not calculated in terms financial, but in levels of compassion, community, tolerance, and justice. Show me a church that is long on compassion, big on the building of community, patiently tolerant of human differences, and sensitive to fair play, and I will show you a church that is rich in what ultimately matters.

We didn't dream up these values. They come from the Lord of the Church, whose resurrection is our hope, our sustenance, and our joy. If you want to find the risen Christ, it is in these bottom line arenas where he will be found. When you are moved by compassion, drawn by what creates genuine community, joyful over the colorful diversity of our world and impassioned by what is equitable, you can say: "The Lord has risen indeed, and he has appeared" to me.

It's never been expressed more eloquently than Albert Schweitzer did in *The Quest of the Historical Jesus*:

> *He comes to us as One unknown, without a name, as of old by the lake-side He came to those who knew Him not. He speaks to us the same word, "Follow thou Me," and sets us to the task which He has to fulfil for our time. He commands. And to those who obey Him, whether they be wise or simple, He will reveal Himself in the toils, the conflicts, the sufferings which they shall pass through in His fellowship, and, as an ineffable mystery, they shall learn in their own experience who He is.* [2]

Luke says of those huddled post-Resurrection disciples that "in their joy they were disbelieving."

Is all this too good to believe? Yes, it is. But believe it anyway — for the simple reason that it's true!

---

1. James Evans McReynolds, "Afraid of Easter" (*Alive Now!* March/April 1978), p. 58.

2. Marcus J. Borg, *Jesus, A New Vision* (San Fancisco: Harper & Row, 1987), p. 19.

A Tireless And Timeless Image

Images are highly influential. They become emblazoned on the wall of our minds and they evoke a wide range of responses. Millions of people will remember the fireman carrying the baby out of the ruins of the Murrah Federal Building in Oklahoma City. World War II veterans, particularly the ones who served in the South Pacific, will always remember Mount Surabachi and the Marines who raised an American flag at its summit, as well as the image of General MacArthur returning to the Philippines. Neil Armstrong taking that first step on the moon in the early '70s is frozen in many memories, too. If you were old enough to watch and understand television in 1963, you probably remember young John F. Kennedy, Jr., at the casket of his father Jack. Much closer to our own time, many of us will long retain the image of students running out of Columbine High School with their hands over their heads. Some images are immensely powerful and have a tenacity that is tireless and timeless.

If there is one image associated with the Christian faith which, more than any other, has found an enduring place within the collective life of the Christian church, it is the image of Jesus as the good shepherd. Even if you weren't reared in an agrarian culture, the chances are excellent that you have a very firm grasp of what a good shepherd is. The imagery is in our hymns, in stained glass windows surrounding Christian sanctuaries, and in paintings. In the Bible, there are over 500 references to sheep. You might be familiar with the confession found in the book of Isaiah (53:6) that runs: "All we like sheep have gone astray ..." And in one of our classic prayers of confession, we tell God that "we have erred and strayed from thy ways like lost sheep."

Even if people have never heard of shepherds and sheep, it is an easy matter to acquaint folks with both. To understand matters that attend to being shepherded sheep is to acquaint ourselves with the language of intimacy.

Shepherded sheep certainly were the beneficiaries of *security*. Shepherds, in a variety of ways, saw to the security of the sheep. They did that with rods and staffs. A rod was a stout piece of wood, around three feet long, with a lump of wood at the end about the size of an orange. With it, the shepherd fought the battles of the sheep; he would use it to drive off wild animals and defend the flock against robbers. A staff was a long crooked stick, and if a sheep showed signs of straying, the shepherd would use that staff to pull it back. The psalmist says of the two items, "Thy rod and Thy staff, they comfort me." Obviously those tools attended to the security and therefore the comfort of the sheep.

Additionally, when the sheep were resting for the night in a cave, the shepherd would recline in its entrance. This made it possible for him to intercept any intruder from the outside, while at the same time stopping any sheep from leaving.

Ideally, when children are young, they have regular occasions when they are safely tucked into bed, and then sent off to sleep with words and gestures from both Mom and Dad, indicating they are loved beyond measure and totally safe within the boundaries of parental care. That's security — and it's a wonderful feeling.

The shepherd/sheep relationship was also marked by *affection*, sometimes playful affection. Here's one recorded observation: "I once watched a shepherd playing with his flock. He pretended to run away; the sheep pursued and surrounded him. Then he pretended to climb the rocks; the goats ran after him; and finally all the flock formed a circle, gamboling round him." Writes William Barclay: "The shepherd literally talks to his herd in a voice and a language that they can understand."[1]

The securing of *food* for his flock was also an ongoing shepherdly activity. You will easily remember the words we enjoy from *Messiah*: "He will feed his flock like a shepherd." Pastures and wells were in short supply, and the good shepherd led his flock to both. In a fast food culture, it is easy to lose sight of the culinary rhythms that are so rich in symbolic value. When most of us go to our places of employment, we do not think of going forth to provide food for our loved ones. Maybe we should recover the beauty of that simple, and yet profound, act. I can tell you this: Parents and children being routed from their homes anywhere in the world are not taking this rhythm of going forth, securing, and then preparing food lightly at all.

Empathy also marked the shepherd's bearing toward the sheep. If there were little lambs who could not keep pace with the flock, the shepherd would carry them by hand. That empathy was also reflected in the fact that every sheep in the flock had a name; a shepherd and a sheep could be together for as many as eight years, and over that time a strong relationship developed. Those of us who have had pets for animals know much about how all that happens.

It nearly goes without saying that shepherds had to have *tenacity*. Sheep were in constant need of supervision and care, like infants and young children need the constant supervision of Mother and Dad. That which is tenacious holds firmly, strongly, and persistently. If you have ever seen a sheep dog at work, you have seen what is virtually an artistic rendering of tenacity. I have also seen, and you have too, a parent whose lovingly tenacious ways with a young child can approach artistry. Such a parent cabins and curbs, but not jerkingly, and certainly not violently. Effective parenting means a child is loved, yet controlled; given freedom, but not so much as to be endangered; free to explore, with only with the bounds of what is safe and friendly.

Then also there was an *evaluation* dimension to shepherding. An important part of knowing the sheep was taking their measure. A shepherd would not demand from the sheep more than their strength could deliver. He knew the limits of their endurance and how far to push them.

Part of the shepherd's evaluation of his flock was the practice of having each of the sheep pass "under the rod." At evening, as the sheep entered the fold through a narrow entrance, they did so one at a time and as they did this, the shepherd would hold his rod near to the ground and demand that each sheep pass under that rod. As they did so, the shepherd was able to give each sheep a quick examination to make sure the sheep had not sustained an injury during the day. Ezekiel uses this imagery in referring to God's relationship with his people: "I will make you pass under the staff, and will bring you within the bond of the covenant" (Ezekiel 20:37).

Here, then, is what the shepherd provided: security, affection, food, empathy, tenacity, and evaluation. In short, the shepherd provided safety for the sheep.

This tireless and timeless image is a blessed one for the community of faith and serves us in at least two very vital ways.

It gives tremendous substance to what it means for the Christian community that Jesus is, as it is expressed in the book of Hebrews, "the great shepherd of the sheep" (Hebrews 13:20). Who is the risen Christ for us? He is one who attends affectionately to our security; who feeds us; who has great empathy for us; who, like the good shepherd going after the one even though the 99 are safe, is tenacious in his endeavors to bring us into the fold of God's care; and one who takes the measure of our hearts, and leads us toward the throne of grace. Hence we sing the old lines, "Savior, like a shepherd lead us, Much we need Thy tender care." And we say with the psalmist: "Know that the Lord is God. It is he that made us, and we are his; we are his people, and the sheep of his pasture" (Psalm 100:3).

Secondly, the image provides us with some clues regarding what it means that the church is to be a pastoral presence in the world. Day care centers, medical clinics, programs of calling and support, housing, education, financial assistance, food pantries — all these and so much more represent expressions of the church's pastoral outreach. These are all consonant with the church's understanding of how we as God's people have first been shepherded by God in Christ. The experience of being shepherded leads us to, in turn, shepherd. A shepherdless flock is an endangered and very vulnerable one.

You have come today because you are a part of this flock and want to be cared for in a pastoral way ("pastor" being the Latin word for shepherd). You will leave in a few minutes and tomorrow some of you will be in classrooms, some of you in offices, some of you in shops, and all of us in neighborhoods and homes. Into those places you will not carry rods and staffs. But you can carry with you the rod of informed judgment and the rod of language; and you can carry with you the staff of affection and caring. There are sheep out there needing care; you have skills that can make you a modern-day shepherd. Please take upon you this tireless and timeless image. You will be surprised how warmly, welcomingly, and gratefully you will be received. And your exertions will bring joy to the heart of God, who will always be your shepherd.

---

1. William Barclay, *Jesus As They Saw Him* (New York: Harper & Row, Publishers, 1962), p. 194.

Together, But Not Enmeshed

Jesus describes the community gathered in his name — and that would be all of us — using the imagery of the vine. We, individually, are the various branches of the vine. Jesus is, as John describes him, "the true vine." And God is the vinegrower. Jesus is shaped and empowered by God, and we — as branches — are shaped, empowered, and nourished by the presence of the risen Christ.

We are strongly impacted by images; no surprise here. Early in the Bush administration when Vice President Cheney left the hospital after treatment for chest pain, it was obviously extremely important, from the standpoint of image, that he walk out confidently under his own power. Imagine the fallout if, by contrast, he had been pushed out in a wheelchair and helped into his waiting automobile. Whenever possible, we want to project the best image we can.

The images we have of ourselves are also powerful, both with regard to how we behave and how our behavior affects other people. There is a world of difference between a husband who sees himself as a loving helpmate to a wife who is his co-equal, and a husband who sees himself as the lord and master of his home and, by implication, his wife as a subordinate. A manager who moves by fiat and intimidation is a very different cat from a manager who builds consensus and is secure in her authority. A teacher who sees her classroom as a garden is very different from a teacher who views his classroom as an assembly line. To whom do you warm: a minister who is always in your face, or one who helps you save face? A supervisor who acts like Attila the Hun, or one who resembles your favorite aunt or uncle, and while supportive, also holds you to a reasonable standard?

And what of our image of God? Some view God as a capricious, vindictive, and erratic presence whose delight is our miserableness. The souls of those who so believe are going to exhibit a climate quite at variance with the souls of those who understand God to be one whose love for us is profound, and whose judgment is for our growth, not destruction.

In the imagery of John, God is the vinegrower. Chances are there are vines very near where you live. Typically they grow along the ground and up walls. What's more, they are tenacious. God is the planter of the vine.

I believe God is planting seeds all the time. We call them by different names of course — hunches, ideas, senses, inklings, and the like. Nevertheless, when those seeds issue in fruit that is indeed kingdom fruit, we know full well who has been doing the planting.

What's more, God often plants seeds in us so that we can carry those seeds of hope, insight, strength, and perseverance to others. Paul puts it rather neatly in his first Corinthian epistle. Writing of his work with that congregation, Paul says: "I planted, Apollos watered, but God gave the growth" (1 Corinthians 3:6).

A simple example of seed planting is something that parents do (or should be doing) with a small child. Perhaps the child has a difficulty with a classmate and comes home upset. Mom and/or Dad listens, comforts, and then comes up with a suggestion to make matters better with this classmate. That's planting a seed.

Every congregation was begun by a person or group, who planted a seed. There was a perceived need, that need was articulated and presented, and in that way a seed was planted. The result was the church of which you are presently a member.

God, John tells us, is the vinegrower. And Jesus is "the true vine." It is this connectional theology that provides us with an understanding of who we are and how we live. We define what for the Christian community is this special relationship to God all the time. We do that through what becomes our glib use of a five-word phrase: "through Jesus Christ our Lord." The phrase points to the particular lens through which God comes for us more fully into focus. Looking through the lens that is Jesus, God's compassion, grace, overtures, hope, and mandates become visible to us. Every time we use that five word phrase we are reminding ourselves, and others, how it is that we can see most clearly. This is the vine that nourishes us and enables us to grow.

God the vinegrower. Jesus the true vine. And now we, the branches, nourished by God in Christ, so that we can be fruitful.

To be nourished — that's why you came this morning, that's why we read the Bible, that's why we trouble ourselves to be involved in programs of adult education, that's why we read theological literature, and that's why we spend time with others who are on the same journey. Doing all this is what is meant by "abiding in Christ." But it's not absorption for absorption's sake; it's absorption for exertion, fueling for propulsion, ingestion for action.

There is a significant portion of the Christian family that believes God is the grand collector, a collector of human souls. Jesus is the bait God uses to capture and collect those souls, and the ultimate purpose of God is to gather as many souls as God in Christ can. What's important is to be part of the gathered; and once one has been gathered, one waits with others who have been gathered until all die and live in heaven with God forevermore. The gathered are the redeemed and happy in Christ, and what fuels this portion of the Christian family is the ongoing repetition of invitation and ingathering.

The image of Christian believers as branches off the vine does not square with this understanding of God as the great gatherer. God is not so much the gatherer as God is the sender. Declares Jesus: "I am the vine, you are the branches. Those who abide in me and I in them will bear much fruit ..." (v. 5). Said differently, we are not the shelved heirs of salvation; we are the heirs of salvation charged with bearing fruit, and read "bearing fruit" to mean getting out there on the highways and avenues and making a beneficent difference for God by working for what is fair, graceful, beautiful, lovely, and wholesome.

Pruning, too, is a part of this imagery. Pruning involves cutting off what is dead, and sometimes what is living, too — all with a view to increasing fruitfulness.

Churches are quite reluctant to put members on inactive lists, and even less inclined to take measures whereby one is dropped from membership. Ministers spend a fair share of time over the years chasing after inactive church members. But sometimes there comes a point where it is better to allow people to drift way, because not to do so can mean we are neglecting those already here, and on the way in.

Then, too, pruning what is living means realizing we have too many balls in the air; and trying to keep them all in the air means in effect that we will soon be able to keep none of them in the air. So we prune in order to increase effectiveness and fruitfulness.

God the vinegrower; Christ the true vine; and God's people as Christ's branch managers, who manage themselves in such ways as to produce fruit. Together the elements establish the picture of a vibrant organism that is continually replenished and productive.

Now, one more observation. When Jesus talks about "those who abide in me and I in them," he is talking about togetherness, but a togetherness that serves a common good — and that's the reign of God.

There are two kinds of togetherness, a good one and a bad one. Family systems theorists term bad togetherness *fusion* or *enmeshment*. A family that is enmeshed looks like a can of worms, or like a string of Christmas lights that has become hopelessly entangled. There is constant reactivity and unspoken rules govern family life, rules like you can't be angry, or men in the family can't be scared, but the women can. This kind of togetherness does not well serve the kingdom.

But that is not the only kind of togetherness. God is well served by allowed and encouraged variety. No one in a congregation has a corner on the total truth. Therefore through vigorous debate and the sharing of various ideas, a collective wisdom emerges that is better than anything less. A congregation is richer because of variety. What's more, in congregational life it isn't required that everyone be interested in the same aspect of faith.

There was wide press coverage of the female doctor who developed breast cancer while serving with others in a geological survey of the South Pole. Part of the coverage included the housing arrangements. You may recall that there was a rather large external structure, but within that structure there were several smaller modules, each with its own purpose.

Any mature grouping of people looks like that. The outside structure might be the family, but within the family there are individuals. The outer structure — the family — is really richer and healthier when adequate attention is paid to the development of its constitutive parts.

The same holds true for the family that is the church. We are a congregational family, and our outer structure is healthier and happier when our constitutive parts flourish.

Take a church choir. Can you imagine the sounds that would emanate if we asked the sopranos to sing like basses, the basses like altos, the altos like tenors, and the tenors like sopranos? That would be idiocy. The choir sounds like a choir because its singers are true to their voices.

Together, but not enmeshed. When that happens, we are infinitely happier; but more to the point, God is better served.

Called To Love, Not Like

The humorist Will Rogers told us that he never met a man he didn't like. In the musical that celebrated Rogers' life, there is a song by that title and in that song Rogers admits that one man "put him to the test," but never pushed him finally to the point where his ability to like evaporated. I don't know what your response is to Rogers' disclosure, but I am led to think he was — to utilize an overworked phrase — "in denial." Come now, can any of us stand and say that we have, without exception, always liked every single person with whom we have ever come into contact? I appreciated the honesty of a well-seasoned cleric who confessed: "There are some people to whom I couldn't warm even if I were cremated with them!"

Let's get this on the table before we go a step further. Christian men and women are not called to like everyone. The old camp song is titled "They Will Know We Are Christians By Our Love," and not, "They Will Know We Are Christians By Our Likes and Dislikes." If there are folks to whom you do not warm, know please that you are not in violation of any Christian norm.

We are not called to like, but we are called — and this is the burden of our text — to love: "This is my commandment, that you love one another as I have loved you," says Jesus.

Love, as it is defined by our faith, is both a revered panacea, and an underemployed practice. To say that the answer to the world's problems is for people to love each other more is both right and banal at the same time. It sounds wonderful and grand. Who would argue with the contention? But when you sit eyeball to eyeball with another person — especially one who is cantankerous, obnoxious, difficult, unlovely, and seemingly unlovable — it is anything but an easy task. There will be more than a few times when we say with Jeremiah: "O that I had in the desert a traveler's lodging place, that I might leave my people and go away from them!" (Jeremiah 9:2).

Frederick Buechner has observed: "In the Christian sense, love is not primarily an emotion, but an act of will."[1] What is this saying to us about our faith's distinctive understanding of love?

First, it says that love in the Christian sense has a cognitive dimension. When Jesus commands that we love, it is with the qualifier, "as I have loved you." Christian love is referentially learned. We know something about the mandates of love because we have first been loved. At no place in the New Testament is this referential nature of love more aptly put than in 1 John: "... everyone who loves is born of God and knows God" (4:7).

When you stop and think about it, all love is referential. We learn what it's about when we become its beneficiaries. The love of a parent, or surrogate parent, or grandparent, or uncle, or friend, or fellow believer are all ways in which we first learn what it's like to be loved. Remember Elizabeth Barrett Browning's words in *Sonnets From the Portuguese*?

> *The face of all the world is changed, I think,*
> *Since first I heard the footsteps of thy soul*
> *Move still, oh, still beside me; as they stole*
> *Betwixt me and the dreadful outer brink*
> *Of obvious death, where I who thought to sink*
> *Was caught up into love and taught the whole*
> *Of life in a new rhythm.*[2]

For the Christian community, what makes us experience "the whole of life in a new rhythm" is the unfettering and grace filled love of God as we have come to know it in Jesus Christ.

We live in a culture that loves to quantify. We weigh, measure, time, photograph, and generally assess just about anything we can get our hands on. What's more, I am not sure we much like that which we can't quantify and therefore control. Maybe that's why it is so hard for us to grasp the love of God: it is both uncontrollable and immeasurable.

A young boy once asked for the autograph of a young lady. She obliged and wrote the following: "Yours till the ocean wears rubber pants to keep its bottom dry." The love of God is love of that duration and it is not our task to understand nor comprehend that love, but instead our joy to acquiesce in it. "We love because he first loved us," announces 1 John 4:19.

Because God's love for us is this peculiar and unfathomable love, it follows that our exertions too will be in the direction of a love that is peculiar. Hence Kierkegaard's comment: "If anyone thinks that by falling in love or by finding a friend he has learned about Christian love, he is in profound error."[3] In his classic work on love, this Danish theologian takes pains to point out that Christian love is marked off from what he calls "spontaneous love" because Christian love endeavors to do its work on a level that is distinctive from the need-ridden life of erotic love. Writes Kierkegaard:

> *All other love, whether humanly speaking it withers early and is altered or lovingly preserves itself for a round of time — such love is still transient; it merely blossoms. This is precisely its weakness and tragedy, whether it blossoms for an hour or for seventy years — it merely blossoms; but Christian love is eternal ... Christian love abides and for that very reason is Christian love. For what perishes blossoms and what blossoms perishes, but that which has being cannot be sung about — it must be believed and it must be lived.*[4]

Were we briefly to sketch out what makes Christian love distinctive and special, it would include the following.

Christian love sees through walls and around corners.

Being under the mandate of God to love means also we are under a mandate to love others by looking through the walls they place in our way, and around the corners where they are hiding. This isn't always, or even very often, fun, but it is what the gospel calls us to do. It is the work of love.

155

W. Paul Jones, a Roman Catholic priest, has written about what he calls "love as formative imagination" and how it is vital, in our love exertions, to try to enter the lives of others, the better to understand them.

In trying to love especially difficult people, our imagination can provide the transportation beyond those walls and around those corners. What must it feel like for Jan to believe she must erect a wall? What must it be like for Jim to peek at me, as if barely, with just one eye, around the corner? What fear must be rampant? What excessive reservation gives such pause? And how can I gain Jan and Jim's confidence so they will take down the wall or emerge fully around the corner?

Christian love, as Paul so beautifully reminds us, is also patient. Waiting for the Jans and Jims to take down walls and turn corners doesn't happen overnight. It may take months, sometimes years. But consistent patience eventually pays off.

In a culture that blindly salutes doing and worships acceleration, patience can come off as a quality that is anachronistic. But the speed we demand of our machines, and by implication our people, is neither always healthy nor realistic. To be patient and honor another's timetable is a manifestation of Christian love. As John Milton once reminded us, "They also serve who only stand and wait."[5]

Christian love has bifocals. It sees the people we would love in two ways: It sees them close up (the way they are right now) and it sees them way down the pike (at a place where we would eventually like them to be).

If, as example, we are working with a student population training eventually to enter a particular field, the educational experience will be enhanced if we treat them not only as students, but also as though they were already in that field for which they are training. If we lower the bar and expect less than we should, we will raise the probability of future failure.

And Christian love, while unconditionally offered, is at the same time intolerant of love's enemies in the lives of those whom we would love. Unconditional love does not equate to a blanket acceptance of all behavior.

An older gentleman paid regular visits to his physician, but between visits was not always good at following his physician's directives. At times the physician would become exasperated and say to the man: "Larry, I love ya'! But you gotta stop doing that!"

Christian love is just like that. It's what Paul calls "speaking the truth in love" (Ephesians 4:15). Like that doctor, we will say: "John, I love you, but you have to part company with alcohol because you are addicted to it." "Martin, I love you, but you've got to stop riding roughshod over people's feelings; think before you speak." "Carol, I love you, but you've got to stop your carping, because it's driving a big wedge between you and your children." "Mary, I love you, but you've got to stop behaving like a doormat; there are more important things than being liked by everybody on the face of the planet."

Christian love is a tall assignment. It's not easy work. But we worship, and are called to love, by One whose enacted love for us is seen in the suffering love of the crucified Jesus, who has become for us the exalted head of the Church.

Jennifer Woodruff has penned some poignant words that speak to our exertions in love. They come under the title "With the Drawing of this Love and the Voice of this Calling":

> *Not only what we thought we could afford,*
> *Not only what we have the strength to give*
> *is asked of us; the grace that makes us live*
> *calls for a death, and all we are is poured*
> *Onto an altar we did not design*
> *and yet which holds us in his perfect will*
> *And in both flames and darkness keeps us still*
> *and is the strength, the pillar, and the sign*
>
> *Of all that never fails, though we are weak,*
> *of he who calls, and asks us to embrace*
> *our weakness, and our cross, to see his face —*
> *and, made most strong in weakness, he will speak.*[6]

---

1. Frederick Buechner, *Wishful Thinking* (San Francisco: Harper, 1973), p. 63.

2. Elizabeth Barrett Browning, *Sonnets From The Portuguese* (Kansas City, Hallmark Cards, 1967), p. 9.

3. Soren Kierkegaard, *Works of Love* (NewYork: Harper & Row, 1962), p. 69.

4. *Ibid.*, pp. 25, 26.

5. John Bartlett, *Familiar Quotations* (Boston: Little, Brown and Company, 1955), p. 251.

6. Jennifer Woodruff, "With the Drawing of this Love and the Voice of this Calling" (*Weavings*, Volume XIV, Number 3, May/June, 1999), p. 26.

Ascension Of The Lord
Luke 24:44-53

A Friend In High Places

What we want to talk about is not, I am extremely sure, a theme that dominated your breakfast conversation this morning. It is not, I am equally confident, a theme that came up in any church conversation around here in the last little while. It is not even, I am still confident, something that you have ever thought much about at all. And I am sure it is not something you have heard homiletically addressed more than once, if at all. I am talking about the ascension of Jesus Christ into heaven. If by chance it rings a theological bell within your memory, chances are that bell was rung by the creedal line that runs: "... and the third day he rose again according to the scriptures: And ascended into heaven, and sitteth on the right hand of the Father...."

Before you zone off, thinking that this theme has nothing of value to add to your soul's nourishment, let me be heard to say that the ascension does have a contribution to make; it does say something that can speak to our hearts and bring us closer to God.

Now I know what you are thinking, because I have already thought it. When Luke describes Jesus as being "carried up into heaven," often our penchant for knowing the "how" of a matter immediately takes precedence over the meaning of the matter. And finding the mechanics of the event to be incredulous, we dismiss the matter as fanciful, merely a product of exuberance. End of story. Physics has euchred theology.

Strangely, in other areas of our lives, we don't seem to have the same problem. We can hear Elizabeth Barrett Browning say of her beloved, Robert, that he "lifted me from this drear flat of earth where I was thrown ..." and we know precisely what she means. Not for a moment do we think that he brought in some kind of crane and lifted her from one place to another. Rather, she is speaking poetically about a moving experience of soul that vivified and restored her.

Similarly, Luke is describing the post-resurrection estate of Jesus. The Jesus who was, is now again the Jesus who is, but in a new and expansive way.

The imagery bespeaks permanence. There is a wonderful line from the thirteenth chapter of Hebrews that is really a statement about the ascension of Jesus. It goes like this: "Jesus Christ is the same yesterday and today and forever" (Hebrews 13:8). What Jesus did, he did forever. The pattern of his life, the substance of his teachings, his role in bringing us closer to God — all of that is permanent and will never change.

People familiar with New England will remember seeing ruggedly beautiful stone walls that mark off property lines; they will also call to mind the rock-bound coast of Maine. Either image will convey the permanence of stone. A boulder is like a silent sentinel, guarding those in its shadow from the ravages of a tempest. Little wonder that people of earlier generations used to warm to Augustus Toplady's hymn, "Rock Of Ages," and gladly sing, "Rock of Ages, cleft for me, Let me hide myself in Thee...."

We desperately hunger for what is forever. This hunger is so commonplace that it goes unrecognized for what it is. The insecurity of children, the childishness of adults, the behavior of hedging — all these are reflections of our hope to be connected to what is permanent and our disquietude when we are disappointed because that permanence can be so evasive. How many children really believe — and feel — that the love of their parents is unconditional and will always be there? How many adults really believe — and feel — that the love of a mate or best friend is unconditional and will always be there? This hope we all have, and our despair when it is promised and then either not given or taken away is profound.

In our adult maturity, of course, we come to a time when we realize that the ultimate and only permanent permanence — if I can speak that way — is the permanence of God's eternity. Sam

Miller once wrote an essay on this theme provocatively titled "Beginning Eternity Now." Wrote Miller:

> *There is a sense in which we begin eternity here and now. It is not something that we will easily add on to the end of life when we die. Eternity is mixed invisibly with the stuff of the earth. With every new coming of springtime across the earth, some men will continue to live the old, old life they have always lived while others will see that most amazing stuff we call the soul that shines with potential surprises able to begin again no matter how far it has gone, stretching itself toward that peace which is only known in the endless dimensions of God's eternal purpose.*[1]

The ascension is about the permanence of God in Jesus the Christ. And it is also about the ultimate object of our adoration. Following Jesus' ascension, Luke tells us that his disciples "returned to Jerusalem with great joy; and they were continually in the temple blessing God" (Luke 24:52). To gather regularly for public worship to sing our praises to God makes perfect sense, because if we fail to worship God here, we will worship at some other altar. Should we do that, it is guaranteed that eventually we will succumb to the most profound of disappointments.

We are, by our very nature, worshiping people. And there is no end to the golden calves before which we willingly lie prostrate. Said differently, we will regularly make our way to one temple or another, of this we can be certain. You and I both know about the golden calves that wait to seduce us; preachers have been cataloguing them forever. Money, cars, houses, bank accounts — these are always in top ten idol lists. But often idolatry is more subtle; it has us in its snare and for a long time we might not even notice it.

There can come a time, for example, when in rightly caring for our bodies we move from stewardship to idolatry. Exercise can become worship of the body, the gym our temple. When the exercise and development of one's "abs" becomes absolutely and ultimately important, we can easily cross over the line into the territory of idolatry.

161

Debbie Parvin writes about an even more insidious form of body worship:

I buy the market's products
because I've bought
the market's definition
of my self and beauty.

Dear God,
sit with me
when I look in the mirror.
Forgive me for falling
for the market's cheap tricks,
for I have given them
my sense of worth
along with all my money.

Help me believe again
that I am beautiful,
that you have made me good,
and that there may be a little bit
of loveliness in me
to linger
even when I'm gone.[2]

The ascension is not the province of physics; it is, however, the province of theology. It speaks to the sense of permanence we ardently seek, and the worship we would gladly give. It announces that we have, so to speak, "a friend in high places," who is our rock and redeemer, alone worthy of our unbounded praise.

---

1. Samuel H. Miller, *The Life of the Soul* (New York and Evanston: Harper & Row, Publishers, 1951), pp. 152, 157.

2. Debbie W. Parvin, "Make-Up" (*Alive Now*, January/February, 1997), pp. 26-27.

Entrustment

Over thirty years ago, the late David H. C. Read preached and published a sermon series on the National Radio Pulpit that he titled *Overheard*. In that creative volume, he addressed a series of faith issues one might conceivably have overheard at that time. We overhear comments regularly. We might be riding on public transportation and overhear an amusing or telling conversation between two people, perhaps a parent and child; or we might be standing in a church lounge after worship and hear some people commenting on some dimension of church life, and our ears suddenly perk up.

In our text for the morning, we overhear Jesus — just prior to his betrayal and arrest — praying to God. It is often referred to as a high priestly prayer, and is an exceedingly personal moment between Jesus and God, much in keeping with the intimate relationship between Father and Son that is painted by John. Being invited by John to overhear Jesus praying to God can be very helpful to us.

At the outset, one is struck by the ease with which Jesus talks to God. It is a pure outpouring of heart. By contrast, it is common to have people indicate that they don't know how to talk to God; you may be among that number. Why might that be so? I suspect for the same reasons that people often don't know how to talk to other people in their lives. Among the questions that retard the tongue would be the following: Will what I say be accepted? Will I be allowed my own convictions? Will the person get angry with me? Can the person be trusted to keep a confidence? What words shall I use? Will the person be a good listener? Will I be belittled, upbraided, or laughed at? This window on the priestly prayer of

Jesus can serve as a reminder that all the contents of any heart can be poured out before God and given a compassionate listening. There is nothing we need fear in doing that.

If words come hard for us, our thoughts can initially be our words. And if giving the contents of our hearts verbal shape continues to perplex us, there is no reason we can't use others' words in giving shape to heartfelt concerns.

Thumb through the Psalms sometime in the next few days and note how many times the psalmist speaks for you. Then the next time you want to speak to God, go ahead and speak with and through the psalmist. If you want to thank God, join the psalmist in saying, "It is good to give thanks to the Lord, to sing praises to your name, O Most High; to declare your steadfast love in the morning, and your faithfulness by night" (Psalm 92:1-2). Or, should you feel inconsolable, let the psalmist speak for you: "I cry aloud to God, aloud to God, that he may hear me. In the day of my trouble I seek the Lord; in the night my hand is stretched out without wearying; my soul refuses to be comforted. I think of God, and I moan; I meditate, and my spirit faints" (Psalm 77:1-3).

But more specifically, this priestly prayer is a prayer of entrustment. It is found in John between the accounts of Jesus' last supper with his disciples, and his betrayal and arrest. He knows what's coming and he entrusts both his life and legacy to God. The dominance of this theme is striking.

Entrustment is both necessity and release.

While we have no conscious control over the decision, at birth God entrusts us to parental care givers. Houses of faith acknowledge and ritualize this through services of baptism or dedication, whereby moms and dads publicly acknowledge the receipt of that entrustment. Parents, in turn, entrust their children to other care givers and eventually to school systems.

Nor does entrustment end when children become adults. Adults also entrust themselves to others. When we marry, we are making a statement about the trust we have in our helpmate. Every time we board an airliner, we entrust our lives to pilots. In surgical suites, we entrust our lives to a medical team. In fact, every time we leave the house to go off somewhere is an act of entrustment.

Arguably, entrustment (or faith if you prefer) is the most important resource we can develop. Without it, we would all hole up somewhere, with our only excursions beyond being those of absolute necessity.

The obverse dimension of this is, of course, the cultivation of trustworthiness. It is as our entrustment is vindicated that we develop the capacity for more of it.

I don't know who taught you to swim, if ever you learned, but I do know that you would not have learned to survive in the water if there weren't a teacher present whom you trusted to make the learning environment a wholly safe one for you.

I don't know who taught you to ride your first two-wheel bicycle, but I do know that in all likelihood you would not have learned were it not for that trustworthy other who ran along side of you, as you wobbled from side to side, on that day when the training wheels were first removed.

A child would not be able to take the first step onto a school bus and leave Mom and Dad behind were it not for the fact that, preceding the first school bus ride, there were firmly in place a series of successfully completed developmental tasks, reflective of the child's experience that others in her life have proved themselves trustworthy.

Ironically, this reliance on the trustworthiness of others eventually leads to the ability to trust ourselves — our little inside voices, senses, and intuition. We can swim. We can ride the bike. We can go off to unfamiliar territory, establish ourselves, and be successful. Louise Kaplan has written beautifully about this process:

> ... we manage to hold together when the world lets us down. Although we feel temporarily abandoned and vulnerable, constancy prevails. We retain enough of a sense of our personal worth and the worth of others eventually to convert disenchantment and disappointment into challenge. Constancy enables us to bend with the shifting winds and still remain rooted to the earth that nourishes us.[1]

Entrustment is necessity; but it is also release.

Summer is still the traditional time for vacations. Often families and individuals begin to think about summer travel plans early in the new year. They consult the Internet and their favorite travel agency. A decision is eventually made and excitement about the vacation builds as the date for its actualization draws closer. What makes the vacation even sweeter is the ability totally to walk away from one's place of employment, utterly confident that what one does there has been entrusted to someone else who can capably handle what needs to be handled while we are away. One is thereby released from day to day concerns, free now to enjoy a time of re-creation.

Caregivers also need times of respite. We all know people who have primary responsibility for a loved one. Their devotion to that loved one is in no way diminished by their need for release from those responsibilities; in fact, respite from those responsibilities maintains, and can improve, the quality of that devotion. How wonderful it is that there are programs and people to whom these care givers can temporarily entrust the care of that loved other.

In this priestly prayer of Jesus, though, entrustment is elevated to its ultimate level. When all that we can do is done, when all that we can say is said, and when what we can give we have given, we entrust matters to God. This experience happens repeatedly in life, up to and including those moments when we entrust, through death, our loved ones — and eventually ourselves — to God's care.

I suspect that what makes ultimate entrustment possible is all the little entrustments that we learn to make all along the way. We hope wisdom is cumulative, and the more we learn to entrust in matters small, the more graceful we become in our ultimate entrustments.

Our goal, I believe, is to come to that point where we can say with Walt Whitman:

> My terminus near,
> The clouds already closing in upon me,
> The voyage balk'd — the course
> disputed, lost,
> I yield my ships to Thee ...

My hands, my limbs grow nerveless;
My brain feels rack'd, bewildered;
Let the old timbers part — I will not part!
I will cling fast to Thee, O God,
though the waves buffet me;
Thee, Thee, at least, I know.[2]

1. Louise Kaplan, *Oneness & Separateness: From Infant to Individual* (New York: Simon and Schuster, 1978), p. 41.

2. Walt Whitman, *Leaves of Grass* (New York: Doubleday, 1997), pp. 275-276.

Sermons On The Gospel Readings

For Sundays
After Pentecost
(First Third)

David G. Rogne

*This is for all those Patient Saints
who continued to love the Preacher
while the Preacher learned his craft*

Chosen

It is a difficult thing not to be chosen. I can still remember what a relief it was to be appointed by the teacher as one of the two captains who would choose team members when our class would be divided for softball. It meant that I would be, in effect, the first one to be chosen. What agony it was, however, when others were doing the choosing. As an uncoordinated youngster, with very little to offer toward the team's success, I was likely to be chosen last, and the humiliation was keenly felt.

Perhaps the disciples of Jesus experienced similar anguish when they contemplated the task that was before them following the death of Jesus. It must have been helpful to look back to that last meal they shared with Jesus before his death, and remember that he had affirmed that he had chosen them to be on his team. I think that it is fair to say that, as Jesus chose the members of that first team of disciples, he continues to choose the current members of his team, and to deploy them in ways that serve his plan. Look with me at this passage from the Gospel of John so that we might all learn what Christ chooses for his disciples to do.

For one thing, he says that he has chosen us to witness. Most of us don't like that suggestion. We have had people witness to us in ways that were not very winsome. Witnessing has a bad name. It conjures up images of people who make us uncomfortable. But really, a witness is simply a person who honestly shares his or her perception of reality. And it may persuade someone who is uncommitted.

Dave Dravecky, the former Giants pitcher, tells of having a speaking engagement at a church one evening, but he really didn't feel like going through with it. He was still struggling over the loss of his pitching arm to cancer. He felt lousy, but he went anyway. "I felt so unworthy to be standing there in front of all those people who looked up to me," he wrote. He felt that if they knew what he was really like, they would get up and walk out the door. But nobody walked out.

In fact, one fellow came forward who felt that he was making a mess out of his life. He wanted to change his life, but he wasn't sure how. He was involved with another woman, but was trying to put his marriage back together. There was something in what Dave said that spoke to him. He wanted Christ to come into his heart and to change his life. That night the man went home to his wife. In the weeks that followed, his co-workers, his neighbors, and his wife noticed the change in him. Five weeks later he was involved in a truck accident that killed him.

A few months later Dave Dravecky was speaking on a radio program. During the call-in segment of the show, the man's widow called in to say that those five weeks were the best days of their marriage. Tearfully, she thanked Dave for what his words had done for her husband and for herself. Sometimes, our words fall on fertile ground.

But witnessing is not only about words. Selwyn Dawson has written:

> The living truth is what I long to see:
> I cannot lean upon what used to be,
> So shut the Bible up and show me how
> The Christ you talk about is living now.

Cecil Northcott tells of a group of young people from many nations who were discussing how they might witness to Christ in our day. Some spoke of television, some spoke of radio, some spoke of distributing literature, and still others of holding mass meetings. Then a girl from Africa spoke: "When we want to take Christianity to one of our villages, we don't send them books. We take a Christian family and send them to live in the village. They make the village Christian by living there." We have been chosen to bear witness.

A second thing we have been chosen to do is to bear fruit. This statement comes on the heels of Jesus's description of himself as a vine and of his disciples as branches. A healthy plant has to put down roots so that the whole plant will be sustained. Most of us are acquainted with the Japanese art of raising and styling dwarf trees called *bonsai*. The Japanese simply cut the tap root, and as a result, the tree must live on small surface roots only. What would otherwise become a great oak or pine remains a little tree, perhaps twelve or eighteen inches high. The result may be pleasing and decorative, but it hardly allows the tree to develop to its full potential.

It is possible for people to remain dwarfed in their spiritual lives, decorative, but never reaching full potential, because their initial faith has not been nurtured. They are too puny themselves to bear any significant fruit.

Jesus invites us to participate with him in a life that will enable us to grow and to fulfill the potential which God has placed in us. Jesus gained his own strength from being rooted in God, and through Jesus, Christians are brought into contact with the Eternal. Jesus describes himself as being the true vine. He describes those associated with him as branches. The branch needs to have an intimate relationship with the vine in order to benefit from the life-sustaining nourishment.

I have a friend who for many years has been a grape farmer in the San Joaquin Valley of California. The branches of his vines are tied to long wires that run between the plants. The wires are attached to posts. Every few years he has to go through the vineyard and replace the posts. The branches stay in contact with the living root and they are sustained from year to year. The posts are placed in the same ground, right next to the vine, but having no root, not only do they not grow, they begin to rot.

Christians need to stay in contact with the one who gives life and sustenance to their spiritual growth. We do that when we make time for prayer, when we make time to read the Bible and reflect on its implications for us, when we spend time in meditation and ask questions like, "What does God expect of me?" When we do those things, we find that our spirits are sustained and our spiritual lives continue to grow.

But we have been chosen, not simply to develop personally, but to bear fruit. That is, our Christian faith should show some results. It is possible for a tree to look good but to be unprofitable. We used to have an apricot tree in our backyard. It was one of the nicest-looking apricot trees you'd ever want to see: healthy leaves, long branches, well-developed trunk. The only problem was that it didn't produce apricots.

The same thing can happen to people. A few years ago the psychology department of Princeton University conducted an experiment. Immediately after an ethics seminar, a class of forty ministry students left to attend a peace rally. Unknown to them, the department had hired an actress to stand along the route the students would take and pretend that she was choking, unable to catch her breath. The actress leaned helplessly against the wall of a building in plain view. The future ministers hurried by her; some of them did glance uneasily at the woman, but none of them stopped to help her. At one point she even fell to one knee for greater effect. But still no one stopped. Later, when the students learned of the experiment, many of them gave the peace rally as an excuse for not stopping. Each one felt that surely someone else was better equipped to spare the time to help the woman. After all, the peace rally was important.

It is important that Christians grow in the faith, learn to pray, become familiar with the Bible, as were those students, but if that is where it stops, we are no more than ornamental decorations — bonsais — healthy in ourselves, but stunted and unuseful. We are to bear fruit.

William Penn, who was eventually to become the founder of Pennsylvania, was once asked by an acquaintance to take him to a Quaker meeting in London. The young Quaker did so. When he and his friend had sat through about an hour of silence, the friend asked Penn in a whisper, "When does the service begin?" Penn's answer was, "The service begins when the meeting ends." It is still that way today. We worship, study, and pray so that we may become useful.

A third thing we have been chosen to do is to love. It sounds like a high calling, and for the most part, we are glad to be part of the team chosen to express it. But even something as noble as love can be trivialized. A while back there was a popular commercial on television showing a group of fishing buddies sitting around a campfire, "bonding" over their experience. One of the guys becomes quite emotional, moves close to another fellow seated around the fire, throws his arms around his friend, and chokes out the words: "I love you, man!" Instead of being touched, however, the friend is cautious. "That's great, man," he says, "but you still aren't getting my Budweiser!" Too often, love has been reduced to a device used to help us get what we want.

The love for which Jesus has chosen us involves giving rather than getting. I read recently about a devout nun who works in a hospital in New York City. Before her shift she would spend an hour on her knees in adoration of God and in preparation for her work. Late one afternoon, toward the end of her shift, she was bathing an abusive patient who was dying with AIDS. A man passing through the ward saw her and said out loud to a companion, "I wouldn't do that for all the gold in Fort Knox." The nun, hearing the remark, gently replied, "Neither would I." The visitor apologized profusely. With a warm smile, the nun responded, "It becomes possible when one prays, 'Lord, help me to remember that there is nothing that you and I together cannot do.' "

The love to which Jesus calls us is an inclusive love that helps us to see others as part of God's family.

A rabbi asked his disciples how one could tell when the night had ended and the day had dawned. One replied eagerly, "It happens when you see an animal at a distance and you are able to tell whether it is a cow or a horse." The rabbi shook his head in disappointment. A second disciple said, "Day has begun when you can distinguish an oak tree from a cottonwood tree." Again the rabbi gave a thumbs down. "How then, Rabbi, would you tell?" they asked. He replied simply: "Day has begun when you look in the face of a stranger and there see a brother or a sister. But if you cannot do this, it still remains night."

In his book, *Who Speaks For God?* Jim Wallis tells about a reporter who was covering the conflict in Sarajevo. He saw a little girl shot by a sniper. He rushed to a man who was holding the child and helped them both into his car. As the reporter raced to the hospital, the man in the back seat said, "Hurry, my friend, my child is still alive." A little later he said, "Hurry, my friend, my child is still breathing." Still later he said, "Hurry, my friend, my child is still warm." Finally, he said, "Hurry. Oh, God, my child is getting cold." When they got to the hospital, the little girl was dead. The man who had been holding the child then said to the reporter, "This is a terrible task for me. I must go and tell her father that his child is dead. He will be heartbroken." The reporter was puzzled and responded, "I thought she was your child." The man looked at him and said, "No, but aren't they all our children?"

They are all our children. They are all God's children, and Christ has chosen us to love them. Can we do it? Can we witness to God's presence in life? Can we demonstrate our faith authentically enough to attract people to Christ? Maybe not, if we are left to our own devices. But Jesus indicates that there is a power available to help us move beyond ourselves and our own interests. That power he calls *paraclete*. It is a Greek word, translated variously as comforter, counselor, advocate, helper. Literally, it means "one called to our side to help." One understanding of the word is that it comes from ancient warfare. When Greek soldiers went into combat they went in pairs, so that when the enemy attacked they could draw together back-to-back, covering each other's blind side. One's battle partner was the paraclete. What one cannot accomplish alone can be accomplished because we have a helper, the Holy Spirit of God. We have been chosen to be on the team, but God himself is the backup. Let's get involved in the game.

He Came By Night

I came upon Jesus quite by accident. We didn't travel in the same circles, so it was unlikely that we would ever have met socially. I was passing through the marketplace in Jerusalem one day when I heard him speaking to a handful of people who had stopped to listen. "Just another wandering street-preacher," I thought to myself. But as I passed by I heard him talking about the Kingdom of God, and about God himself, in such unsophisticated terms, uncluttered with a lot of theology, that I could see he was having an impact upon his audience which we more learned scholars could never have. He spoke of God in terms of personal experience, and he appeared so warm and approachable that I was immediately attracted to him. My name is Nicodemus. I am a professor of religion at the university in Jerusalem.

When I got back to the university, I mentioned the young teacher to my colleagues and suggested that we should invite him to share some of his thoughts with us. My colleagues opposed the idea. What could this uneducated teller of stories possibly contribute to our understanding of religion? All of us were experts in the field. They ridiculed the idea and ridiculed me for suggesting it. Moreover, street-preachers were known to turn into demagogues and radical leaders. Better to stay as far away from them as possible if I valued my position, I was told.

It was obvious that I wouldn't get anywhere with my colleagues, but I felt that what the young teacher was saying could provide a breath of fresh air in our rather stuffy academic surroundings. So I continued for several days to go and listen to Jesus. I would stand on the edge of the crowd or pretend to be considering the purchase of some item from a merchant. That way I wouldn't appear to be one of his followers or appear to be lending my endorsement to what he was saying.

But there were some ideas that Jesus had which I wanted to pursue more in depth. I could have asked questions in the market-place, but that would have been unseemly. After all, *I* was the professor of religion; *I* was the one who answered other people's questions. What would people think if I should be asking Jesus questions about my field? So I decided to go to him privately, at night. I found out where he was staying and I went one evening to engage him in conversation. That conversation with Jesus helped many of my ideas to fall into place, and I'd like to share them with you. But let me tell you about myself so that you will understand the significance of what I received from Jesus.

I've already told you that I am a professor of religion. In fact, when I met Jesus he already knew of me by reputation. I am also a member of the Judicial Council, known as the Sanhedrin, which attempts to govern the people and rule on civil matters so that our people may be governed as much as possible by our Jewish laws, rather than the different laws of the Roman occupying forces. There are only seventy of us on the Council at any one time, so the position carries with it a certain level of authority and prestige.

I am also a Pharisee. A Pharisee is a member of a very select group. There are only about 6,000 of us in Palestine at any one time. We are a strict religious party that stands for all that is good in Judaism. We are not much interested in politics because we feel that politics tends to corrupt people. We are the "separated ones." That is what the name means: separated from the sinful ways of the ignorant and uninformed people who do not keep the law. We take our religion seriously. Our scribes have for centuries been working out the implications of the laws of Moses so that there is a ruling for every conceivable situation in which a religious person might find himself. We Pharisees have memorized those regulations and committed ourselves to the keeping of all of them. You can understand the feeling among my Pharisaical brothers, then, that if anyone is going to make it with God, it would be the Pharisees. From our point of view, no one was trying harder.

Yet, in spite of all this, I was not satisfied. I had mastered the rules of conduct, but something was still lacking. I guess that that is why I was attracted to Jesus. Whether he knew the rules or not, he didn't seem to make them the focus of religion, and he had a living relationship with God that all of my books and schooling had never given me. It was that relationship with God that I wanted for myself. It was all this that prompted me to go and speak with him on that night I told you about.

The first thing Jesus said to me was that it was necessary to be born again. He said, "No one can see the kingdom of God without being born anew." I didn't understand how that was to be accomplished. Did it involve starting one's physical existence all over again? For me, as an old man, that would be just fine, but how would I go about it? As we talked, it became clear that Jesus was talking about some kind of a spiritual rebirth. But even that was hard to accept. After struggling for all these years to arrive at the point where I now was, I was being told to break with the past and to start over. I questioned whether I could really do that.

But as Jesus continued to speak, it occurred to me that he had purposely chosen a word with more than one meaning, for the word means not only "born anew," but also "born from above." I've come to the conclusion that what he was driving at is the necessity of being reborn into a new point of view. Each of us inherits a physical nature from our parents. That nature is related to this physical world; it possesses certain animal needs and drives. It is from below and its attitudes tend to dominate us. In fact, we often operate as if that is all there is to life; satisfying ourselves, our own ego needs, our own passions. And for some people, unfortunately, that is all there is. Surely, you know what I am talking about. It is the attitude that religious people call "sin." It ignores God, and it alienates people from God, from one another, and from a better self of which we are all capable. It promotes self-seeking to the point where we bring misery to ourselves and to others. It was that sense of separation from God and from others that had driven me to seek out Jesus in the first place. My religion had given me a set of rules

179

to keep, but all that did was to show me where I was going wrong. Now, I heard Jesus saying that there is a birth from above. It is the birth of a spiritual outlook generated by God's grace, not by our own achievements. I heard Jesus saying that no matter what we have made of life, no matter how entrenched our habits, no matter how old we are, God can change our point of view.

I wanted some formula which could be used to make this happen — to capture the Spirit — but Jesus likened the Spirit to the wind. In fact, that was another play on words, for in our language the word for "spirit" and the word for "wind" is the same word. Jesus said, "The wind blows where it chooses, and you hear the sound of it, but you do not know where it comes from or where it goes." The Spirit of God is like that — it can't be captured in a formula — it breaks into our lives, freshens them, and cleanses them in ways we cannot predict or demand. At the heart of religion there is mystery, a divine action that can give birth to a spiritual nature in a person whether we understand how it happens or not. Each of us needs to be born anew, from above. There is in each of us a spiritual nature, a higher nature if you will, which is brought to life when we reach out beyond ourselves, beyond our own immediate passions and desires, beyond our self-serving, this-world point of view.

When I again asked, "How does this happen?" the second thing Jesus did was to refer to an incident in the history of my people. Centuries ago, as the people of Israel were making their way from Egypt to Palestine under the direction of Moses, they were troubled by a plague of serpents which bit the people and caused many to die. The people interpreted this as punishment for certain sins they had committed. They confessed their sins and asked Moses to help them. In keeping with the imitative magic of that day, Moses formed a serpent out of bronze and had it put on a pole. Whenever people were bitten, they were told to look upon that bronze serpent in faith, and they would live. You can believe what you want about the details; the important thing is that people were saved by their faith.

Jesus went on to make the point that, as Moses had lifted up the serpent in the wilderness, so that people could be saved by looking to it in faith, so the Son of Man would have to be lifted up, so that whoever believes in him could have eternal life. What Jesus was saying was that somehow the healing, the wholeness, the salvation which people seek is going to come about through faith or trust in someone called the Son of Man. In identifying this saving person, Jesus again used a word with more than one meaning. He said, "The Son of Man must be lifted up." I took that to mean "exalted," "raised up so that all people could gather before his throne." I thought he was referring to the Messiah, who was expected to come in great power and glory, and I was ready to agree that the Messiah certainly would bring people to God.

I have subsequently come to believe that the "Son of Man" in whom one is to put trust is Jesus himself. And his being "lifted up" is not in "glory" and "power," but "lifted up" on a cross. Here indeed is an illustration of the unpredictable way in which God's Spirit works. We expect that when God speaks to us it will be in thunder and lightning, in expressions of power and glory. But instead, Jesus was "exalted" by first being lifted up on a cross. God speaks to us through weakness and agony and says that victory is to be found by enduring the ordeals we face, not in avoiding them. Somehow our rebirth, our salvation, is tied to our faith in the crucified one even as the healing of the children of Israel was tied to an object of faith in the wilderness.

There is a final statement from that late-night conversation which still sticks with me. I don't remember now whether Jesus himself said it or one of his associates, but it goes like this: "God so loved the world that he gave his only Son, so that everyone who believes in him may not perish but have eternal life."

There were several thoughts in that statement which were new for me; for example, the declaration that "God loves." You see, my religious training caused me to picture God as a righteous judge who demanded obedience on pain of punishment and death. I could envision God loving, but only in response to right conduct. If a person did the right thing, I could imagine that person loved by God. But Jesus was teaching that God loves first — that the initiative is with God — that back of everything is the love of God, who is seeking to win us, not to destroy us.

It was also a new concept for me to think of God loving the world. A few individuals, I could believe, though even they would have to be Jews, and quite likely Pharisees, like myself. But for God to love the world! That includes Gentiles; it includes sinners, the foolish, the ignorant, those who love God, and those who do not; those who are repentant, and those who are not; those who think of God as I do, and those who do not. I had to think about that for awhile before I could really allow God to love all people indiscriminately. Perhaps you are like that. You think you know who God should and should not love. It takes a considerable change of attitude to come around to the view that God loves all God's children.

In fact, it wasn't until I saw Jesus die, that I could accept such a loving God. I am aware that some people set the sternness of God on the one side and love of Jesus for humanity on the other, as though they have different attitudes. I have come to see Jesus as an expression of the love of God. I believe that in the actions of Jesus we can see the mind of God. When Jesus willingly died in order to further his message of God's love, I believe that he was showing the lengths to which God will go to win us to himself.

So we are told that belief in Jesus leads to "eternal life," or to the "Kingdom of God," or to "rebirth" — you can call it what you want. The important thing is that you take Jesus seriously. I did that. Not all at once, but eventually, so that when he was crucified I was among those who were unafraid to claim his body and prepare it for burial. I had learned from him that I didn't have to be afraid or cautious any longer. I can say now that I am not ashamed to call him my teacher and to believe what he said. I am convinced that Jesus makes known to us the love of God, but we are the ones who have to decide whether to believe him or not. You can take it from me, that decision makes all the difference, for now and for eternity.

Keeping Sunday

One of the churches where I served was located next to a Jewish synagogue. That synagogue was served by a rabbi who quite typically walked to the synagogue on the Sabbath, though his house was some distance away. It was not that he didn't have a car, but that for him it was improper to drive on the Sabbath, for that constituted work. Sometimes I would see him riding a bicycle to synagogue. I suggested to him that that was a lot more work than simply turning on the ignition in an automobile. He said that when a person is riding a bicycle on the Sabbath, the person is not tempted to go shopping or run errands, or to pick up something at the cleaners. However, when one is driving a car, it is easy to do many more things than one intended to do, and thus, the special nature of the day is lost. He was, of course, attempting to live up to the requirements of the third commandment: "Remember the Sabbath day, and keep it holy." Some people would honor his attempt to live by the requirements of this commandment. Others would see it as an unnecessary concern for an outdated concept.

In Jesus' brief ministry, he was repeatedly running into the requirements generated by this commandment. While he was often at odds with the religious authorities over how this commandment was to be observed, he did not discount its religious value. In the passage of scripture we are dealing with, Jesus attempts to balance the validity of sacred scripture with human necessity. In that balance there are lessons for us.

The first thing this passage says to me is that religious people tend to get focused on regulations. Consider the Jewish people of

183

Jesus' day. The Sabbath was very special to them. One reason for this is that according to the teachings of Israel, the day was ordained by God to provide for the rest and refreshment of humans. It is interesting to note that the prohibition against killing takes only four words, but the commandment about the Sabbath takes 94 words. The requirement to observe the Sabbath is so contrary to human activity that it required an extensive explanation. One explanation given is that God created the idea of rest on the seventh day of creation. Therefore, a Sabbath rest is built into the very structure of the universe; there is a basic rhythm of activity and rest in all of life.

André Gide tells about an incident that took place some years ago when he made a journey into the interior of the Belgian Congo. His party had been pushing ahead at a fast pace for a number of days, and one morning when the Europeans were ready to set out, their native bearers, who carried the food and equipment, were found sitting about, making no preparation for the new day's trek. Upon being questioned, they said quite simply that they had been traveling so fast in the last few days that they had gotten ahead of their souls and were going to stay quietly in camp for the day in order that their souls could catch up with them. In their primitive way they were describing the need for a rhythm in life between activity and rest.

But for Israel in particular, the Sabbath was a sign of their unique relationship with God. The Sabbath became a weekly reminder of the Passover, the time when God had delivered the Israelites from slavery in Egypt and made them his people. In his book, *East River*, Sholem Asch quotes the words of an old Jew, Moshe Wolf, in regard to observing the Sabbath. Wolf says, "When people labor, not for a livelihood, but to accumulate wealth, they become slaves. For this reason God granted the Sabbath. For it is by the Sabbath that we are taught that we are not working animals, born to eat and to labor. We are humans. It is the Sabbath which is our goal, not labor...."

Unfortunately, as with everything in which people are involved, the Sabbath had the possibility of excess within it. The sincere dread of profaning a day called "holy" began to haunt the Israelites. All kinds of petty regulations were set up to safeguard the Sabbath. Ultimately, the *day* became the important thing, not the *people* for whom it was created.

By the time of Jesus, the Sabbath had become a burden, not a blessing. Strict rabbis had drawn up a lot of rules over the years, regulating everything. Some were ridiculous. For example, it was taught that there could be no work on the Sabbath, so a person must be still; he must not shave or ride horseback; if his ox fell in a ditch, he could pull the ox out; if he fell in a ditch, he had to stay there. Eggs laid on the Sabbath could not be eaten; the hens had been working. If a flea bit a person on the Sabbath, he must not scratch it, but let it bite in peace, for to try to catch the flea would be hunting on the Sabbath. Once fire broke out in Jerusalem on the Sabbath. The Jews, afraid to work on that day, let it burn, and three people were killed. The day became more important than the persons it was designed to serve. But when Jesus came, he reversed the idea, reminding people that human life was more important than rules or regulations or days. For this they sought his life.

Christians, too, have been tempted to focus on regulations. Requirements about the observation of the Sabbath were eventually attached to Sunday. The early Christians were responsible for some of the change. They had no special day of worship at first; so they observed the Sabbath along with the Jews. But as the resurrection of Jesus assumed increasing significance among them, it seemed appropriate to have a day to remember that distinctly Christian happening. Therefore, the disciples chose the first day of the week rather than the seventh day, so that they might have a weekly reminder of Easter. In 321 A.D., Constantine made Sunday an official day of rest for the Empire, and with that there began to develop an increasing series of rules to regulate that rest.

Subsequently, Sunday observance followed the pattern of the Jewish Sabbath before it. Strict laws were set up for its observance. In England, in 1653, a law was passed saying that any person above the age of seven caught walking in the streets on Sunday would be whipped and fined. In one of our American colonies a law said that a woman could not wear a red dress on Sunday. A sea captain returned to his home in Massachusetts after many months at sea. His wife met him at the gate and he kissed her. But it was Sunday, and it was illegal to kiss one's wife on Sunday, so the captain was jailed.

Some of us know the blue laws which governed Sunday activities as we were growing up. The enforced piety which made Sundays so long and dull was enough to turn any healthy child from religion. Moreover, the implication was that being a Christian was equated with keeping the rules. It was that kind of legalism that Jesus was challenging in this passage.

The second thing this passage says to me is that human beings are more important than regulations. In the first situation that is described, the religious leaders fault Jesus' disciples for pulling off handfuls of grain as they passed through a field on the Sabbath and popping the grain into their mouths. They contended that this amounted to working on the Sabbath. Jesus justified his disciples' actions by reminding his hearers that when David was fleeing for his life, he and his men went to the tabernacle at Nob and asked for food. They were told that there was no food except for bread which had been offered as a sacrifice to God, and which was to be eaten only by the priests. Nevertheless, David, who was looked upon as Israel's great hero, took the bread, ate it, and shared it with his men. The implication is clear that in time of need, human necessity takes precedence over the requirements of law.

In the other situation described in this passage, Jesus is in a synagogue on the Sabbath. A man comes in who has a paralyzed hand. Jesus seizes the initiative and invites the man to step forward. He then asks the religious authorities whether it is lawful to do good on the Sabbath. When they refuse to answer him, he heals the man. The religious authorities interpret this as work, are convinced that Jesus has willingly broken the commandment, and seek to kill him. Again, the implication is clear: human life is more important than rules. The religious leaders have lost sight of this because, for them, religion is keeping the rules.

In spite of Jesus' statement that "the sabbath was made for humankind, and not humankind for the sabbath," the Christian church, too, has attempted to regulate how the Sabbath is to be observed. Over the centuries, Sunday has been identified with the Sabbath and the church has sought to apply Sabbath restrictions to Sunday activities. Over the years this had the effect of forcing people to go to church. And they might as well, for there was nothing else to do. If they did find something else to do, the church prevented them from enjoying it by heaping up guilt over desecrating the Sabbath. As Christians have become more affluent, however, they have managed to acquire more of life's amenities: vans, trailers, motor homes, boats, cabins, leisure. Weekends, of course, are the logical times to enjoy these amenities. The church has been reluctant to acknowledge this because it might seem to give people permission to stay away from church, and if they stay away they will get out of the habit of going to church, and the church will be weakened. So it has served the interest of the church to interpret statements about keeping the Sabbath holy as meaning, "Thou shalt attend church on Sunday." The Bible does not require that. And people eventually get tired of being made to feel guilty and they stay away anyway. There are numerous valid reasons for Christian people to gather for worship, but the requirement to keep the Sabbath holy, is not one of them.

Having said all that, the third thing that occurs to me as I consider this passage is that there are, nevertheless, some principles involved in Sabbath observance that are important for us to keep in mind. One of those principles is rest. Dr. William Dement, a Stanford psychiatrist, says that our cultural demands push us so hard that we are creating a "national sleep deficit." More than half the workers he surveyed admitted to falling asleep on the job. They get sick, lose productivity, have serious accidents, become depressed, and make bad decisions because they haven't provided themselves with adequate rest. This is dangerous for everyone. He points out that the nuclear disasters at Chernobyl and Three Mile Island both occurred in early morning hours, in the middle of overnight shifts, when workers were at a mental low. The *Challenger* shuttle disaster followed an all-night discussion by exhausted launch officials. Pennsylvania's Peach Bottom nuclear power plant was shut down a few years ago after the Nuclear Regulatory Commission inspectors found shift workers dozing. Some of this problem

Dement attributes to Thomas Edison. Before the light bulb was developed, people went to sleep when it got dark. Moreover, Edison didn't help matters any by giving his own opinion that a good night's sleep was a waste of time.

Too many people act as though a day of rest will lessen their return from life. I read an epitaph once which someone had written for a person who worked himself to death. It said, "Born a man, he died a grocer."

Actually, a time of rest enhances our ability to enjoy the remainder of life. Winston Churchill stayed rested and alert during the difficult days of World War II by scheduling cabinet meetings around his naps. Albert Einstein believed that regular naps refreshed his mind and stimulated his creativity. The recurrent Sabbath reminds us that the rhythm of activity and rest are built into the scheme of things.

A second principle involved in the observance of the Sabbath is the reminder that we are human. One of the biblical reasons given for observing the Sabbath is that God himself rested from his creative activity. If God rested, who then are we, that we should attempt to go on day after day, from one activity to another without pause? A few years ago *The New York Times* carried an article about a chess Olympiad which was being held in Germany. It mentioned a certain change in the schedule of play which would be helpful to two players, Fischer and Reshevsky, because neither would play on Friday night or Saturday. Fischer was a member of a strict Christian sect and Reshevsky was an orthodox Jew. Both observed the Sabbath. Here were two people involved in an international competition, who were saying to the rest of the world, "Time out, while I observe the Sabbath." They were demonstrating their freedom to choose how they would conduct their lives. They were free to choose activity, but instead they sought stillness. They were free to keep right on competing, but they chose to take an upward look. The Sabbath principle involves remembering that we are creatures, not gods; we cannot do everything, nor ought we to expect ourselves to, for that smacks of pride, and we do better humbly to recognize our limitations.

A third Sabbath principle is worship. Ralph Sockman once wrote, "Six days a week we sit at the loom. On the seventh day God calls us to come look at the design." Difficult as it is for me to say it, not all worship takes place in a church, and not all that takes place in a church contributes to worship. A young boy, coming reluctantly into the sanctuary of his church, noticed a plaque on the church wall. "What's that?" he asked his father. "That was put up in memory of all the brave people who died in the service," said the father. "Which service," asked the boy, "8:30 or 10 o'clock?"

The Sabbath principle is that when people get quiet, they begin to think seriously about God, about life, and about God's purpose for that life. Wherever that takes place it becomes worship. Marcus Bach, in his book *The Power of Perception*, tells about a Sunday when his father defied his strongly conservative mother and cut church to take young Marcus fishing. It was a glorious spring day, but Marcus' joy in it was marred by thoughts of a wrathful God. As they bicycled past the cemetery, with its awesome reminders of mortality, his pleasure in the outing seemed to ebb completely. But then, out in the country, it came back again. "A flash of secret wisdom told me I knew things," he writes, "that even my preacher uncle did not know. I knew them because I felt them on this beautiful spring morning. God liked fishing. Jesus liked fishermen. God liked this Sunday morning world ... God's world was life and freedom. God's world was the open road and the farmyards and the young corn coming up in clean, cultivated fields. God's world was the man-sized bike and the legs that made the wheels go round. God's world was Dad and I and Lodi's Mill. God's world included people going to church or going fishing, just as long as they really loved the Lord." Later, as the boy stood by the pond, watching the green flakes of algae, the shimmering lily pads, the beds of watercress, the silent mill wheel, and the other fishermen standing around the bank, an old hymn started ringing in his mind:

> *Come, Thou Almighty King,*
> *Help us thy name to sing,*
> *Help us to praise!*

Father all glorious,
O'er all victorious
Come, and reign over us....

Oh, that those gathering in church could have a worship experience half so authentic!

As meaningful as such a private worship experience may be, it is in worship with others that most of us find our faith encouraged, challenged, and disciplined. Someone has pointed out that private worship is like singing an aria in the shower; family worship is like the same selection sung together around the piano; public worship is like singing that aria in a choir at a concert. All enrich, all supplement, all are needed.

I am aware that the experience of worshiping together may not always be stimulating. A preacher was visiting one of his shut-ins, an elderly lady, who was bemoaning the fact that she could not come to church to hear his sermons. The preacher, trying to console her, said "Mrs. Jones, you aren't missing anything." "Yes," she replied, "that's what everybody tells me." Well, even if the sermon sometimes misses the mark, somehow the fellowship of like-minded persons can provide us with strength for the long haul, inward reinforcement, clearer vision of duty, and restored faith and courage.

I read recently about a strange custom in the British Navy. If there is a disaster aboard ship, "the still" is blown. The particular "still" is not a place where whiskey is made, but rather, a whistle which calls the crew to a moment of silence in a time of crisis. When the still is blown, every person knows that it means "Prepare to do the wise thing." That moment of calm, it is said, has helped to avert many catastrophes and kept people from foolish actions. The principle of the Sabbath is the blowing of the still. It is a reminder that God said, "Be still, and know that I am God."

Proper 5
Pentecost 3
Ordinary Time 10
Mark 3:20-35

Is Anything Unforgivable?

One morning I was roused from sleep around 3 a.m. by the ringing of the telephone. The person on the other end of the line was distraught because, she said, she had committed the unforgivable sin. It is interesting to me that such calls often occur at such an hour, after the bars have closed. The woman went on to say that at some point in her life she had really been angry about something, and had said, "Damn the Holy Spirit." Now she was remorseful, but she knew that Jesus had said that blasphemy against the Holy Spirit is unforgivable. Therefore, she was sure that there was no hope for her, either in this world or in the next.

Her situation is certainly not unique. The eighteenth century poet, William Cowper, suffered recurrent attacks of insanity due to his belief that he had committed the unforgivable sin. After one such terrible bout he wrote:

> *Damned below Judas; more abhorred than he was,*
> *Who for a few pence sold his holy Master!*
> *Twice-betrayed Jesus, me, the last delinquent,*
> *Deems the profanest.*
> *Man disavows, and Deity disowns me....*

There, indeed, is despair — the despair of one who feels disowned by God.

It has been my experience that there are still individuals who feel that they have done some deed so heinous that they cannot be forgiven by God. Seeing the distress caused by such an idea, one would like to dismiss it as unsound and damaging to human life. But, unfortunately, we cannot get away from the fact that Jesus did mention it. He said: "... whoever blasphemes against the Holy Spirit can never have forgiveness, but is guilty of an eternal sin." It seems so unlike Jesus to suggest that any sin in unforgivable. In fact, some scholars doubt that he ever said it, or that if he said it, he said it quite so emphatically. As for myself, if I had a list titled "Things I Wish Jesus Had Never Said," undoubtedly this saying would head the list. But three Gospel writers thought it important enough to include it, so we had better try to discover its meaning.

The setting in which these words were uttered gives us a clue to their meaning. At the beginning of the chapter Jesus has healed a man who had a paralyzed hand. In the passage we are looking at, religious authorities have apparently come down from Jerusalem to observe the various things Jesus was doing and to discredit them. They saw his obviously good acts in behalf of others, and they said that Jesus was able to accomplish these things because he was in league with Beelzebul, the ruler of demons. Jesus counters by saying that if illness and demon possession are the domain of Satan, Satan would hardly be consenting to this abridgment of his powers. He then goes on to draw the conclusion that something about the attitude of the religious authorities is unforgivable.

The first thing that I would like to point out is that Jesus draws a distinction between blasphemy in general, which he says is forgivable, and blasphemy against the Holy Spirit, which he says is not forgivable. Christians reading these word are likely to understand Holy Spirit in the sense of the third person of the Trinity, and feel that, somehow, it is possible so to offend the Holy Spirit as to be forever unforgiven. I think that we need to understand the Holy Spirit as Jesus' Jewish audience would have understood it, for no idea of Trinity had yet been introduced. For them, the Holy Spirit of God had two functions. One was to bring God's truth to people, as when a person was inspired to speak a word in God's behalf. The other function was to enable people to recognize and accept that truth when they were exposed to it. For them, the Holy Spirit was an inner light, given by God, which resides in every person, enabling us to recognize goodness and truth. To sin against the

192

Holy Spirit, therefore, would be to go against the light we have been given.

What Jesus was talking about was spiritual atrophy. We know that people lose those faculties which they do not use. Certainly that is true of our physical bodies. Whenever I take a vacation, my body says, "I want a vacation, too," which means, "I don't want to do that usual regimen of morning exercises." I give in, but when I return to the regimen, I discover, all too painfully, that certain muscles are no longer able to do what they used to do. They have to be educated all over again. If the disuse were to go on for an extended period, the atrophy might become permanent.

This is also true for our minds. I took four years of high school Spanish, and came away with good grades, but I do not have much occasion to use it. When I communicated with the Spanish speaking gardener, telling him how I would like the bushes trimmed, I came back to find that he had understood the opposite. When we don't use a language, we lose it.

This is especially true in the area of esthetics. Charles Darwin tells how, as a young man, he loved music and poetry. But he so gave himself to biology that he completely lost that love, and as a consequence, in later life he wrote that poetry meant nothing to him, and music was only a noise.

This has its application in the spiritual realm as well. In the scripture we are dealing with, Jesus has healed a man, and apparently cast out demons. These were good acts, and any unbiased person would have declared them to be so, but the vision of the religious authorities was so distorted by anger, fear, and hatred that they called these good works evil. They called the light darkness, and they tried to persuade others that actions which were obviously good were evil, and done by an evil person for an evil purpose. In this they demonstrated their own blindness.

In Mammoth Cave, Kentucky, the waters in the farthest recesses of the cave are completely dark. The fish that swim there are blind. The structure of their eyes is intact, but the optic nerve has atrophied. They have eyes, but cannot see. If they were to swim out into the sunlight, they could not tell the difference between that and midnight. Jesus was suggesting that if a people shut their eyes and ears to goodness long enough, they eventually come to the place where they can no longer tell the difference between good and evil. They have extinguished the light that is within them. Those religious authorities could look at goodness, and instead of being moved by it, they could call it evil. The sin against the Holy Spirit, about which Jesus spoke, is the act of so consistently refusing to see God at work in the world that, eventually, God's work can no longer be recognized, even when it is fully displayed.

Still, one must ask, what makes this particular situation unforgivable, when other, seemingly more heinous acts, are forgivable? I do not think that Jesus is in any way limiting the desire or ability of God to forgive. The situation is not unforgivable because God refuses to forgive it. There is nothing that God cannot forgive if the person involved humbly seeks such forgiveness. That is precisely why those who worry about whether they have committed the unforgivable sin are the ones who needn't worry about it. Their consciences are still sensitive to right and wrong, goodness and evil, or else they wouldn't be worrying. And if they are sensitive, they are not blind to the light.

It is this very awareness that we are not all that we could be, that our conduct leaves something to be desired, that leads to our salvation, to our right relationship with God. This awareness is a sense of sin, and it is a healthy thing to have. It doesn't have to be the conviction that one is the worst person who ever lived, or that one is utterly unlovable. It is simply an awareness that we have, thus far, missed the mark, and that our relationships with our better self, with other people and with God, could be better than they are. When such an awareness exists, God has a channel through which to approach us.

I am acquainted with two women who were good friends with each other until one said some hurtful things to and about the other. Their relationship came to an end. In time the offended person found it in her heart to forgive the offender, but she couldn't get through the barrier which the other had erected, so they had no benefit of a relationship with each other. All they knew was alienation, in spite of the fact that forgiveness was available. Years later

194

they resolved the difficulty, but there were all those years of alienation which could have been years of restored relationships, if one of them had been willing to open the channel through which forgiveness and reconciliation could flow.

God has already forgiven us, already accepted us, and desires to share with us the kind of relationship for which we were intended. What separates us is not God's unwillingness or inability to forgive, but our unwillingness to accept what God offers.

If we already know that God accepts us, and we have availed ourselves of that acceptance, is there any message for us in these words of Jesus? I think that there are two messages.

For one thing, these words hold out a warning. The warning is that we must beware of ascribing evil motives to the good actions of others. When the Roman Catholic Church considers elevating a deceased person to sainthood, an actual trial is held in which one person attempts to propose all the good things that the person did in his or her lifetime. There is another person who is appointed to be the devil's advocate. It is this person's job to call into question everything which the person under consideration has done, especially to discredit his or her motives. It is a poor occupation to be a devil's advocate. And yet, we are too often just that when we seek to protect our advantages or to defend our security. We are tempted to discredit someone else's good work or generous act by finding a bad motive, so that the person will not be such a threat to us. Such an attitude eventually leads to moral blindness, the discrediting of goodness, and hardness of heart.

In the play *Amadeus,* the eighteenth-century composer, Antonio Salieri, is depicted as a pious and devout man who seeks to glorify God by his music. As he becomes acquainted with Mozart, he becomes more and more consumed by jealousy and anger over Mozart's greater brilliance. He does everything in his power to discredit his great contemporary. Eventually, Salieri commits himself to the destruction of Mozart and to enmity with God. In seeking to protect his own advantage and security, a good person loses his own soul. Jesus is warning us about this.

There is also a positive message to be learned from these words. The lesson is that we must keep ourselves alert to the way God is working in the world. Remember that those who were seeking to discredit Jesus were religious people. Their problem was that they just didn't expect God to be acting as Jesus said he was acting, so they missed the movement of God in their midst, and in fact, they called it evil. Today God may be speaking to us in causes that are unpopular, or in political events that cause us to feel threatened and insecure. The cries for justice and fairness in the world may come from quarters that we are not accustomed to listen to. We need to exercise diligence so that we don't miss the voice of God today just because it happens to be spoken by unfamiliar lips.

I once sat in on a class my wife was taking in music appreciation. The instructor was asking the class members to listen for the recurring theme as it was passed from one instrument to another and was modified. I quickly lost it, but others in the class, who had benefited from their training, were able to keep track of the theme and even state which instrument was playing it. It is a law of life that we hear what we have trained ourselves to hear. What we must do is to train ourselves to listen for the voice of God in areas where we have not expected to hear it. We hear that voice only by attentive listening: by asking ourselves whether there is a valid message in those things which make us uncomfortable.

Jesus spoke of an unforgivable sin, not because any act is unforgivable, but to warn us that our own hardness of heart can close the channels through which God's forgiveness flows and, as a consequence, leave us feeling alienated. Let us, therefore, affirm the good that is in others, so that our own hearts become generous and accepting of others, even as God is generous and accepting of us.

It's Happening!

In an effort to stimulate their thoughts about the nature of God, I invited a group of teenagers to join me in watching the movie, *Oh, God!* In the course of the movie, God, in the person of George Burns, has prevailed on Jerry, the assistant manager of a supermarket, played by John Denver, to carry God's message to the world. Toward the end of the film, Jerry is lamenting to God that nobody seems to be listening to the message. He tells God that he thinks that they have failed. But God doesn't see it that way. "Oh, I don't think so," God says. "You never know; a seed here, a seed there, something will catch hold and grow."

This is the message of the Gospel passage we are looking at. Jesus has been talking about the Kingdom of God, the time when God's reign will be manifest upon the earth, and people will live in conformity to God's will. It was apparent that it wasn't happening then. It would be even more difficult at the conclusion of Jesus' ministry for his disciples to believe that the Kingdom of God had come any closer to being a reality. They would be a small, discouraged group of fugitives without a leader. Now was the time to provide them with a message that would give them hope in times of discouragement and sustain them in the face of future persecution. His words have a message, not only for his original disciples, but for us as well.

The first thing these words of Jesus do is to remind us that we are called to do something. He spoke of seed to be scattered. If the Kingdom of God is to become a reality, we who are aware of God's grace have seeds to sow. The seeds may be seeds of witness.

In a restaurant, a family of five bowed their heads in prayer before beginning to eat. One of the children, a girl of about ten, expressed thanks for the entire family in a hushed voice, her head bobbing expressively. A few moments later a couple, on their way to pay their check, paused at the family's table. "It's been a long time since we've seen anyone do that," said the man, extending his hand to the father. The father smiled and replied, "It was strange at first, but we always express thanks at home before we eat. The children continued it when we went to restaurants, so we just went along with it, and now it's our way." The woman who had come up to the table patted the little girl on the shoulder and, obviously touched, looked at the mother and said, "Don't ever stop. It means a lot to those around you." It seems like such a little thing, but it was a witness. The seeds of the kingdom are little, and we are called to scatter them.

The seeds may be little acts of kindness which take root and bear fruit. Oscar Wilde tells of an incident that had profound meaning for his life. He was being brought down from his prison to the Court of Bankruptcy, between two policemen, when he saw an old acquaintance waiting in the crowd. "He performed an action so sweet and simple that it has remained with me ever since," wrote Wilde. "He simply raised his hat to me and gave me the kindest smile that I have ever received as I passed by, handcuffed and with bowed head. Men have gone to heaven for smaller things than that. It was in this spirit, and with this mode of love, that the saints knelt down to wash the feet of the poor, or stooped to kiss the leper on the cheek. I have never said one single word to him about what he did ... I store it in the treasure-house of my heart ... That small bit of kindness brought me out of the bitterness of lonely exile into harmony with the wounded, broken, and great heart of the world." We plant the littlest of seeds and it helps the Kingdom to grow.

The second thing these words of Jesus do is to remind us that while we are called to do something, we are not called to do everything. We scatter the seed, but the growth is up to God. As a child during World War II, I contributed to the war effort by planting a victory garden in the backyard of our home. It was a good experience for a child to be involved in. I had to prepare the ground, plant the seed, water the rows, and eventually, attend to the harvest. The hardest part was the waiting. At the first sign of sprouting, I felt that I had to pull up a few radish and carrot plants to see how things were going below the surface. Naturally, that was the end of those plants. As scatterers of seeds, we have some responsibilities, but the maturing process has its own timetable, and we are not in charge.

Certainly, we see that in the development of human beings. A number of years ago *Family Weekly* carried a story about a couple who were called to the office of the principal of the high school their son was attending. "I know how disappointing it is for you to hear these things about your son," said the principal, "but I've talked with his teachers, and we think you should let him drop out of school." The parents, both successful in their fields, were not surprised. For years they had been despairing over their son's poor report cards. "In other words," the father said sorrowfully, "you're telling us he'll never amount to anything."

On a June afternoon, nineteen years later, they sat in the gymnasium of a large university watching as their son received an honorary degree. Today, at the age of 42, his statements are frequently quoted in newspapers, and his income is six figures.

How did this come about? One evening he came home from his job as a gas station attendant and announced that he was going to finish high school and go to college. From then on he amazed everyone by the turnabout of his attitude and accomplishments. He explained the change by saying, "Somehow, while I was washing a blue two-door sedan, all the bits and parts fell into place, and I was grown up."

People grow and mature at different rates. Thomas Edison's teacher said he could never amount to anything and advised his mother to take him out of school. Winston Churchill was admitted to school in the lowest level classes and never moved out of the lowest group in all the years he attended Harrow. Albert Einstein seemed so slow and dull that his parents feared that he was mentally deficient. One observer has said, "Great minds and high talent, in most cases, cannot be hurried and, like healthy plants, grow slowly."

It is so with God's Kingdom. We scatter the seed, but we are not ultimately responsible for its growth. We cannot make things happen. The process by which the kingdom of this world becomes the Kingdom of God proceeds very slowly, and it exasperates us. But, at the same time, if we have faithfully scattered the seed, we are not to blame for its failure to appear in its fullness. We are being cautioned, in these words of Jesus, to be patient.

A third thing these words of Jesus do is to call us to hope. We are ignorant of the process, but the word of Jesus is that growth is taking place. "The Kingdom of God is like a mustard seed," he said, "which, when sown upon the ground, is the smallest of all the seeds on earth: yet when it is sown it grows up and becomes the greatest of all shrubs...." The seed is becoming a bush. God's Kingdom is growing in its own way, from seemingly inconsequential beginnings. All the great music in our culture begins with eight notes. The great literature of our language begins with 26 letters.

Whatever God's Kingdom may one day become, it starts out as the smallest of things. The great advances of the race have often started without any trumpets sounding or anybody being aware that anything exceptional was taking place. On the one hundredth anniversary of Abraham Lincoln's birth, John McCutcheon drew a famous cartoon. He showed two Kentucky backwoodsmen standing at the edge of a wood in the winter. One asks the other, "Anything new?" The other man replies, "Nothing much. Oh, there's a new baby over at Tom Lincoln's. But you know, nothing significant ever happens around here."

Centuries before that someone might have asked in Bethlehem, "Anything new?" And the answer might have been, "No, nothing new. Oh, they say a woman named Mary had a baby in a stable last night. But nothing significant ever happens around here." And when that child grew up and taught, he taught about little things: a cup of cold water, a person with one talent, a widow's offering, a lost coin, kindness done for "one of the least of these." So many of the greatest happenings begin in just such a fashion. They are no more than the planting of a mustard seed. Yet, in God's good time, the seed becomes a plant and puts forth its branches for the benefit of all.

Bishop Bevel Jones tells a story about an experience of Andrew Young, former ambassador to the United Nations, when Young visited South Africa at the invitation of Nelson Mandela several years ago. For years Mandela was a leading opponent of apartheid in South Africa. In 1964, the white establishment locked him up for life. But as his legend grew, there was international pressure to set him free. He was released in 1990, and in 1994 he was elected president of South Africa.

Thirteen months later, Mandela invited Andy Young to be his guest when South Africa hosted the Rugby World Cup Tournament. Rugby was a white man's game, and the South African team was all white, though South Africa is about eighty percent black. Even though the world championship was being played in Johannesburg, there was deliberate absence of support for the team.

As the tournament approached, there was controversy over the South African team symbol — a leaping gazelle called a springbok. Most of the white Afrikaners said, "The springbok has been a symbol of every rugby team we've ever had." Most black South Africans said, "Exactly! It reminds us of South Africa's racist history, and we want it changed." It was an explosive situation.

A few days before the opening game, Mandela visited the team and then called a press conference, at which he wore a team jersey and athletic cap with the team mascot, a springbok, on it. He said that until the elections, he and most other black people in South Africa had always supported whoever was playing against the Springboks. "But regardless of the past," he said, "these are our boys now. They may all be white, but they're our boys, and we must get behind them and support them in this tournament."

The next day, instead of holding a practice, the Springbok's coach took his team out to Robben Island, to the prison where Nelson Mandela had spent nearly three decades of his life behind bars. The coach and every player on the team walked into Mandela's cell. As they stood there, the coach said, "This is the cell where Nelson Mandela was imprisoned. He was kept here for 27 years by the racist policies of our government. We Afrikaners tolerated his imprisonment for all those years, and yet he has backed us publicly. We can't let him down."

The tournament opened, and the Springboks outdid themselves. To everyone's surprise, they won their first game. In fact, they made it into the final game against New Zealand, a rugby powerhouse. At the end of regulation, the game was tied. President Mandela was in the stands, wearing a Springbok jersey. During the timeout, he brought a South African children's choir out of the stands. They sang an old African miners' song which to them is like "Swing Low, Sweet Chariot" was to the slaves in America. Within minutes, 65,000 people in the stadium were standing and singing this black African miners' song. Andy Young said, "I don't know anything about rugby, and I don't understand the words of the song, but I was in tears."[1]

When the Springboks took the field, they were unstoppable. They won the World Rugby Championship. And for the next 24 hours, whites danced with blacks in the streets of South Africa. One of the most divided nations on the planet was united by something some people might consider insignificant — a rugby match. But God used it to heal a nation.

We are not to lose hope when the Kingdom tarries. The seeds have been scattered. Small as they may appear to be to us, the Lord of the harvest will bring them to flower.

----

1. Taken from *Homiletics,* Volume 9, Number 2, p. 48.

When The Boat Begins To Sink

In the Gardener Museum in Boston hangs Rembrandt's painting of *The Storm on the Sea of Galilee*. The artist recreates the scene so powerfully that a viewer can sense the danger the small craft is in and the panic of those who are on board. The small boat is being lifted on the crest of a giant wave; sail and lines are torn loose from the riggings and flailing wildly in the gale. Five disciples are struggling to reef the sail while they hold on desperately to the mast. The rest are in the stern of the boat, clustered around Jesus, some frightened almost to death, one miserably seasick, hanging over the side, and others frantically waking Jesus from his sleep. It is apparent from the calm expression on the face of Christ that this is the moment when he says, "Why are you afraid?" Fourteen figures are in the boat: the twelve disciples, Jesus, and Rembrandt himself. There he stands, clutching one of the stays, holding his head in terror. That is where the artist saw himself. And it is there that many of us find ourselves, with little hope and much fear, as the furious storms threaten to sweep us overboard also.

It is to such persons as we are that this incident is directed. The Gospel writers felt that this incident was important enough for three of them to include it. Though they were reporting an incident from their close association with Jesus, they were aware that the significance of the event went beyond the experiences of that day. I think that the story has several things to say to us today.

In the first place, it tells of the fury of the storm. The Sea of Galilee is as dangerous as it is beautiful. W. M. Christie, who spent years in Galilee, tells of an occasion when a company of visitors were standing on the shore of the Sea of Galilee, and, noting the glassy surface of the water and the smallness of the lake, expressed doubts as to the possibility of such storms as those described in the Gospels. Almost immediately the wind sprang up. In twenty minutes the sea was white with foam-crested waves. Great billows broke over the towers at the corners of the city walls, and the visitors were compelled to seek shelter from the blinding spray, though they were 200 yards from the lakeside!

Such was the experience of the disciples in our story. The day had been a busy one. Mark states that Jesus had preached his message to the people using many parables. Being exhausted, he left the crowd, took his disciples with him, and got into a boat. Jesus went to the back of the boat, stretched out on a pillow, and went to sleep. Suddenly, a strong wind blew up the waves, and water began to spill into the boat. The disciples panicked and rushed to wake the sleeping Jesus.

Certainly the early Christian church heard this story gladly. They saw the boat as the church trying to make its way in a turbulent time. They saw the sea as the realm of evil, dominated by demons. They saw the storm as the persecution they were undergoing in the time of Nero. Sometimes it seemed to them, too, that the Lord was asleep or uncaring. They needed to be reminded that their Lord was with them in a time of persecution, and he would rise to strengthen their faith at the critical moment. This incident became for them an allegory, designed to bring them comfort and hope.

And, of course, we too are confronted with storms. We may stand for something we believe to be right, only to discover opposition, ridicule, a storm of protest. Headlines tell us that it happens today: "Holdout Juror Results in Hung Jury." "Union Activist Fired." "Whistleblower Demoted." We may find ourselves standing there, seemingly alone, clutching for life to some guy wire of integrity, not knowing whether it will hold us.

We may discover that those things we previously relied on for security are swept away: "Merger Leads To 5,000 Layoffs Locally." "Church Divides Over Abortion Issue." "Families Lose Life Savings In Investment Scam." When those headlines are about us, it feels as though everything is falling away beneath us. The boat is beginning to sink. Trusted landmarks have disappeared; navigation is out of control.

The second thing this story takes note of is the fear in the disciples. They shared the world view of their time. As far as they were concerned, every kind of trouble, disaster, or disorder was due to demonic forces. These forces were personal; they were creature-like servants of the evil one. Nature was governed by powers which possessed personalities and wills. Disease, deformity, and mental disturbances were signs of demonic possession. Storms, earthquakes, and natural disasters were the raging activity of demons. When the storm suddenly arose from nowhere, the winds beat against them, the lightning struck, and the waves whipped about them, threatening to capsize their little boat, they must have thought that a whole legion of demons had attacked them. Their cry for help is not only the cry of persons afraid of dying, but of persons afraid of falling into the hands of the evil one.

Now, what does this have to say to us today? We are too sophisticated to believe that demons have any power in our world, aren't we? Maybe, but there is still plenty of superstition to go around. My neighbor changed newspapers because the one she was reading didn't carry the daily astrological forecast. I took an elevator to the fourteenth floor of a modern office building without ever passing the thirteenth floor because none was listed. I have been instructed that the proper way to hang a horseshoe over a door is with the opening up, so that all the good luck doesn't pour out. No matter how educated we become, there is a feeling that there may be some forces at work in the world which have a say in what befalls us, and we are concerned about their power. Like those disciples, we too have fears about who, or what, is in control.

Fear, of course, is ruinous of life. It robs us of the ability to enjoy life. Recently, all the television news programs devoted themselves to the story of a man in Atlanta, Georgia, who killed twelve people and himself in an upscale business neighborhood. He was a day trader in the stock market, and had recently lost more than $100,000 in a week of trading. He was enraged, but also frightened about what this meant for him and his family. He couldn't face the future without his money, so he went home and killed his wife and two children, in order to spare them the agony of fear he was experiencing. Of course, the man was unbalanced, but fear causes people to do crazy things.

Whoever we are, these words about the fury of the storm and the fear it can create still speak to us. The movie *Titanic* captured the interest of people of all ages. One of the things that was obvious to moviegoers was that many of the lifeboats that were lowered were only half full. Yet hundreds of people were left behind to drown because of fear on the part of those in the boats. Survivors told of a swimmer who succeeded in making his way to one of the half-empty boats. He clutched the side and tried to climb in, but no one lent him a hand. In fact, one woman took an oar and pounded his hands until he couldn't hold on any longer, and he slipped back into the sea. She did it, not because there was no room in the boat, but because she was brutalized by fear. Fear can cause us to do things we would never have done if we felt secure.

One could go on and on describing the things that make us fearful and what happens to us as a result. Suffice it to say that fear is a common human experience and that it often robs life of its fulfillment.

In their fear the disciples cried out, "Teacher, don't you care?" Of course they knew that Jesus cared. But at this moment, as they fought for their lives and Jesus slept, it appeared that he didn't care. They got sucked into the panic of the moment, and they asked the question, "Don't you care?"

That is a feeling that is frequently expressed by us when life becomes stormy and we don't know if we can hold on. It is interesting that the word in this story that is translated "great storm" is also the word for "earthquake." As a Californian, I can certainly relate to that! Those who have not experienced earthquakes have certainly seen news footage over and over again of people who have had everything they have struggled to accumulate turned into rubble. Doesn't God care? Elsewhere, the problem is wildfire. People pray that it will not come near them, but it does come to many, and it brings devastation in its wake. Doesn't God care? For others, it is the rising of a river. The whole community turns out to fill sandbags and to patrol the levee, but the water breaks through anyway. Doesn't God care? Each of us knows from one experience or another, what it is like to be caught in a storm, to feel alone, and, like those disciples, to be afraid.

The third thing the story mentions is the response of Jesus. "Peace, be still," he said. There are those who say that he was really addressing the frightened disciples, that he was telling them, "Hush, get hold of yourselves!" Then, when they did get hold of themselves, they settled down, and when the storm ended as abruptly as it began, as is often the case on that lake, they felt that Jesus had brought it to pass. When they got calmed down because of his calm manner, they were able to cope with their situation. Certainly, there is something to be said for such an interpretation, for frequently, when we cry out in our distress, we find that we are not delivered from the situation, but are given grace to endure, given a new attitude that makes it possible to cope.

Such an interpretation appeals to me because that is the way I have found life to be. When we are in trouble, we pray for God's miraculous intervention to get us out of it. There is nothing wrong with that. That is the way children respond to difficulty, and we are children of the heavenly father. But I do not see God regularly interfering in the course of nature to set things right for his favorites or for those who have prayed for deliverance. If that were the case, deeply religious people would never have to face the consequences of their acts or suffer the risks that everyone else must deal with. To think that God could and should keep the rain off of our parade, no matter what is happening to others, is an assumption of arrogance which the life and teachings of Jesus do not support. Jesus, in prayer, asked to be spared the agony of the cross. That is a normal, human request. But he was not spared. Instead, he was strengthened to go through it. In the storm mentioned in this passage, the disciples were being reminded that whether their lives were spared or not, they could not fall outside of God's concern.

The next thing Jesus says is: "Why are you afraid?" God was silent and that made the disciples feel that God was asleep or unaware of their plight, so they were crying out for assurance. Richard Carl Hoefler tells of a little boy who was taking a train ride across the country with his parents. When it came time to go to bed, his mother put him in an upper berth and told him not to be afraid because she was there, Daddy was there, and God was there, and they would all look after him. When the lights were turned down, the little boy called out, "Mommy, are you still here?" "Yes, dear." "Is Daddy still here?" "Yes, dear." "Is God still here?" "Yes, dear." About five minutes later the voice was heard again, "Mommy, are you still here?" "Yes, dear." "Is Daddy still here?" "Yes, dear." "Is God still here?" "Yes, dear." Five minutes later it was the same thing and on through the night until about one o'clock, the little voice was heard again: "Mommy, are you still here?" Whereupon a great gruff voice from the end of the Pullman car roared, "Yes, your mother's here. Your daddy's here. Now shut up and go to sleep." There was a moment of silence and then the little voice spoke up once more, "Mommy, was that God?"[1] Surely, sometimes God must feel like responding to us just as that man did in the Pullman car. We keep asking for assurances because, frankly, we're not that convinced that God is there.

So Jesus asks the disciples: "Have you no faith?" Faith is not the conviction that everyone is going to have things work out in their favor. We often talk about faith as though that is what it means. No wonder we are disappointed. In a world that makes sense, everyone cannot have everything work out favorably for them. A ministerial colleague tells of a conversation he had one day with a female medical assistant in a doctor's office, as he was waiting to see the doctor. The woman recognized him because she had occasionally attended his church, though she was a member of another church. "I want to tell you about my experience," she said. "I got saved in the Assemblies of God Church ... I gave my life to God ... and guess what? ... Life tumbled in! I developed a heart problem. My husband lost his executive job ... and he recently died of cancer." The minister says he tried to mumble a few theological sounding explanatory words about God's mysterious ways, thinking that was what the woman wanted. But she went right on with her story, indicating that she had repeatedly asked God, "Why me?" "And what do you think God told me?" she continued. " 'Why not you?' That's what God said. 'Why should you be spared all the crises of

208

life that everyone else must go through?' " Then she wound up her story saying, "One day I said to God, 'Lord, you've forgiven me. Now I forgive you.' "[2]

There is a woman who, from my point of view, has a healthy faith. Her faith is not a series of propositions, it is a relationship, and as in all relationships, it is one that changes and can tolerate challenges. It is vital because it is honest.

In so many ways our experiences are like those of the disciples: We know what it is to go through stormy times. We know what it is to feel afraid and at the mercy of unfriendly forces. We know what it is to cry out at what feels like an unfriendly universe.

How shall we respond to the question of Jesus: "Have you no faith?" In a devotional article, Milward Simpson, a former governor of Wyoming, tells of flying in a plane that developed engine trouble. When the pilot announced that they were going to try to make an emergency landing, the governor took the hand of his wife and together they offered a simple statement of faith they often shared:

> *The light of God surrounds us.*
> *The love of God enfolds us.*
> *The power of God protects us.*
> *And the presence of God watches over us:*
> *Wherever we are, God is.*

In the article he added that they knew that asserting this affirmation would not make everything turn out all right. But, he said, saying what they said was their way of declaring their confidence that, living or dying, they were in God's care.

Where is God when our boat begins to sink? Right there in the boat, as Jesus was with the disciples. God's presence is not a guarantee of protection, but an offer of maximum support. Support to calm the storm in us, support that helps us to realize that, whatever we are called to go through, at the heart of the universe is Love, and that Love is seeking to find expression through us.

1. Richard Carl Hoefler, *There Are Demons In The Sea* (Lima: CSS Publishing Company, 1978), p. 101.

2. *Pulpit Resources*, Volume 16, Number 2, p. 43.

The Healing Touch

Recently, when I renewed my driver's license, I was presented with the opportunity to renew the accompanying organ donor card. I decided to renew, but I subsequently asked a doctor what organs were likely to be harvested. He mentioned many that I was aware of through stories of successful transplants. Then he pointed out that there is a continuing need for the largest, oldest, most sensitive, most protective organ of the body. When I asked what that was, he replied, "Your skin." I never had thought of it as an organ, but he pointed out that this is the organ that puts us most in contact with the world. Through it we get messages of heat and cold, pain and pleasure, and even love and friendship. It keeps us in touch with ourselves, with others, and with our environment. Touch plays a big part in our well-being.

The passage of scripture before us contains two instances which have something to say about touch. Jesus has just stepped off a boat after crossing the Sea of Galilee, when a man by the name of Jairus, the president of the local synagogue, approaches Jesus and asks him to come to his home, because Jairus' daughter is at the point of death. Jesus agrees to go with him, but as they make their way through the street crowded with spectators, a woman, who has been suffering from a hemorrhage for twelve years, sneaks up behind Jesus with the hope of just touching him, for she feels that just a touch might be enough to heal her. She is considered unclean because of the hemorrhage, and is not even supposed to be out in public, but she is desperate. She succeeds in touching Jesus, and she immediately perceives that she is healed. She hopes to get away unnoticed, but Jesus, feeling that power has gone out from him, stops in his tracks, turns around to face the crowd, and asks, "Who touched my clothes?" The woman falls trembling at Jesus' feet, admitting that it was she who made the contact. Jesus tells her that her faith has made her well, that she is to go in peace, and that she is healed.

While Jesus is still speaking, one of Jairus' servants comes to inform him that his daughter has died, and that there is no need to trouble Jesus further. When Jesus hears this, he urges Jairus to have no fear, but only to believe. When they arrive at the house, Jesus takes the girl by the hand and urges her to get up. She immediately gets up, and gives evidence of being very much alive.

There are many things to be gotten from these two incidents, but what I want to focus on in both of them is the power of touch. People have long felt that touch is important in healing. Bruce Larson tells about a program at Syracuse Upstate Medical Center where they operate on the theory that well people have a reservoir of power that can be tapped to bring healing to the sick. A course is offered in the laying on of hands on the premise that healthy people have a life force called "prana" that can be transferred to persons who are ill.[1] In Lloyd C. Douglas' book *The Robe,* the idea is carried forward that even the clothing worn by Jesus has power to heal, just as the woman in the first story believed.

In his book *Caring, Feeling, Touching*, Sidney B. Simon, a teacher at the University of Massachusetts, speaks of a "skin hunger" felt by all, which is a deep-seated need for the touch, the feel, the concrete reality of human contact. He points out that every human being comes into the world needing to be touched, a need that persists until death. Further, being touched in tender, caring ways can be healing and therapeutic. I have a friend who eats breakfast out most days. One morning he was sitting at the counter in a restaurant, apparently feeling sorry for himself, when a woman came in and sat next to him. They entered into conversation, and the woman told him that he looked like somebody who really needed a hug. She said everybody needed at least ten hugs a day.

He acknowledged that he hadn't had a hug for a long time, whereupon she slipped from her seat and opened her arms wide. He accepted the embrace, and was so energized by it that he went about from that point on offering hugs to everybody.

Andy Rooney points out that there are a lot of hugs that really don't qualify as hugs. He speaks of the "A-frame hug," where two people come together and their heads touch — but nothing else. He says that the effect is a massive leaning, so that the people look like a ski lodge. Another non-hug he calls the "chest-to-chest burp." Chest contact is made, but this makes people so nervous they start patting each other on the back as if they were burping a baby. He says that is our way of reducing the other person to a safe, infantile status. A real hug, Rooney says, is a full body hug that collapses the A-frame and doesn't include the burping. The people coming together take time really to look at each other. I recall being present once when a naval officer who had been at sea for a year, surprised his young son by stepping out of a closet. The boy flew across the room and embraced his father with arms and legs. That was the kind of hug that heals a lot of things. It was a therapeutic touch.

There are, however, other kinds of touching. My unabridged dictionary listed 25 uses of the word touch that go beyond the tactile experience. These include such words as affect, impress, move, inspire, contaminate, stir to pity, and so forth. Jesus asked, "Who touched me?" It is a question we also would do well to ask, and its answer will remind us that each of us has much for which to be grateful.

We have been touched by those who create beauty. In his book *When Iron Gates Yield*, Geoffrey Bull, an English missionary who endured the torture of Chinese communist brainwashing, tells how one day in Chunking, after his captors had taken away everything important, and he was facing death, he heard Beethoven's "Emperor Concerto" coming from a radio being played somewhere outside his prison room. The beauty of the music, he says, sustained him, and he was able to survive. We have been touched time and again by the creators of beauty.

We have been touched by those who have preserved the beauty of nature for us. In Yosemite National Park there is a bronze plaque attached to a huge boulder. The plaque features the outline of a man, and under it are the words: "Stephen Ting Mather. Born July 4, 1867. Died January 22, 1930. He laid the foundation of the National Park Service, defining and establishing the policies under which its areas shall be developed and conserved for future generations. There will never come an end to the work he has done." Here was a man whose work continues to touch us.

We have been touched by a heritage of faith. Norm Lawson shows us how that heritage is passed on. In 1858 a Sunday school teacher named Mr. Kimball led a shoe clerk to give his life to Christ. The clerk's name was Dwight L. Moody. Moody became an evangelist in England, and in 1879 he awakened the heart of Fredrick Meyer, at that time pastor of a small church. Pastor Meyer came to America and, while preaching on a college campus, won J. Wilbur Chapman to Christ. Wilbur Chapman became a YMCA worker and picked up a former baseball player to do evangelistic work. That player was named Billy Sunday. At a revival in Charlotte, North Carolina, Sunday so excited a group of local men that they engaged Mordecai Hamm to come to their town. In a revival with Mordecai Hamm, a young man heard the gospel and yielded his life to Christ. His name was Billy Graham. How many lives have been touched by that man? All of us are what we are because our lives have been touched by others.

The scripture passages we are considering remind us that touching people creatively can cost us something. In the encounter with the woman who touched him, Jesus was aware that power had gone out of him. At Jairus' house Jesus was laughed at when he said that the young girl was not dead. Those who reach out to touch others will find that there is a price to pay. For example, the writer who hopes to leave something for posterity is aware that one doesn't just sit down and write whatever comes to mind. Writing is ten percent inspiration, but ninety percent perspiration. Hemingway was lucky to write three pages a day. I have seen the pages of poets as they write, rewrite, cross out and write again, looking for the right word, the right cadence. It does not come easily.

Helen Hayes, America's first lady of theater, participated in a television commercial some years ago in which she reminded us that good acting involves cost to the actor. Remember, she said, that when we speak of acting, we say that the actor gave a fine performance. Those who truly touch us, whether as actors, writers, or preachers give of themselves.

This is also true of those who serve. I am reminded of Father Damien, who gave himself unselfishly to serve the unfortunate lepers on Molokai. One day when he stood to speak to his flock, he began his remarks by addressing them as "We lepers." He had touched them so intimately as he bound their wounds, that he himself contracted the dreaded disease. If we seek to touch the hurting places of the world, we need to be prepared for the fact that there are costs involved.

And yet, this is the way the power that was in Christ continues to get out to a hurting world. All through our lives others have touched us through their gifts, and those gifts are to be passed on as we touch others. God has chosen to use the human network to tie the generations together. We don't have to preach or pressure anyone. All over this hurting world there is need for a healing touch that is uniquely ours to give.

We are often doubtful that anything we can do can make a difference in the lives of others. I am reminded of that movie *It's A Wonderful Life*, which continues to get replayed every Christmas. A man who is about to lose his business and the savings of a lot of other people as well, wants to take his life, but his guardian angel won't let him. Instead, he is granted his wish that he had never been born. When he revisits his hometown he discovers that nobody knows him, because he had never been born. He finds many things left undone because he had not been there to do them. His brother had died because he wasn't there to save him in an accident. Many bad things had happened because he wasn't there to prevent them. He saw how many lives had been touched by his, and it gave him a new appreciation for how much poorer the community would have been without him.

It would be the same in our community without the touch that each of us can bring. To borrow a phrase, "Reach out and touch somebody," as only you can.

---

1. Bruce Larson, *The Communicator's Commentary: Luke* (Waco: Word Books, Publisher, 1983), p. 157.

You Are Free To Fail

Following his service as Prime Minister of Great Britain during the dark days of World War II, Winston Churchill was invited to speak at Harrow, his boyhood grammar school, from which he had been graduated some seventy years before. As he stood at the lectern, looking out at his young audience, he said, "Young men, never give up! Never give up! Never! Never! Never!" With that he sat down. The audience was stunned. The message was so brief. Yet, in this succinct message, the man who had kept England going in such difficult times was stating the philosophy of perseverance that had led to victory. It is a characteristic that we admire, and which we have been taught to emulate. But does it pertain to every situation we may encounter?

I heard about a woman golfer who finished last in the Shawnee Invitation for Ladies in Pennsylvania some years ago. When she teed off the sixteenth hole, her drive went directly into a nearby river. She gamely set out in a rowboat to play the ball. When she finally succeeded in stroking it out of the water, it landed in a dense woods. From there she drove the ball into the rough, then into a sand trap, then back into the rough. Two hours later she arrived on the green, having taken 166 strokes on a four-stroke hole. She had perseverance, but was it a virtue?

W. C. Fields once said, "If at first you don't succeed, then quit. There's no use in being a fool about it." I think that the reality is somewhere between the two.

In the passages we are looking at from the Gospel according to Mark, there are some useful lessons to be learned about failure.

The first thing I learn from these verses is to accept the fact that sometimes we are going to fail. Some people give the impression that failure is unacceptable. They make it hard for us to live with failure when it happens. Some years ago there was a story about a student at the University of Michigan who, having failed his courses, climbed into the attic of a church and stayed there for many months. He didn't want his parents to know about his failure. At night he would come down into the church in Ann Arbor to get clothing from the church rummage sales and food from church supper leftovers. He suffered terribly from loneliness. Eventually he was discovered, and experienced acceptance from the church. Somewhere he had gotten the notion that is all too prevalent in society that failure is unacceptable.

When Jesus went back to his hometown of Nazareth, he stood up to teach in the synagogue, but the townspeople were offended that this one who had grown up among them should presume to teach them anything. "Isn't this the carpenter?" they said. "Don't we know his family? What does he know about anything?" I've heard it said that an expert is someone who is forty miles from home who shows slides. Jesus was at home and had no slides. Familiarity with Jesus and his background made the hometown folks contemptuous. We read that Jesus could do no deeds of power there because of their unbelief. It was a noble effort, but Jesus experienced failure.

I think that we have to make peace with the possibility of failure, because there are times that we are going to meet up with it. I like the attitude of Harry Truman. When a reporter asked him if he were afraid of making mistakes, he answered: "No. If I were, I could never make a decision. I have to make a decision every day, and I know that fifty percent of them will be wrong. But then, that leaves me fifty percent right, and that's batting 500." "How do you handle the fifty percent wrong?" asked the reporter. Truman replied, "I laugh at them, and at myself, and so does Bess."

I once saw a banner hanging in a church sanctuary that gave me much comfort. It said, "You Are Free Today To Fail." We have to accept the possibility that we may fail, and learn to accept the grace that makes it possible to go on.

A second thing these verses say to me is that our failure is not always our responsibility. Jesus called his disciples together and sent them out two by two to extend his ministry. But he told them right up front that they might not be accepted. "If they refuse to hear you," he told them, "then shake off the dust that is on your feet as a testimony against them." In Jesus' day it was a sacred duty to be hospitable. The village was to offer hospitality to strangers. The Jewish law said that the dust of a Gentile and of a heathen country was defiled, and that when a Jew entered Palestine from another country, he must shake off every particle of dust of the heathen land. Jesus was telling his disciples that when they were not accepted by a town, they should treat that town as a Jew would treat Gentiles.

What I understand Jesus to be saying is that those who are his disciples are to do the best they can to extend his ministry, but that it is not always in our power to succeed. A man called in to one of those late-night radio talk shows. He achingly told about his inability to establish a relationship with his two adult daughters. He and his wife had divorced after 21 years of marriage, and he claimed that the minds of his daughters had been poisoned against him unfairly by his former wife. He said that his life was meaningless without their love. The only contact with them had been at their respective weddings, where he was asked to foot the bills and was given the honor of giving them away. However, before and since, the daughters had not wished to see him, and whenever he tried to establish contact by telephone, they were verbally abusive and hostile. The advice of the radio host was that all he could do was to wait and hope that the girls would one day accept his overtures. There are times when we do what we can, and after that it is out of our hands.

A member of a local church tells how a woman with psychological problems began to attend her church. The pastor and congregation determined to love her into health and happiness. All of their attempts met with failure. When the woman was admitted to the state hospital, many members of the congregation sent cards expressing their concern. The hospitalized woman sent back the cards with criticisms and rejections written on them. When one member of the congregation was asked what she would do next, she responded, "The only truly loving thing there is to do. I'm going to accept her rejection of me." We may fail in what we set out to do, but it does not mean that we are failures. We are simply recognizing that success is not always in our hands.

A third thing I learn from this passage is that when we experience failure, we are to move on. Jesus told his disciples that when they experienced failure in one place, they were to leave.

Sometimes, the best thing we can do is to move on to another place. Lawrence Welk began life in a Dakota farmhouse with sod floor and walls. He was one of eight children born to parents of German ancestry. They were farmers, and expected Lawrence to take up farming as well. From his earliest years, Lawrence was interested in music. His father played the accordian for the family's amusement. When he was a teenager, Lawrence bought a cheap accordian, but it soon fell apart. He saw a more expensive one, and proposed to his father that he would work on the farm for four years without pay if he could have that accordian. The deal was made.

After years of practice, he rented the local opera house and tried to sell tickets for a concert, but it was a dismal failure. No one thought that the local farmboy could be very entertaining. He tried unsuccessfully several times later, but few tickets sold. Even his own family wouldn't come to hear him play. His father told him that music was all right as a pastime, but not as a life work.

Lawrence decided that he would have to leave home to find a place where his music would be accepted. His father warned him that he wouldn't last six weeks, but on his twenty-first birthday, Lawrence left his hometown to test his dream. It was only then that he found success as a maker of music.

Sometimes the best thing we can do is to move on to another field. Paul Harvey tells the story of Joe, who was born into a family of Sicilian immigrants, a family who had a 300-year history as fishermen. Joe's dad was a fisherman. His brothers were fishermen. But Joe was made sick by the smell of raw fish and the motion of a rocking boat. In a family where the only acceptable way to earn a living was by fishing, Joe was a failure. His dad used to refer to his son as "good for nothing." Joe believed his dad. He believed that his attempts at other types of work were an admission of failure, but he just couldn't stand the smell of the fishing business. One thing that Joe could do was to play baseball. Giving up a field where he could not succeed, Joe DiMaggio moved to another field and became one of the great successes of baseball.

Sometimes the best thing we can do is to learn from our failures and try a different approach from the one we've been following. Thomas Edison claimed that he probably had more failures than anyone ever did, yet we do not remember him as a failure. He patented 1,093 inventions in his lifetime, that would lead one to believe that he couldn't have had too many failures. The truth is that he failed quite frequently. But he didn't look on them as failures. When something didn't work he would say, "Now we know one more thing that doesn't work. We're that much closer to finding one that will."

What all of this says to me is that failure is a part of life, but God can redeem even failure and work it into the pattern that God is weaving. Jesus failed to turn the world or even his own people to his understanding of God and God's place in our lives. His enemies seized him and killed him. But God was able to use even Jesus' apparent failure — his crucifixion — as a way to capture our attention, and to woo us toward reliance on God's grace. If God could use such an apparent failure to accomplish his purposes, what may God yet do in those areas where we have failed? We may lose some battles, but God is able to use them to win the "war."

The Fox

I know that I don't have much status up here in Gaul, but will you do me the favor of listening to me? I've had an awful lot of time to think during these years I have been in exile, and I need to share my conclusions about life with someone.

My name is Herod. The problem is that our family is so extended, and so many people bear that name, that I should really use my given name, which is Antipas. My circumstances used to be far different than they are now. It's not that Lyons is such a bad place to end up, but I became used to a lot more luxury when I was Tetrarch of Galilee and Perea in Palestine. All that has been taken from me now by the Emperor, and I am consigned to remain here on the fringes of the Empire for the rest of my life.

My family has exercised power in Palestine for many years. My father, Herod the Great, was King of the Jews. He wasn't even a Jew; he was an Idumean. My mother was a Samaritan, so I don't have a drop of Jewish blood in me. My father's second will named me as his successor, but his final will gave the kingdom to my brother Archelaus, along with the provinces of Judea and Samaria. Another half-brother, Philip, was made ruler of Trachonitus, and I was made Tetrarch of Galilee. A tetrarch is a person who rules a subsection of an area. I contested the assignments, but Caesar upheld the will, and that is how I wound up where I did.

I decided to make the best of it. I built a wall around the city of Sepphoris and made it a metropolis. I built the city of Tiberius, overlooking the Sea of Galilee, and named it after the Emperor. I established another city in Perea, south of the Sea of Galilee, and

223

named it Livias, after the Emperor's wife. For myself, I built the fortress of Machaerus, near the Dead Sea. All that was a long time ago. Reflecting on the events which brought me to where I am now has taught me some important lessons about life. I'd like to share those with you, if you will listen.

The first lesson is: "Control your passions." When I was Tetrarch, I married a certain Nabatean princess, whose father, Aretus, ruled the Nabateans, an Arab people, from his capital in Petra. In the year 35 of the current era I went to Rome to visit my half-brother, named Philip, who was living as a private citizen in Rome. His wife, Herodias, who was also his niece, was my hostess, and she entertained me very well. In fact, I was so enamored of her, that our passions overtook our senses. I seduced her and persuaded her to divorce my brother. My problem was that I was still married. I divorced my wife and married Herodias. This was not uncommon in Rome, but the marriage was against Jewish law, for one is not to marry his brother's wife while his brother is living. Nor did they like the fact that Herodias was my niece. But I didn't feel that I was bound by Jewish laws.

When I brought her back to Palestine, my first wife departed and complained to her father in Nabatea. He was irate at my treatment of his daughter, and he attacked my province with his army. He was successful and defeated my army. I would have lost everything if the Romans had not intervened and put a stop to it. His attack, however, brought great suffering to many of my subjects, and that produced unrest among them. I allowed my passions to take control, and they were leading me into difficulty.

A second lesson I would offer is: "Be considerate of critics." About this time a strange fellow was preaching in the Jordan Valley. The people called him John the Baptist. He dressed peculiarly and called people to repent and to be baptized. I was interested in hearing what he had to say, so I invited him to come to my palace for an audience. He had the audacity to point his finger at me and tell me that it was wrong for me to have my brother's wife. I was ambivalent toward him. On the one hand, I certainly didn't like his criticism of me; on the other hand, it was refreshing to hear someone state courageously what he felt to be the truth. A ruler gets very little of that. As a consequence, I heard him often.

Herodias, however, was enraged by him. Perhaps she felt that he might persuade me to send her back to Rome. She pointed out that he was a real menace. The people heard him gladly, and many considered him to be a prophet. It had been several centuries since a recognized prophet had been heard in the land, and the people were listening for the voice of God. Herodias pointed out to me that he could easily lead the people in an insurrection, especially since the war with the Nabateans had created such hardship.

I acceded to her request and had John arrested and placed in prison. She wanted him killed as a nuisance. I, on the other hand, wanted him protected, and gave orders that he was not to be harmed. Periodically, I sent for him. In listening to my critic, I believe I was doing the wiser thing. I recommend that course to you. Unfortunately, in my situation, that is not where it ended.

Another lesson I would offer is: "Be careful with promises." One day, on my birthday, I was holding a celebration at my fortress, Machaerus. I had invited various officers, courtiers, and leaders in Galilee. Herodias was present. The food and wine were abundant. As a special entertainment, Herodias announced that her daughter, Salome, who was also my niece and step-daughter, would dance for me and my guests. Of itself, this was unusual. Such dances are generally very suggestive and provocative. They are performed by women of questionable background, prostitutes and such. For a young woman from a noble family to engage in such an activity was unheard of. Nevertheless, we were all sufficiently "under the influence" that we cheered her on. Salome was about seventeen at the time, and a very well-endowed young woman. She really knew how to captivate an audience. As others were expressing their appreciation, I sought to outdo them by saying that her performance was so great that I would offer her whatever she might ask, even up to half of my kingdom. I intended it as hyperbole. She left the hall and consulted with her mother about what she should ask for. Herodias saw her chance to make me do something I hadn't wanted to do. She told Salome to ask for the head of John the Baptist. The girl came back in to the festal hall, and before all my guests, she asked for the head of John the Baptist. You could hear a pin drop. All the guests waited to see what I would say. I had foolishly given my word. I didn't expect the girl to take advantage of it, but my guests were waiting to see if I would live up to my promise. I had not wanted any harm to come to John, but I was caught in a dilemma. It was important that my guests see me as a person who kept his word. So I ordered a soldier to go to the dungeon and return with the head of John the Baptist. He left, and a little while later returned with the head of the Baptist on a platter. He gave it to Salome, and she gave it to her mother. I was saddened and sobered by the whole affair. I learned the importance of being careful with promises.

Another lesson I would offer is: "Be prepared for the power of conscience." A person in a position of power frequently has to make decisions he doesn't necessarily want to make. Then, in the wee hours of the morning, those decisions can come back to haunt him. I experienced that over the order to kill the Baptist. Not long after John's death, I began to hear about another itinerant preacher who was called Jesus. He, too, was attracting attention among the poor. When I inquired about him, I learned that some people felt he was a prophet, like one of the prophets of old. The people listened to him, because they wanted to hear an authentic word from God. Others said that he was Elijah, the prophet of old who was expected to return as a herald and forerunner of the Messiah. Still others suggested that he was actually John the Baptist, raised from the dead. That was the explanation that I tended to accept. My conscience was already troubling me, because I had had a person executed who did not deserve it. I told my soldiers that I wanted to see this Jesus, so I could decide for myself who he was, but he eluded me. Some reported back to me that when townspeople told him of my desire to see him, Jesus referred to me as a fox. I didn't get to see him at that time, but his presence kept my conscience in turmoil. Anybody who has to make unpleasant decisions had better be prepared for the same.

The next lesson I would offer is: "Be cautious about making judgments in areas that are not your business." Sometime after the event with the Baptist, I was in Jerusalem during the Passover.

Jesus had been arrested and brought before Pilate, the governor, for judgment. Pilate was apparently being pressured by the Jewish authorities to find Jesus guilty of some matter of Jewish law. As a Roman, Pilate apparently didn't feel that the charges against Jesus called for the death penalty. He was looking for a way out, or looking for someone else to make the decision. There had been bad blood between us for some time, and neither of us cared much for the other. But I think that Pilate saw a chance to use me. He discovered that Jesus was from Galilee, which was in my jurisdiction, so he had Jesus sent over to where I was staying, hoping that I would pass judgment, and thus relieve him of the obligation of imposing an unpalatable sentence. I was glad to have the opportunity to see this Jesus, for whom I had so long been searching, but I was certainly in no mood to get involved in making another judgment. I interviewed Jesus and satisfied myself that he was not John the Baptist resurrected, and then I had him taken back to Pilate with no recommendation from me. From that point on, Pilate and I had a greater respect for one another. I appreciated his acknowledgment of my jurisdiction, and he appreciated my ability to avoid a politically charged situation. I am sure that I acted rightly, and I urge others not to make judgments about things that don't concern them.

One final lesson, perhaps the most costly of my life, that I would pass on, is "Practice contentment." Philip, who governed the area north of me, died. I thought that perhaps I could add his province to mine, but before I could act, the new emperor, Caligula, gave the province to Agrippa, who happened to be Herodias' brother. With the province, Caligula also gave Agrippa the title of king. It was a title I had sought earlier, when my father's kingdom was divided among my brother and me. I could live with the emperor's decision, but it galled Herodias to hear her brother called king, when I was called but a tetrarch.

Herodias couldn't leave it alone. She wanted to be called a queen. She continually urged me to go to Rome to offer the Emperor money for the title of king. She said that we should take lots of money and be prepared to spend whatever it took to get the title. "The purpose of money is to make us happy," she said, and it was apparent that she would not be happy until she had the title queen. Reluctantly, I gave in, and we went to Rome.

In the meantime, Herodias' brother, Agrippa, concerned about our intentions, sent messages to the Emperor, stating that I was untrustworthy, that I was in league with the Parthians and planning an insurrection. The Emperor believed Agrippa, took our money, took away my provinces, sent us into exile here in Lyons, and gave my provinces to Agrippa. Obviously, I had overstepped my bounds. I was seen to be too assertive. I should have been more content with what I had. My advice to you, therefore, is to be slow to push for more recognition. Do your job in the best way you can, and learn to be content.

Perhaps you think that what I have told you only applies to rulers, such as myself. I think that these lessons are applicable to everyone, and I urge you to take them to heart. Control your passions, give consideration to criticism, be careful with promises, be prepared to deal with your conscience, be cautious about making judgments, and practice contentment. Perhaps the best thing that I can do is to have my life be a lesson for you.

Proper 11
Pentecost 9
Ordinary Time 16
Mark 6:30-34, 53-56

Making Compassion A Verb

The Superintendent of Schools was having a bad year. Some contentious issues were being dealt with by the school board. One Sunday, during the coffee hour after church, I heard the Superintendent say in a particularly loud voice, "For crying out loud, it's my day of rest, too!" Someone had approached him about a concern in the school district, and he felt that there was no place he could go to get away from it. I learned right then not to approach people about business matters when they are not on duty.

Jesus was able to deal with such intrusions more graciously. In the passage we are looking at, Jesus has been rejected by the people of his hometown, his disciples have just returned from a mission he sent them on, and he has been informed about the murder of his cousin, John the Baptist. People were pressing in on him, seeking all kinds of help. Jesus felt that it was time to withdraw and get some rest, so he and his disciples got into a boat and set out for a more quiet place some distance away. Unfortunately, some of the townspeople heard where Jesus was going, and they hurried there on foot. When Jesus and his disciples arrived, a crowd had already arrived and needy people were already standing around, waiting to present their needs. Any person seeking a rest would have been justified if he expressed exasperation under such circumstances. Mark tells us, however, that Jesus had compassion for the crowd, because they seemed to him to be like sheep without a shepherd.

What does it mean to have compassion? Mark spends the remainder of the chapter showing us. Jesus proceeds to teach the people, then to feed them, then to comfort his disciples and allay their fears, and then to heal people who are sick. The work appears to be never-ending. Those first century disciples experienced first-hand the mission and ministry of Jesus. They learned by observation what compassion meant. Then they were called to put it into practice. So are we. If we are to put compassion into practice, we need to know what is involved.

In order to be compassionate, at the very least, we need to be sensitive to the suffering of others. Some people's hearts have become hardened. A number of years ago a television company ran an investigation into the allegation that certain ambulance companies would not transport apparently poor people to hospitals without payment up front. The television production team called an ambulance company and asked them to send a team to a staged emergency. When the ambulance team arrived, they found a shabbily dressed middle-aged man lying on the floor of an apartment, his eyes closed, writhing in pain, gasping desperately for air. The driver and attendant looked on impassively. "He's gotta have 38 bucks, or we don't take him," one of them snapped to the stricken man's roommate. Pointing to two one-dollar bills on the kitchen table, the roommate pleaded: "That's all I can find. But he's got a job, and he's good for the money." This wasn't good enough for the ambulance team. Visibly annoyed, the attendants helped the roommate prop the victim in a kitchen chair. Then they departed, but not before one of them pocketed the two dollars from the table.[1] Those who are so hardened to the suffering of another certainly invite our contempt.

Fortunately, most people are capable of more compassion than that. Mencius, a Chinese philosopher who lived several hundred years before Christ, and was eager to show that there is good in everyone, said, "All people have a capacity for compassion. If people see a child about to fall into a well, they will, without exception, experience a feeling of alarm and distress. This is not because they know the child's parents, nor out of desire for praise ... nor out of dislike for the bad reputation that would ensue if they did not go to the rescue. From this we may conclude that without compassion one would not be a human being." Mencius was right to say that compassion is a component of true humanity, but alas, recent wars have shown us that there are also those who would as soon throw a child into a well as to pull one out. Some people are so self-occupied that they don't even notice those who are suffering. The compassion of which we are capable needs cultivating if it is to find expression.

Following Christ is one way to nurture that characteristic. Flannery O'Connor, the insightful Roman Catholic writer, lifted up the Christian dimension when she wrote: "You will have found Christ when you are concerned with other people's sufferings and not your own." The beginning of compassion involves becoming aware of the suffering of others.

But it is not enough simply to *see* the suffering of others, we need to *feel* it. It is possible to see suffering, but not to feel it. Dewitt Jones tells about a photographer who walked down the street one day and came upon a man who was choking. "What a picture," he thought. "This says it all: A man, alone, in need. What a message!" He fumbled for his camera and light meter until the poor fellow who was choking realized that help was not forthcoming. He grabbed the photographer's arm and gasped, "I'm turning blue!" "That's all right," said the photographer, patting the fellow's hand, "I'm shooting color film." Just noticing suffering isn't enough.

The word "compassion" means to "suffer with." Throughout his ministry, Jesus involved himself in the sufferings of others. The passage we are considering reminds us that he fed the hungry, healed the sick, and taught the ignorant. He put his hand out and touched lepers. Even Sunday school children know the shortest verse in the Bible: "Jesus wept," which reminds us that Jesus not only saw, but entered into the sorrows of others.

In his book *The Human Comedy*, William Saroyan noted: "Unless a man has pity, he is inhuman and not yet truly a man, for out of pity comes the balm which heals. Only good men weep. If a man has not yet wept at the world's pain, he is less than the dirt he walks upon, because dirt will nourish seed, root, stalk, leaf, and flower, but the spirit of a man without pity is barren and will bring forth nothing...." Good people feel the pain of others, and they weep.

Will Rogers was known for his laughter, but he also knew how to weep. One day he was entertaining at the Milton H. Berry Institute in Los Angeles, a hospital that specialized in rehabilitating polio victims and people with spinal cord injuries and other extreme physical handicaps. Very soon, Rogers had everybody laughing, even patients who were paralyzed; but then he suddenly left the platform and went to the restroom. Milton Berry followed him to make sure he was all right. When he opened the door, he saw Will Rogers leaning against the wall sobbing like a child over the tragic situations he was seeing. Berry closed the door, and in a few moments Rogers appeared back on the platform as jovial as ever. Christians are called to a ministry of compassion, and if we are faithful to it, it will cause us to weep with those who weep.

But it is not enough simply to *feel* the pain of others, we also need to *act* to relieve it. In Albert Camus' novel, *The Fall*, an established, impeccable French lawyer has his world totally under control until one night when he hears the cry of a drowning woman and he turns away. Years later, ruined by his failure to act, he winds up reliving the experience in an Amsterdam bar: "Please tell me what happened to you on the Seine River that night, and how you managed never to risk your life," he says to himself. "(Go ahead), utter the words that for years have never ceased echoing through my nights ... 'O young woman, throw yourself into the water again so that I may have a second chance of saving both of us!' " When we fail to act in behalf of someone in distress, something inside of us knows, and will not let us forget, for we have been less than God intends us to be.

Too often, we are content simply to talk about a situation rather than to do something about it. In a book titled *Get Out There And Reap!* Guin Ream Tuckett chronicles the activities of a character named Marsha, who is a forward-thinking Christian in a stodgy, tradition-bound church. One time, quite by accident, she influenced her junior high Sunday school class to challenge the status quo. They talked about an upcoming church dinner. Marsha observed that there was always an abundance of food at such gatherings. She casually remarked what a witness it would be to share their abundance with others. On the evening of the next church supper, the tables were filled with food as usual. During the pre-meal prayer, a loud noise erupted as two dozen disheveled teenagers of all sizes, colors, and appearances rumbled down the stairs. A boy from the junior high class, Jason, went running up to the young people and greeted them enthusiastically. Jason's father worked at the local youth social center. Jason and the class had taken Marsha's words to heart and invited all the kids from the social center. These newcomers were kids who didn't have healthy family structures, and paid little attention to table manners. But they were enthusiastic about the church program, and they gratefully shoveled down food as though they had never had a full meal in their lives. The church members were shocked, and many stared accusingly at Marsha throughout the evening. At the next meeting of the class, Marsha scolded her students for not warning her of the grand scheme. Then she realized where the problem lay. "That's the trouble with you kids," she said. "You take your religion seriously!" Then she realized what she was saying. She and the older church members had been content simply to talk about hungry people. The kids had acted.[2]

Writing about another time and place, Leo Tolstoy said, "I beheld the misery, cold, hunger, humiliation of thousands of my fellow human beings ... I feel, and can never cease to feel, myself a partaker in a crime which is constantly being committed, so long as I have extra food while others have none, so long as I have two coats while there exists one person without any ... I must seek in my heart at every moment, with meekness and humility, some opportunity for doing the job Christ wants done." The job Christ wants done. He set the course; we are to do the rowing.

When World War II ended, the members of a church in Frankfurt, Germany, began reconstructing their bombed-out sanctuary. One of the main objects to be restored was a statue of Christ that had been sorely broken apart. All the pieces were found except the hands. After long debate, the congregation decided to leave the figure without hands. Under it they inscribed the words: "Christ has no hands but our hands." The job that Christ wants done still involves compassion. We are the ones called upon to show it.

1. Stan Gooch, *Total Man* (New York: Holt, Rinehart and Winston, 1972).

2. Guin Ream Tuckett, *Get Out There And Reap!* (St. Louis: Bethany Press, 1976), p. 80.

Sermons On The Gospel Readings

For Sundays
After Pentecost
(Middle Third)

Stephen M. Crotts

Dedicated
to
George Byron Crotts

My Father,
My Mentor,
My Friend.

I still think he is ten feet tall!

Foreword

William Butler Yeats, an Irish poet, wrote of "The Lake Isle of Innisfree," a quiet natural reserve he retreated to for peace and inspiration.

My Innisfree is on Lake Macintosh in the midlands of North Carolina. There I have in the Good Lord's provision a tiny Walden-like cabin secluded in the shade of maples, dogwoods, and beeches.

It is here the Lord Jesus speaks to me. It is here I pour over his Word. To the sound of lake water lapping on the shore I pray and meditate. On long walks down country roads I ponder. And there in my rocking chair I scribble the words that become books.

These words come from Jesus, from the Bible as inspired to me by the Holy Spirit.

These words have shaped me, goaded me, corrected me, and healed me.

I have seen them do the same for others in the life we keep together called church. It is my prayer they will do the same for you and yours.

Through the gift and grace of Christ Jesus we no longer stumble in darkness but walk with open eyes in the bright of day.

Stephen M. Crotts
Innisfree

**Proper 12
Pentecost 10
Ordinary Time 17
John 6:1-21**

The Hillside And The Basket

There is a certain rock known as a geode. From the outside it is but a dull-looking stone. Yet crack it open and one discovers a breathtaking array of crystals in a hollow core.

I feel like I'm holding an uncracked geode in my hands when I look at a Bible text. I know there is a powerful blessing in the passage. It must simply be opened to the light by preaching.

So to the text, the story of the feeding of the multitudes, we now turn.

There Was a Need!

Our text begins with a human need.

Jesus had been busily ministering from Jerusalem to Galilee. The healings, the preaching, the conflict left him spent. So he got in a boat with his disciples and sailed across the lake to take a break. But the throngs of people had not had enough of the Master's words and deeds. They wanted more. So they tramped around the lake's north shore, perhaps a distance of fifteen or twenty miles, in order to be where Jesus was.

The text tells us it was the time of Passover. So the roads would have been filled with pilgrims on their way to Jerusalem. How quickly word spread of Jesus and his whereabouts. And so it was that the crowd swelled as men, women, and children detoured to have a look at Jesus. They were looking for Passover bread and found Jesus instead!

So, there stands Jesus atop a hillside overlooking Lake Galilee. The crowd he sought to be rid of has followed him and even grown into the thousands. By now it is late in the day, supper time nears and stomachs begin to rumble for want of food.

But, wait! There's more need than for a meal. The sick are in the crowd. The ignorant are present. So, too, are the lonely, the adulterous, the confused, the lost, the misguided. All these Jesus sees as he looks over the vast throng gathering at his feet.

Such needs are still with us today. We see the teeming refugees of Rwanda on the evening news. Day after day the papers print accounts of the gunshot and bleeding victims of inner city crime. The famine-ravaged throngs are vividly heralded in our weekly news magazines. Through the miracle of modern mass communication we see more needy crowds than Jesus did in his day. Sociologists are beginning to identify in people a syndrome that is a direct result of the information age. It seems we see so many hurts and can do so little about it that we feel powerless. So we avert our eyes, stop our ears to the wails, grow calloused in our hearts. The result is the poor hurting masses become increasingly invisible to us.

I have a friend who ministers in a large western city among the Chinese. He shares with me how church groups call and ask for their group to be allowed to tour the Chinese ghetto. He obliges, showing them up close and personal the poverty, the ignorance, and the depravity that breed like flies in the ghetto. One group saw all this, sat for a moment in sullen silence, then all but spoke in unison, "Can you tell us where the best Chinese restaurant in town is so we can go eat?"

It is so easy to see and not see, to hear and not hear, to become so self-absorbed in what we want that we miss what others need.

So many times I speak with ministers who desire a change, a larger church. It's just not "happening" where they are. They want to move. But, open your eyes! We each pass by more hurting people, more potential ministry in a single day than any one person could do in a lifetime!

There on the hillside where you stand, do you see the throngs of hurting people all around you? Jesus did. Ask Christ to open your eyes to the lost there in your factory, in your neighborhood, at your family holiday gathering.

There Was An Inadequacy

The text further points out that there was an inadequacy. "Lifting up his eyes, then, and seeing that a multitude was coming to him, Jesus said to Philip, 'How are we to buy bread, so that these people may eat?' This he said to test him for he knew what he would do. Philip answered him, 'Two hundred denarii would not be enough bread for each of them to get a little' " (vv. 5-7). "Two hundred denarii" is equal to roughly half a year's wages. In other words, Philip surveyed the multitude, and, standing right beside Jesus declared the situation hopeless. "There is nothing that can be done!" he said.

Notice the text reveals how Christ had set up this situation and used it to test Philip. John 1:44 tells us Philip was from this region. He knew the towns, the valleys, the roads, and the lake. He would have known what local resources could be brought to bear on the needs, so Jesus queried him, "How are we to buy bread so that these people may eat?" And Philip did the math in his head. Standing beside Jesus he looked at the hillside crowd, surveyed the contents of his own purse, and declared his resources woefully inadequate.

Philip wasn't the first to feel inadequate in the face of life. The children of Israel stood on the edge of the promised land and listened to their returning spies describe the giants. "We seemed as grasshoppers to them," they moaned. And immediately there was a move to return to Egypt. They simply couldn't see God for the giants.

Solomon, newly crowned Israel's king, besought the Lord. He confessed, "I don't know how to go in and out before this people."

I knew when my first church had 47 people in it that it was too big for me.

Inadequacy. That's what a missionary in Zaire feels as he walks through a village smitten with the Ebola virus. It's what the parents of an angry teenager feel. And it is what Philip felt standing beside Jesus looking at a hungry crowd of 5,000.

And it was a test. Would Philip stress the difficulties presented or the resources possessed? Would he measure his powers or his problems? Would he focus on the hillside of people or the basket?

Would he count the crowd or the loaves? Would he look at his ability to begin the work or his inability to finish the work?

Jesus was testing Philip, even as he still tests you and me today. He was educating the disciples to do what they could and leave the rest to God. He was illustrating the universal law: Resources and powers are given to those who use what resources and powers they have.

There Was An Offering

So, Philip flunks the test. He can't see Jesus for the crowd. He considers his and the area's human inadequacy to meet the need, never once considering God. And so he is pessimistic. "Half a year's wages would barely give each a morsel. The situation is hopeless. Nothing can be done."

Meanwhile there is Andrew. In the crowd he discovers a lad with five barley loaves and two fish. This he carefully explains to Jesus. Then he despairs, "But what are they among so many?"

To be sure, Andrew sees the crowd, the hunger, the expense. But he also sees Jesus. To be sure he sees the daunting task, but he also sees a way to begin.

Andrew could say, "I am only one. I can't do everything. But I can do something. And just because I can't do everything, I will not fail to do that which I can do."

We are told in the text that the little boy carried with him a picnic lunch of five barley loaves and two small fish. Barley bread was the cheapest sort of food. And the fish were likely pickled, not unlike today's sardines.

This is what Andrew found. This is what the lad offered to Jesus in the midst of 5,000 rumbling stomachs. There was a huge need! There was a woeful inadequacy! And these few loaves and fishes were the paltry offering.

But see what happened next!

There Was A Miracle

Jesus received the scant fish and bread, and, causing the masses to be seated, gave thanks to God, and began to break the loaves and distribute them. The Bible says the crowd ate until they were "filled"; in the Greek they were literally "glutted."

And Philip so pessimistic, Andrew so full of questions, the little child so naive, and the multitude so full of hunger all learned of God's caring provision even for their stomachs. And they learned the spiritual law that God can do a lot with a little if he has it all. They learned that little is much when God is in it. They learned not to look at the multitudes or the lack or what lines one's own pockets. Look at Jesus. Give him what you can. And leave the rest to God.

I asked a church that had recently hired a new pastor, "How is it going?" And I'll forever remember the answer. "Stephen, things are going great! Our new pastor is asking God for things our former pastor didn't even know he had!"

Poor Philip. Isn't he so like you and me? Here we stand beside Jesus looking out on a need so vast that our own yearly salary couldn't satisfy even one meal. All the while standing beside us is Jesus, the God who sees the need, who is never inadequate, and who is willing to receive what we've got, add his own blessing to it, and make it enough!

Rembrandt could take a two-dollar canvass, paint a picture on it, and make it a priceless masterpiece. That is art. John D. Rockefeller could take a worthless check, sign his name to it, and make it worth a million dollars. That's capital. A mechanic can take a piece of scrap metal and bend and shape it into a $500 automobile part. That is skill.

Jesus Christ can take the commonest bread and pickled fish, bless and multiply it, and make a banquet for 5,000! That's a miracle.

Likewise can God Almighty take a vile sinner, wash his sins away, fill him with the Holy Spirit, and make him a blessing to humanity. That's salvation, and something of what it means to be a Christian.

You see, it is not what we are in and of ourselves. It is what God does in us and through us.

God can take our paltry offerings in his hands; God can receive our lives, our faith, inadequate as we are, and make us enough on every hillside in every land in every generation.

Conclusion

In the Old Testament, a sign of a king's prowess was how many people he could feed. Pharaoh and Joseph fed all Egypt during a famine. Moses fed Israel for forty years in the wilderness with manna from heaven. And here Jesus acts as the father of the table spread out along a vast hillside.

There is some debate over the exact nature of this miracle. Some Christians see it as a simple and mighty act of divine multiplication. Just as Jesus turned water into wine at the wedding feast of Cana, just as God rained manna and quail in the wilderness, so Jesus fed the 5,000 by doing a miracle.

Others say, "Not so fast!" At his temptation Jesus refused to turn stones into bread. Instead he opted to bring the world spiritual bread. Earlier in this century German theologian Rudolph Bultmann sought to deny the miraculous of the Bible. He would cynically see Jesus storing a hillside cave with bread, guiding a crowd out there, and having a disciple quietly hand the bread out to him so he could give it to an adoring crowd.

Still others point to something else, perhaps even more of a miracle. These persons point out that the crowd was not stupid. They would not have started a Passover pilgrimage without provisioning themselves. So, when 5,000 souls gathered to Jesus on a hillside and supper time drew near, the food was really there. It's just that no one wanted to pull theirs out for fear others would mooch off them and their personal provisions would be seriously eroded.

So, as the story goes, meal time comes and no one wants to share. There is bread enough but it's being hoarded selfishly. And Jesus shames the crowd with the child's sacrificial trusting offering. And the secret stores of food are opened and passed around. Thus the miracle was not in fish and bread, but a greater miracle of the human heart. For no mere fish were changed, nor even the loaves, but selfish men and women were changed.

I love the story of a Christian missionary hiking the high Andean trails to a remote village in Peru. He found a rock along the road, a curious geode, and put it in his pack as a souvenir.

That evening he strode into the village to a very unfriendly welcome. No one offered him a bed. No one asked him to sojourn by their fire. He learned that a famine had hobbled the Indians for over a month. And the people were starving. Each was simply afraid to share amidst so much deprivation.

Praying to Jesus how to help them, he got an idea. Calling the Indians around a campfire he preached God's loving care in Christ. Then he said, "I'm going to feed you by making some stone soup. Ummm! It's tasty! I grew up on it! And you'll like it just fine!" Then he opened his rucksack and produced the rock he'd found that morning.

The Indians demurred, "Stone soup! Why that's the stupidest thing I've ever heard!"

"Trust me," the missionary soothed. "See! I've brought the stone. But I'm going to need a pot to put it in."

An Indian woman quickly volunteered her pot.

"And I'll need about two large buckets of water to boil the stone in." A man, his eyes ablaze, quickly brought water.

So, in went the stone, in went the water, and over the fire the pot was suspended.

Curious, now, the villagers began to gather around the pot, peering into its contents.

The missionary began to stir the pot and drool. "You know, stone soup sure is good with carrots!"

To which an Indian said, "I've got six carrots!" He quickly fetched them and they were cut up into the pot.

Then the missionary smelled deeply of the bubbly broth and sighed, "Some potatoes sure would add to the flavor." From pockets and other hiding places came dozens of spuds. They were quickly added to the soup.

Soon people were bringing onions, celery, and bits of meat to top off the pot of stone soup.

And within the hour a community formed around that stew pot. All ate. And all were filled and they heard the story of Jesus Christ.

Believe John 6:1-14 as a miracle of Jesus in multiplying the bread and fish, if you will, or believe Jesus' miracle in the selfish human heart causing the multitudes to share. But above all, remember this: The next time you see a need or feel inadequate, don't look at the hillside, look in the basket. Don't count the difficulties presented. Look at the resources possessed. Don't measure your problems. Measure God's power! Jesus is standing beside you. And you plus Christ are enough!

Proper 13
Pentecost 11
Ordinary Time 18
John 6:24-35

The Dark Didn't Catch Me!

Remember how it was in grade school when your class went out on the playground during recess? Doug and Sam, the two big guys, started choosing up sides to play kickball. And the rest of us just sort of stood around and hoped one of them would pick us for their team. And how affirming, how exciting it was to hear your name called and know that you were wanted.

And it's the same in this big lonesome world that doesn't seem to need us very much. It's easy to feel left out, unchosen. But the Good News of the Gospel is that God is choosing a team, and he has chosen me and in every likelihood he is calling your name as well. Ephesians 1:3-5 says, "Blessed be the God and Father of our Lord Jesus Christ, who has blessed us in Christ with every spiritual blessing in the heavenly places, even as *he chose us* in him before the foundation of the world, that we should be holy and blameless before him. He destined us in love to be his sons...." That's it! Chosen! Destined in love! Holy and blameless before him! Blessed in Christ with every spiritual blessing! This is where I am right now and I want to tell you how I got here.

Now I realize it is unfashionable to talk about oneself. "I, me, my, mine!" "No! Tell us about the Lord Jesus! We'd rather hear about him!" Well and good. But the Bible does say, "Let the redeemed of the Lord say so" (Psalm 107:2). The Apostle Paul shares his testimony in the letter to the Galatians. And in Psalm 66:16 David says, "Come and hear ... and I will tell what he has done for me." So in that spirit today I want to share with you my testimony.

247

In the text Jesus promised, "I am the bread of life; he who comes to me shall not hunger." I have known hunger. But in Christ I've known satisfaction. Here's my story.

What I Was Saved From

Most testimonies begin something like mine. "I was born at a very early age." Seriously, I was born into a Christian home. No greater privilege could one ask for than a mother and father who fear God, who worship Christ, who love each other, who work hard, who provide a loving home, and who exercised their spiritual authority over me by baptizing me into the covenant when I was only a few weeks old. I was baptized not because I loved God as an infant, but because God loved me. It was a covenant my parents made with God for me to train me up in the ways of Christ and encourage me to have faith.

From my earliest memories I can recall church nurseries, flannel board Bible studies in tiny classrooms, children's sermons, family prayer at mealtime, and being pinched when I misbehaved in worship. There were church suppers, youth fellowships, Bible studies, choirs, Christmas plays, and more sermons than I can remember.

By the time I was ten or eleven years old I knew the parables, the Christmas stories, the Easter story, John 3:16, and all four stanzas of my favorite hymn, "Holy, Holy, Holy!" And I wanted more! Not content with the covenant my parents made for me at my infant baptism, I wanted to make my own covenant with God. I wanted to profess my own faith in Jesus, and I wanted to do so publicly!

So, I was enrolled in a Confirmation Class. And there was no more eager student than I. But in Confirmation Class I was not taught the Bible. I was taught the church; instead of being taught Jesus, I was taught John Wesley and John Calvin. But still, in all of this weakness I reached out in faith and accepted all of Christ I could understand and gave him all of me that I knew how to give.

So, a new Christian was born. But in my church home I was not taught how to live the Christian life. No one told me about the Holy Spirit or prayer or how to study the Bible or witnessing. And I did not grow. And slowly I began to move backward, so that by the time I was sixteen I had a teenage body with teenage problems

248

and a twelve-year-old's faith. And the great sadness was that I thought I knew all of God there was to know.

This time of the year doctors are busy inoculating people against the flu. And do you know how inoculation works? A person is given just enough of the flu so that he gets a mild case, builds up his immunity, and can't therefore get the real thing. And if we are not careful the same thing can happen to us in church. We get just enough religion so that we cannot get Christ.

So, here I was a sixteen-year-old with a twelve-year-old's faith. God was in my life, but he was not in control. My knowledge of God was grossly overshadowed by my ignorance of God. And I began to turn to the world and things, giving them the commitment only God rightly deserves.

There were football and getting a driver's license, wearing the right clothes, being accepted by the right crowd, and girls. And by age sixteen I was really into these things as a way of life. And Jesus became just one more thing I had going for me, and a not very important one at that.

Yet deep within I was not at peace. Jesus says he is the Bread of Life and if we eat his bread we'll never again hunger or thirst. And I was missing his bread. And I was hungering and thirsting. I was finding out firsthand that the human soul is so big that all the world cannot fill it. All of the sports, all of the clothes, popularity, cars, and girlfriends can't ultimately satisfy.

So here I was a sixteen-year-old who had it all, and yet deep within I knew that something was missing.

Henry David Thoreau wrote, "Most men live lives of quiet desperation," and I was one of those men.

Imagine for a moment that you are lost in the forest. It's getting dark and you are afraid. With sundown comes the cold. And you look around yourself for an answer. Off in the distance you see a tiny glimmer of light. So you run through the forest, the briers and limbs tearing at your face and hands. Eventually you come to a campfire burning brightly in a clearing. You don't know to whom it belongs, but you don't care. There is light. There is warmth. And with your present needs met you curl up and fall fast asleep.

Some hours later you awaken. And something is very wrong. The campfire has gone out! It's dark again. You are cold again. You are lonely again. And there is nothing left for you there but cold, unfeeling ashes. Off in the distance you see a tiny flicker of light. Running there, you discover another campfire. Quickly you curl up beside it and fall fast asleep. But that fire goes out too. So you're on the run again.

Some people live their lives running from one campfire to another. "If I can just get a new car, I'll be happy!" And you get the car. Then it's, "If I can just get a girlfriend, I'll be happy!" So you get one, and it's now, "If I can just make the team, I'll be fulfilled!" So you make the team, but you're still not at peace. And so it was with me. I was on a search for meaning in life, for fulfillment. Mine was no orgy of sex, a sordid trail of drug abuse, cruelty, or dishonesty. It was more of a quiet clutch of materialism, substituting things for God.

About this time I read a book, J. D. Salinger's *Catcher In The Rye*. It's the story of a young man who flunks out of prep school and takes off on a three-day escape. You can feel how lonely he is. You can feel his confusion. His conversation is full of bragging, showing off, and smart remarks. He never lets on to others how tender he feels inside. And as I read the book I saw myself and was ashamed. "My God!" I cried. "That guy is me! God help me!" I prayed with all my being.

And God answered my prayer.

Over a period of a year the Lord began jealously to strip me of all the idols that crowded him to the corner of my life. We lost the state championship football game. Popularity proved again and again to be a fickle game. Clothing styles changed faster than I could keep up. And all I was left with that was meaningful was a girlfriend who lived 500 miles away. So, come Easter holiday, I sold my ball glove, my tennis racket, my bike, whatever, and bought a ticket to go see her. And while I was there she told me this would be the last date because she had fallen for another guy.

What I Was Saved To

That Easter in Ohio we went to church for no other reason than it was Easter, and that's what people did then. The preacher told the story of the caterpillar who crawled around in the dust when he could have sprouted wings and soared like a butterfly. And he said many of us lived like that as sinners, less than God meant us to be. But if we were born again we could live life abundantly. He quoted Saint Augustine, "Thou hast made us for Thyself, O God, and our hearts are restless until we find our rest in Thee."

There in my seat, in the quietness of my own empty heart, I believed. "God, I want that new birth. I want you where you're supposed to be in my life right now," I prayed.

Most men come to God by a process of elimination. They try drugs and burn out on them and look for something else. Next they try sex or money or power or things or travel and education, moving from one thing to another until they finally come to Christ. Me, I'd half-tried the Lord in my youth, but allowed the world to crowd him out in my teenage years. And now frustrated and unfulfilled, I was returning to him, a beaten and errant lover who'd not kept faith.

Flying home on the airplane with all of these things climaxing in my life, I can only say to you bluntly that the Lord spoke to me. In an undeniable inner way he simply said to me two words, "Why not?" I knew what he meant. His question was, "Why not sweep all this material clutter away and love me and serve me all your life as a minister?" Sitting in my seat I panicked. I wasn't ready for that sort of commitment! "Lord," I answered him, "I'll tell you why not. Because I am young and there's a lot I want to do. There's fun I want to have. When I get out of college I'll commit myself to you then!" God took his hand and surveyed in a flash of insight the rubble of idols in my life — football, popularity, girlfriends, unfulfillment. And I saw that it was no good apart from him. I sighed and with a simple prayer of surrender prayed, "Why not."

There and then a great feeling swept over me. It was as if someone had opened the door of a hot, stuffy attic in August and let in the cool, scented spring air of May. And for the first time since I was twelve years old I was at peace with God.

251

When the airplane landed I was scared to tell anyone what had happened to me. They'd surely think I was crazy or maybe they'd expect too much from me. So there followed months of intense frustration as I tried to live the Christian life quietly, without any edifying fellowship.

Outwardly I became a very moral person. I quit swearing. I tried not to lie or covet or tell bawdy jokes. But inwardly I was growing considerably vexed. I was confused, lonely, tired, and very discouraged.

It was then that God brought into my life a young Christian couple fresh out of seminary. They got me involved in a small group Bible study and in the Fellowship of Christian Athletes. They began to teach me how to live the Christian life. The discipline of worship, prayer, walking in the Holy Spirit, witnessing, and honest fellowship began to be incorporated into my life.

Then I was invited to attend a rally where Bill Glass was speaking. Bill was a pro-football player who had everything I thought was important in life, and, what's more, he was a committed Christian. So I went to listen.

Bill preached on the parable of the sower from Matthew 13. He talked about how some seed fell into good soil and began to grow, but the cares of the world grew up like weeds and choked the plant's life. I knew Bill was talking about me. When he gave an invitation, I went forward asking Jesus to be more than the Savior he'd been to me since my childhood. I went forward asking him to be my Lord. I didn't care who knew it or what they expected, for from then on I was unashamed of loving God.

Isn't it wonderful that God knows exactly where he is in each of our lists of priorities right now? But regardless of where we put him, God always puts us first.

God doesn't wait for you to start loving him before he starts loving you.

He went to the cross to pay for your sins. He thinks you're worth dying for and rising for! He thinks you're worth choosing for his team! You're worth the filling of his Spirit!

It is customary in this part of the nation to greet someone with the question, "How's it going?" And you can fairly ask that of me these thirty years since my commitment to Christ. "How's it going?"

Honestly, it's going hard but happy. The Christian life is the hardest thing I've ever tried to do. But then, again, it is the happiest thing as well.

The big surprise is that the Lord hasn't taken away from my life so much as he's added to it! It's like when I was twelve and played marbles. It was fun. It was all I knew. But then Coach Boswell came along recruiting for the football team. And when he asked me to try out, I said, "Okay, I'll play, but I want you to know I'm not quitting my marbles game!" And he said, "Sure! you can always play marbles if you still want to!" But when I played football I somehow never went back. I'd found something better! And it's been the same with Christ. I've found something better! The old idols of things and sports and popularity are still there. It's just that I never went back. In Christ I've found an involving, freeing, exciting arousal in which green becomes greener, fun becomes funnier, and love lovelier.

Since I've committed my life to Christ there have been many successes: the challenges of college, graduate school, winning people to know Christ, writing books and magazine articles and news editorials, marriage to my wonderful Kathryn, friendships with the Wests, the Smiths, the Brokhoffs, the Hoffmans, and so many others who have mentored me. Then there are my children; meaningful church work in Augusta, Atlanta, Greenville, Virginia, and Burlington; funneling money and people to missions; the inspiring work of the Fellowship of Christian Athletes; traveling in Mexico, Israel, Russia; and even sharing the Gospel of Jesus Christ with the President ... of the Rotary Club of Asheville, North Carolina.

But Christianity is not all rainbows and mountaintops. There have been many failures as well. Oh, the misunderstandings, the conflict, the rejection, and the weariness of it all. Oh, dear God! The intense spiritual warfare, the wounds, the betrayals, the defeats, the casualties. Yes, there have been times I've thought about quitting, times I've wished for death. But in Matthew 10:22 Jesus said, "He who endures to the end will be saved." So I live on in him and he sustains me.

Now it seems the older I get the more precious Christ and his promises become. When I was younger, God's Word seemed to me like water. A few years ago the scriptures were like milk. But now the Word is like fine wine!

Life in Christ with its joys and disappointments is like a beautiful love story in which God pursues me with his affections and gifts, and I learn to respond emotionally, willfully, and intellectually. To so love God and my neighbor as myself is the meaning of my life now.

Life in Christ is also an adventure story. It's like a good book. Page after page, I simply can't put it down until it's finished. Why, with Christ, life is so serendipitous that a simple trip to the supermarket is like a safari through darkest Africa. You just never know what the Good Lord has for you next!

All of this and the Bible says, "Surely goodness and mercy shall follow me all the days of my life. And I shall dwell in the house of the Lord forever" (Psalm 23). Praise the Lord! And magnify him, O my soul!

Conclusion

The first question in the Bible is, "Where are you?" God asks it of Adam and Eve in Genesis 3 as he comes looking for them. And right now, on behalf of the Lord, I'd like to ask that same question of you. "Where are you?"

Where are you in your relationship to God? Are you inoculated so that you've got just enough religion so that you haven't gotten Christ? Are you living a life of quiet desperation running around from one campfire to another? Why not? Why not right now, where you're sitting, turn to Jesus in faith asking him to forgive your sins and come into your life giving you new birth?

Christ offers *so* much more! If you give him yourself, he will give you himself, and he is all that you are looking for!

A few years ago I was flying to Colorado. Seated next to me on the jet was a businessman who was finishing his third martini. We got to talking and he began to brag. "I'm in big business," he volunteered.

"Why, what a coincidence," I crooned, "I am, too!"

"I'm in business with my father," he continued.

"I'm in business with my Father, also," I countered.

"Yes, but my business is so big it takes me all over the country!"

"My business is so big it takes me across the nation and around the world," I said.

"My business last year netted hundreds of thousands in profits."

"Last year we gave away hundreds of thousands of dollars," I said.

"Just what sort of business are you in?" he finally inquired.

"I am a full time minister of Almighty God and the Gospel of his Son, Jesus the Christ," I boldly told him.

Well, the gentleman reddened, took a few more sips of his drink, and fell silent. Then, after a few minutes he sobered up and said, "You know, Reverend, you're not just in big business, you're in the biggest business!"

A Landmark Event!

During World War II allied armies marched into Germany on their way to Berlin. Retreating German soldiers switched road signs and destroyed landmarks in an effort to confuse their enemy. And, to an extent, it worked, for many a G.I. followed a false marker only to end up in the wrong place.

That just goes to show the need for landmarks, the importance of reliable signposts by which to steer.

Here locally, landmarks like the courthouse, the river, the college, or the bridge are important in helping us find our bearings. Why, if some villain came in one night and removed our signposts, the next day would become a bewildering jumble of uncertainties, and we'd all be lost.

The text is about landmarks. It refers to the Jewish custom of setting boundary stones to mark out property. Just as we do today, so our Hebrew forefathers did then. Wells, fords, buildings, and stone sentinels were their guides. Hence the strict law: "Remove not the ancient landmark which your fathers have set."

We live in a day of rapid change, and this law is being grossly ignored. Our history is being bulldozed to clear the way for development. Some professors are twisting the guideposts in the minds and hearts of our students. Traditions are forgotten, manners ignored. The result is a kind of chaos — social confusion and rootless individualism. We live in a society that's lost its bearings and is adrift on a sea of change.

257

The Lord's table is a landmark. For nearly 2,000 years Christians have been gathering to eat this meal. And, for all, it can be the means of getting one's bearings. How do I say this?

The Past

First, in the communion meal Jesus points us to the past. "Do this in remembrance of me," he commands.

What good is memory?

In John Knowles' novel, *A Separate Peace,* a middle-aged war veteran returns to his New Hampshire prep school fifteen years after graduation. He is drawn to that part of the campus where a huge oak tree overspreads the river. Its branches tower above and become lost in the morning fog.

It was in that tree that the man and his schoolboy rival "Finny" dared each other to climb ever higher for a dive into the river below. And it was there that Finny had fallen when our now-aging vet either intentionally or unintentionally shook the limb on which both were perched. Finny had later died from his injuries. For all these years the novel's main character has remembered and wrestled with the guilt of it all.

What about you? Are there fog-shrouded trees growing like spikes in your conscience? Is there guilt of deeds done or left undone? Divorce? An abortion? Ugly words? A theft? Adultery?

Remembrance can be a painful thing. But it can also be a source of solace and joy.

In the Greek, the word remembrance is *anamnesis.* We derive our word "amnesia" from it. Jesus is saying, "Do this so you won't get amnesia, so you will know who I am and who you are."

During World War II a shell-shocked soldier suffering from amnesia was paraded around boxing rings in the hope that someone would recognize him. "Won't someone tell me who I am!" he shouted. Jesus knows the world hits us hard, and we can lapse into spiritual amnesia. We can forget home, brothers, sisters, father, even our own name. So Jesus invites us regularly to come to his house, to sit at his table, to take the blood of his cup, the bread of his body, and remember our sins, remember at what great a price we were bought at Calvary, and to remember whose we now are.

At communion we find our bearings by laying down all our guilty past and becoming immersed in the pleasant memories of all Jesus has done for us. Ah, sweet remembrance!

The Future

The Lord's Supper also points us to the future. In 1 Corinthians 11:23-26 Paul speaks of celebrating communion as a means of proclaiming Christ's death "until he comes." That is a reference to the second coming of our Lord.

A few years ago my family watched the movie, *The Day After*, which was about the horrible aftermath of a nuclear war. One night, soon after my eldest son came to me. "Dad," he confided, "I just don't know about this school work. I mean, why should I work so hard? With the way the world is going it doesn't look like there's any future worth studying for." Indeed, as W. C. Fields put it, "The future isn't what it used to be."

Iraq is rearming itself. Our country sinks deeper into financial debt. Academic levels plummet. Homes split up; churches grow cold. Ah! But for the text we, like the world, could only anticipate a hopeless end. Yet here in Christ, seated about his table, we know an endless hope!

Two words: "He comes."

A young lady, desperately single, aching with unfulfilled longings, shared with me her pain. "I eat alone. I sleep alone. I vacation alone. I'm sick! Do you hear me? Sick of it! Where is my lover?"

I told her of Jesus, the most eligible bachelor in the universe. I explained how we are his bride. And even now Christ is preparing a place for us in heaven. And soon, oh so very soon, the shout will go up. "The Bridegroom cometh!" And we'll each go to live forever in a loving relationship like we've been longing for.

"In this hope we were saved," the Bible says. Such hope makes the Lord's Supper an appetizer. It is but a foretaste of the marriage supper of the Lamb mentioned in Revelation 19.

Robert Frost's poem, "Death of a Hired Man," has a Vermont farmer who discovers the town drunk sleeping in his barn. The farmer has tried to help the old man out many times over the years. But the drunk proved worthless. Why, last time he was there he walked off the farm in harvest time leaving the farmer short-handed.

"Never again," the farmer vowed.

So now he finds the old drunk asleep in his hayloft. And angrily he tells his wife he's going to run him off.

Yet his wife realizes the old man is near death and she pleads with her husband to show mercy. "He's come home to die, Pa. He has no place to go but here. He has no one but you. With nothing to look back on in pride and nothing to look forward to in hope ... he's come home to die."

Perhaps there's one of you here today whose past is nothing more than a guilty spasm of pain and whose future seems but a hopeless end. Come! For such a one as you this church is built, this table is spread. Here at communion Jesus takes your face in his gentle hands and points you to your past — all cleansed, forgiven, and enabled in his grace. Then he turns your gaze to the future as his bride in a paradise so wonderful no tongue can describe it.

The Present

Yes, this wonder-filled table is spread for the past and the future. But what of the here and now? We Christians have our theology of the past well-founded in the cross, all our guilty sins washed away. And our theology of the future is secure in the second coming. But our faith is often like an antique brass bed — rock sturdy at both ends but soft and saggy in the middle. So, what does our theology offer for the here and now?

Jesus said, "This is my Body; this is my Blood." Not was. Not shall be. But is. Now!

John Calvin used to remind the saints that there is no miracle in the bread and wine. The miracle is in us! When we commune with repentant and faithful hearts, the Holy Spirit moves among us and in us, bringing life, growth, bonding, reassurance, comfort, insight, love, strength, and whatever else is necessary to keep us on our feet.

After the resurrection, Jesus showed up at every mealtime. When Peter denied the Lord, it was at breakfast the Lord met him and Peter redevoted himself to the Savior. It was on the road to

Emmaus that two discouraged disciples were drawn into a meal and the reality of the risen Lord. It was while behind locked doors for fear of the Jews that Jesus materialized, eating, and rejuvenating the apostles at the table. And it is in churches like this, at tables like this, in servants like you and me, that the real presence of the Holy Spirit makes himself known.

Conclusion

In the play, *Fiddler On The Roof,* Tevye, the Russian Jew, speaks of the landmarks of tradition in his life: "Because of our traditions, we've kept our balance for many, many years. Here in Anatevka, we have traditions for everything — how to eat, how to sleep, how to wear clothes. For instance, we always keep our heads covered and always wear a little prayer shawl. This shows our constant devotion to God. You may ask, how did this tradition start? I'll tell you — I don't know! But it's a tradition! Because of our traditions everyone knows who he is and what God expects him to do."

So it is that the Lord's Supper is a tradition, a landmark in our lives. Jesus wills us to remember him, to come often, to sit and look to our past, future, and present.

It's been my experience that persons coming to the church have a problem in one of three areas. They've a struggle with the past and guilt, or a struggle with the future and fear, or a problem with the present and strength.

The Gospel touches us in all three areas. Driving over here this morning, didn't you look into your rearview mirror? But did you not as well glance through the forward windshield? And I do so hope you enjoyed the view out the side windows. A safe driver looks all three ways.

And a healthy Christian also has a past secured from guilt — "remembrance"; a future secure in hope — "He comes"; and a present enabled by the Spirit's strength for now.

Today it is fitting we celebrate communion as a landmark in our lives. Forgetting the sins of the past, absorbed in his wonderful grace, remembering the cross and our glorious heritage, let us find nourishment in God's Spirit in this bread and wine, that we might press on into future fruitful ministry until he comes.

To A Life Beyond

The torches burned long into the night in the banquet hall. Their flickering light cast grotesque shadows across the huge table. Most of the seated revelers were slumped in their places sleeping off the effects of food and grog. There were a few murmured conversations, occasional outbursts of ribald laughter. Few but the king noticed when a tiny sparrow flew in the open window, pecked at a table scrap, circled the hall several times, then winged through another open window into the remaining night. The medieval king rose, and to no one in particular, began to muse, "Our lives are like that lost sparrow. We come from the darkness of who knows where, flit through the lighted banquet hall of life snatching at morsels, then we fly out the window of death to who knows where! Who can tell me more of these things?"

The stuporous king's questioning has occupied inquisitive minds from the beginning of time. "Whence have I come? Whither shall I go? Why?"

William Shakespeare's Prince Hamlet called death "the undiscovered country from whose border no traveler ever returns."

Do you ever wonder about death? What happens after you die? Is there life beyond the grave? What is heaven like? In the text, Jesus mentions "eternal life," he will "raise him (us) up at the last day," and how we "will live forever." That's three mentions of heaven! But what is paradise like?

The big issue is: How can one find sure answers to such questions? The best means is for someone to die and return to tell us! And, indeed, scripture records several incidents of death and resurrection.

Lazarus died and was buried several days. Then Jesus brought him back to life. But Lazarus never talked about his experience (John 11).

The Apostle Paul was stoned in the village of Lystra. He was left for dead. But he was revived. Of his death experience all Paul said was, "I know a man caught up to the third heaven. He saw things no man can utter" (Acts 14:19; 2 Corinthians 12:2).

Even Jesus died and rose again. And he was with us forty days before he ascended. Yet he never discussed with his disciples all that lay beyond death's veil.

Answers to questions about death and the hereafter are frustratingly difficult to find until one comes to the concluding book of the Bible. There in Revelation 7:9-17, John is given a vision of heaven which he faithfully records.

"I looked," John wrote, "and in heaven, an open door." Through that door John walked, observing as he progressed. His Book of Revelation is his subsequent attempt to give to the world what he saw. And it is of immense importance in answering our basic questions about death.

Where Are The Dead?

The first question is: "Where are the dead?" Revelation 7:9 observes, "After this I looked, and behold, a great multitude which no man could number from every nation, every tribe, and peoples and tongue, standing before the throne and before the Lamb."

See here! The dead are not in the grave! They are not lying in a cold, musty tomb! They are risen, standing among other people. In the very presence of God!

In the cowboy film, *Hud*, hard times have come to the West. Drought, dying cattle, a father's sudden death, and then there is the somber funeral. An old padre tries to comfort the grieving son, saying, "He's gone to a better place." But the son bitterly replies, "Not unless you believe that breathing dirt is better than breathing air!"

To the naked eye death is horrid. It is the end of all — coffins, airless, decay, skeletons. But John gives us a view from the other side! And to the eye of faith that looks through heaven's open door, death is to be transported ... to live ... before the throne ... with the saints ... always beholding him!

In Bunyan's *Pilgrim's Progress*, Mr. Hopeful is crossing the cold, raging river of death. He calls back to the frightened pilgrims on the bank who must follow after him, "Be of good cheer, my brothers. I feel the bottom and it is sound!" John's Revelation gives us the same firm footing as we face death. It assures us that dying is not merely an exit. It is an entrance into paradise!

Is There Room For Me?

A second question we must ask is: "Is there room for me in heaven?"

I've been asked by the dying as he rolls his head on his pillow, looks me in the eye, and broods, "Preacher, has God got a place in paradise for someone like me?"

I suppose we all remember how when Jesus was born there was no room in the inn. We ourselves have made a long journey, arrived late, and found "no vacancy" signs at every motel. And deep inside, aren't we all afraid heaven won't have room for the likes of us?

Yet look what John saw through heaven's open door! "A great multitude which no man can number" (Revelation 7:9). Surely this means heaven is big enough to hold all of God's children.

Jesus promised, "In my father's house are many mansions. I go to prepare a place for you" (John 14). Hear that? "A place for you." "Prepared." By Jesus. He is doing all this for you right now.

Will We Recognize Each Other?

A third question is: "Will we recognize each other in heaven?" Some say we are like a drop of water returning to a faceless sea. To die is but to merge into obscurity.

An elderly widow once told me, "I don't think I could enjoy heaven unless my late husband was there. Will I see him again? Will we know each other?"

In Revelation 7:9, John points out how the host of heaven could be identified by their nationality, tongue, tribe, and race. And this isn't the only evidence we have. Matthew 17 records Jesus' transfiguration

265

in which the Lord spoke with two men dead now in heaven yet clearly recognizable — Moses and Elijah.

John 20 tells of Christ's resurrection. His voice, his personality, his words, his face, all were recognized by his good friend Mary Magdalene.

Imagine, stepping through that open door into paradise to be greeted by Grandpapa, Mother, friends. And who's that over there? Why, it's the Apostle Paul! And isn't that Mr. George Frederick Handel? And there's David, the sweet psalmist of Israel! Why, heaven's but one glad reunion of familiar faces and names.

What Are They Doing?

A fourth question we must ask is: "What do people do in heaven?"

I love the local newspaper and its typographical errors. My favorite is the obituary that read, "Mr. Joseph Brown has gone to rust." Embarrassed, the editor tried to correct it the next day. But another typo read, "Mr. Joseph Brown has gone to roost." The third day was still worse. "Mr. Brown has gone to roast." Finally, the fourth day got it right. "Mr. Joseph Brown has gone to rest."

This is the popular notion of heaven: rest. Do we sit on clouds, adjust our haloes, and play harps? In Revelation 7:15, John saw, "They are before the throne of God and serve him day and night...."

It would seem, then, that heaven is not an eternal sort of south Florida lazy indulgence in trivia that we call retirement.

"They serve him," the Bible explains. When French impressionist painter Auguste Renoir lay dying, he said, "What a pity! I was just beginning to show promise." If John's Revelation is correct, and I believe it is, then our promise is not ended in death, but progresses as we continue to serve with fulfilling work, as we continue to live our lives amidst a colorful community from every race, tribe, and tongue; as we fellowship without war, divorce, covenant-breaking, sickness, absences, and our general cussedness.

And just look at the worship of heaven! My, but what a great congregation! Full attendance! Singing a new song! Beholding God's face! Faith turned into seeing!

What Is Heaven Like?

Yet a fifth question: "John, when you looked through heaven's door, what did heaven look like?"

John used very descriptive language in the text. God will "spread his tent over us," a mid-eastern sign of hospitality. In his pavilion we "hunger no more," "never again thirst," suffer no "scorching heat," and drink cool refreshment from the "spring of living water."

John goes on to describe how in God's presence there are no more tears, no more sin, no guilt, no more unfulfillment, no broken relationships, no disease, no fatigue, no crippling old age.

Heaven's architectural and artistic beauty are detailed — streets of gold, gates of pearl, incredible worship music. And right in the middle of it all — God's throne!

Some days I come home from a trip late at night. As I round the last corner I see my house all lighted up. My key fits the lock, and I go in to find the familiar smell, my books, my chair, my music, clean clothes. All these things are fine. But what I want to see is my wife's face.

The same with heaven. The streets of gold, the pearly gates, the music, and the people — all these things are nice. But the best of it all is Jesus! And I'll fall on his neck with joy!

Interestingly, Revelation 4:6 describes the area around God's throne as "a sea of glass." Like the lake surface on a perfect summer morning, in God's presence, there is not a ripple of care, pain, doubt, worry, or sin. In short, we shall live in the Lord's presence undisturbed forever.

Who Gets In?

A final question, the most important question of all, is: "Who is allowed into heaven?"

Have you ever read "The Fisherman's Prayer"? It goes like this:

> *I pray that I may live to fish*
> *Until my dying day.*
> *And when it comes to my last cast,*
> *I then most humbly pray,*

267

When in the Lord's landing net,
And peacefully asleep,
That in His mercy
I be judged big enough to keep.
                              Author unknown

How big is a "keeper" in the Lord's eyes? What sort of person gets into heaven?

Revelation 7:9 mentions those in white robes, palm branches in hands, who praise God saying, "Salvation belongs to our God."

"Who are they?" verse 13 asks.

To which verse 14 replies, "They are those who've washed their robes in the blood of the Lamb." They've suffered for Jesus, coming through great tribulation. Now "they serve God night and day."

What a perfect description of a Christian. Their sins cleansed by Christ's blood on the cross. Their new life lived in white-robed righteousness. Suffering, serving, worshiping.

This is not the easy-believism of today's lukewarm church. It is the life-changing faith of Jesus Christ!

Let me ask you a question. If you were to die today and stand before God and he asked, "Why should I let you into heaven?" What would you say?

Would you appeal to the good life you tried to live? God would say, "That doesn't save you!"

Would you offer to buy your way in with a sum of money? God would say, "Your money is no good!"

Would you tout your religion and honors and education? God would still turn you away!

The only way into God's heaven is through Jesus Christ. For when you turn from sin and self to face Jesus, when you ask him for mercy, ask him to come into your life and fill you with his presence that you might serve him, when you begin to worship him actively, then you become a child of God. And there is room in God's house for all his children.

Conclusion

"In heaven." "An open door." "I saw," John wrote.

In 1295 A.D. Marco Polo returned from a long sojourn in China. To his Italian friends he chronicled the adventures of the Far East. Silk! Spices! Fireworks! Pagodas! Printing presses! "You're exaggerating!" his friends hissed. "Behold, the half of it I have not told you!" Polo said. And I can say the same to you about heaven. For you must read John's Revelation for yourself. Even then, words can never do justice to paradise. For as Paul wrote, "Eye has not seen, ear has not heard, nor has thought entered the mind of man as to the wonderfulness of what God has created for those who love him" (1 Corinthians 2:9).

At the beginning of Christianity, when all of this first came to be known, Clement of Alexandria, Egypt, wrote of Jesus, "He has turned all our sunsets into sunrise." And this day may he turn all your fears into faith.

King Forever!

Norman Rockwell has a painting titled *Lift Up Thine Eyes*. Shown in his painting is the magnificent entrance to an urban cathedral. Vaulted high above its carved gothic doors are statues of the prophets, apostles, and martyrs. And right in the center is Jesus Christ, sitting on a throne at the right hand of God. On the sidewalk below the cathedral move the busy throngs of people amidst the noise and fumes of cars and taxis. The pastor of the church has just finished changing the public bulletin board. The sign, written for edification of the passers-by, reads: "Lift Up Thine Eyes!" The irony, of course, is in the scene below. Each person in the passing crowd is caught up with his own thoughts. No one looks up. Most appear gloomy, harried, and depressed. They hurry on with eyes glued to the pavement. Some are lugging their briefcases like millstones.

What a picture of modern life! And today, God's word paints much the same kind of painting for you who have taken time out from counting the cracks in your sidewalks to come into the Church and lift up thine eyes.

In the text Jesus alludes to his resurrection and his return to the right hand of God (John 6:62). The faithful disciples of Jesus struggled to understand that he had the "words of eternal life" and that he was "the Holy One of God." Forty days after the resurrection, the disciples lifted up their eyes to see Jesus lifted up into heaven and they returned to Jerusalem with great joy, and were "continually in the temple blessing God" (Luke 24:53). I wonder: Can you and I glimpse the ascension the same way the apostles did on that hillside near Bethany? Can the ascension make the same

271

difference to us that it made to them? Can we lift up our eyes, witness Christ at the right hand of God, and return to our homes rejoicing and praising God for his salvation? Lift up thine eyes and let's see!

Affirmation

One way to view the ascension is as an affirmation. It's a compliment! In Matthew's Gospel, Jesus' last statement is a transfer of responsibility. The Lord says, "All authority in heaven and on earth has been given unto me. Go therefore and make disciples of all nations, baptizing them in the name of the Father and the Son and the Holy Spirit." This statement is sometimes referred to as the great commission. Now, a king might commission an artist to do a sculpture or a painting. A church might commission an architect to do a cathedral. But who ever heard of God Almighty giving a commission to a man? Yet this is exactly part of what the ascension means. From the cross Jesus said, "It is finished." His work done, Jesus packed up and ascended to heaven. He left. But before he left, he looked to his disciples as he looks to us today, and he said, "Now it is your turn. I commission you to make disciples. Go to work!"

There is an old legend about our Lord's return to heaven. He walked through the gates of Paradise and a group of angels stopped him and inquired, "From whence have you come?" Jesus said, "I've come from preaching the gospel on earth, from dying on the cross for the forgiveness of sins, from resurrecting, and from commissioning my disciples to carry on my ministry." The angels were astonished at Christ's doings, and one of them said, "You gave mere men such an important task? What if they fail you?" Jesus leveled his eyes at the inquiring angel and said, "No. No. They won't fail me. They won't." See what trust the Lord has in you and me that he commissions us to carry on his work? It's a compliment, a divine affirmation! We must not let him down!

Acquittal

Lift up thine eyes! See the ascension? What does it mean? It's an affirmation. It is also the sign of your acquittal. Listen to what

272

Saint Paul wrote about the ascension in Romans 8:34. "Who is to condemn? It is Christ Jesus, who died, yes, who was raised from the dead, who is at the right hand of God, who indeed intercedes for us." Paul was pointing out something that might not be so obvious to us today. What do you think it means when scripture says that Christ is at the right hand of God? It means that he shares God's majesty, God's power and authority. But it means something more! In the ancient world when a king judged one of his subjects who had been brought before him for trial, he sat on his throne with a scribe on each side. If the prisoner were pardoned, the scribe on the right side of the king registered it in his record. But if the prisoner were sentenced, the king turned to the scribe on his left and he wrote the name on his ledger. Jesus is at the right hand of God the Father Almighty. The ascension means that Christ is on the forgiving side of God! It means that one day when you as a Christian stand to be judged, the Lord will intercede for you. He will say, "This is one of my faithful disciples. Calvary was for him. Justice is done." And you will be acquitted.

Lift up thine eyes to the ascension! What do you see? It is an affirmation and an acquittal. But it is also a sign of authority.

Authority

Let me ask you an interesting question. What is the highest point in Washington, D.C.? Is it the Washington Monument? No. Is it the Capitol? No. Washington Cathedral is the highest point in our nation's capital. Divine authority rises higher than any mortal's memorial or any law maker's citadel. The same is true of the universe. In Daniel 7:9 the prophet gets a vision of the throne of God. And he sees a man come and take his seat. Who is that man? Is it Caesar? No. Is it Alexander? No. Is it Napoleon? No. Could it be Adolf Hitler? No. It is Jesus Christ! He sits on the throne and is given power and dominion and authority to be King forever!

What does it mean to you and me today that Jesus is King forever? What does it mean that Christ is given ultimate authority? It means that we should make him in our lives right now what he is in the universe, King of kings and Lord of lords! As a minister I am finding out what it means to live under the authority of Christ.

273

People say, "I want my loved one's funeral this way. It was his last will." And quite often that last will is not in line with the Lord's will. That's when I have to say that the Lord's throne, his authority, outranks that of the deceased. I've had to do the same thing with marriage vows, membership vows, and baptisms. It doesn't matter so much what we want on our authority as it matters what Christ wills himself! He rules the world; we do not!

If we are going to take our faith seriously, we have to take the ascension seriously. Heaven's throne is not up for grabs. Nor is it vacant! Jesus sits there with God. And he is a living, willing ruler. He has plans. And as Christians we are responsible for living under his Lordship, under his authority. He is the King. We are the subjects.

Each Sunday we pray the Lord's Prayer. Do we pray it sincerely when we say, "Thy will be done on earth as it is in heaven"? Do you want God's will for your marriage, for your business? Do you want God's will for your financial life? Does America want God's will for its salvation, its political life?

When George Handel wrote the *Messiah* it became an immediate sensation. The "Hallelujah Chorus" was and still is the highlight. And it has become customary for the audience to stand during the performance of the chorus. When King George II of England attended the *Messiah*, he sat listening with great joy. Then, when the "Hallelujah Chorus" was sung, these words of truth filled the theatre. "Hallelujah, for the Lord God omnipotent reigneth, the kingdom of this world is become the kingdom of the Lord and of his Christ, and he shall reign forever and ever." When the king heard this truth, he rose and removed his crown and bowed his head saying, "Jesus is Lord; I am His subject." God's authority is supreme! Is God supreme in your life? Is Jesus your Lord? Do you bow to him? Have you stood and removed your crown to him? The Bible says that there shall come a day when every knee shall bow and every tongue confess Jesus is Lord (Philippians 2:10). It's not a question of will you bow. It is a question of when. Will you bow now while salvation is offered by grace through faith? Or will you bow as a conquered rebel to be judged by the King?

Assurance

Lift up thine eyes! That's the Word of God to you this day! Lift up thine eyes and behold the ascended Christ. He is a symbol of affirmation, acquittal, and authority. And he is one final thing. He is a symbol of assurance!

I asked a Christian this week, "How are you doing?" The plaintive reply was, "Well, Pastor Crotts, under the circumstances I'm doing fair, I guess." My only reply was, "Under the circumstances? What in heaven's name are you doing under the circumstances? You ought to be on top of them! Jesus rules the world. You work for him. Get out from under things and get on top!"

Under the circumstances! Crime — 23,000 murders last year. Divorce — nearly forty percent of all marriages ending in a divorce. War — Afghanistan, Northen Ireland, terrorism, the Mid-East. Under the circumstances! Live porno shows in town, political graft, inflation, spiraling taxes, the energy crisis, over-population, famine, nuclear proliferation, cancer, sleepy little nations awakening to measure their muscle in megatons! Under the circumstances we ought to be depressed. But wait a minute. Who's in charge here? Look at heaven's throne. God Almighty rules. He's got the whole world in his hands. He's got you and me and baby in his hands. He's on top of it all. He is able. And we can crawl out from under the circumstances, we can crawl out of our churches, our little stained glass fox holes, we can quit talking like cynics, pessimists, and get on top of things. God rules! Hallelujah! I saw a bumper sticker on a car. There amidst the depravity of humanity, the bad news of sin, the sticker said, "Rise above it!" That's God's Word to you today in the ascension. "Rise above it!" Get out from under the circumstances. The news is not all bad, get on top. That is where God is!

During World War II a delightful Christian English lady kept a personal diary. It tells of her husband's death in the war effort. It tells of food rationing and the horrible bombing of London. It tells of her children's evacuation to the countryside. One night during the bombings the woman confessed that she woke up and could not get back to sleep. She kept thinking of Hitler, invasion, and the S.S. troops. She trembled until she suddenly thought, "Where is

Alexander the Great who gobbled up the world? Where is Caesar's dogmatic rule upheld on the tips of spears? Where is Napoleon? They are all in their graves and come to nought," she wrote. "And that is where Hitler will be, too. The same God reigns!" And she rolled over, laughed, and went back to sleep! The Mid-East, terrorism, crime, abortion — is this what your eyes are upon? Are you gazing at the world, and glancing at Christ? Rise above it! Lift up your eyes and see! The same God still reigns. Be assured!

What An Exit!

You must admit that Jesus knew how to make a stage exit dramatically. Sir Lawrence Olivier and Sir John Gielgud could make a grand Shakespearean exit. But only Christ in his ascension could leave the stage of God's drama of salvation in such a way as to leave his apostles throughout history feeling affirmed, acquitted, under authority, and assured.

In Peachtree Presbyterian Church in Atlanta there is a magnificent ascension window over the Lord's table in the chancel. Every time you worship in the place you are reminded of Christ's rise to power and glory. The architects of the church house wanted always to remind worshipers of where the Lord is. The text today wants to do the same thing for you. Is there an ascension window in your mind? Lift up thine eyes! Where is Jesus? Where are you in relation to him? Brothers and sisters, is it faith? Is it faith?

Proper 17
Pentecost 15
Ordinary Time 22
Mark 7:1-8, 14-15, 21-23

The Dangers Of Being Religious

Jeff Foxworthy has made a career of telling "redneck" jokes. For instance, "You might be a redneck if someone asks you for some identification and you show them your belt buckle." The South doesn't have a lock on rednecks. The North has them also. For instance, "You might be a northern redneck if you've ever burned a tire on the hood of your car in winter to help get it started."

Here in the church I'd like to poke fun at some of the straight-laced, self-righteousness that passes for Christianity. So, behold, I bring you the Pharisee joke!

For instance, you might be a Pharisee if you've ever shouted, "Amen!" more than 51 times during a single sermon on somebody else's sin. You might be a Pharisee if you think the only music God listens to is at least 100 years old ... if you're sure nobody has ever had to forgive you ... if your black leather Thompson Chain Reference Bible is so big it takes two hands to hold it up. You might be a Pharisee if you think the world would be a better place if everyone were just like you ... if you think Jesus might have overstepped his bounds when he turned water into wine ... if you think big hair is a sign of holiness ... if you go to church to prove you're good!

Seriously, in the Gospels Jesus issues three bewares to his disciples. Mark 8:15, "Beware the leaven of the Herodians." Such were Jews who went along with the occupying army of Rome that they might prosper materially. To them nothing was more important than property, career, and money.

Jesus also said, "Beware the leaven of the Sadducees" (Matthew 16:6). Theirs was the problem of liberalism. Discounting scripture, such Jews did not believe in angels, spirits, or even the resurrection. (This is why they were so sad, you see.)

The third beware is of the leaven of the Pharisees (Matthew 16:6). Their leaven was legalism. Taking the Ten Commandments and interpreting them, these Jewish believers constructed a code of over 5,000 laws to ensnarl life. By following their code they understood they were earning God's love, deserving salvation, and even putting God in their debt. The depth of their sin was most evident in their refusal to admit their helplessness. They believed they were somehow good enough to earn salvation.

The word "Pharisee" is Greek and literally means "separated ones." At the time of Christ the Pharisetical sect was the most powerful group among all Hebrews. While the Herodians and Sadducee sects were snobbishly standoffish, the Pharisees were the sect of the common people. Theirs was a quest to make the law of God practical daily bread, not cake for special occasions. Never numbering more than five or six thousand in number, the Pharisees did their best to live morally and involve God in every detail of their lives, be it how and what they ate, whom they married, or how they dressed.

In their day, the Pharisees were much admired by the common people. Their zeal for traditional Jewish values, their strict lifestyle, placed them on a pedestal of respect.

When Jesus came and ministered he frequently ran into the Pharisees — in the temple, at funerals, at weddings, in synagogues.

The New Testament tells us that the Pharisees, the best Bible students of their generation, the best behaved, became the constant opponents of Jesus Christ and, in the end, actually plotted Jesus' death.

Today, we who know the scriptures and share a commitment to God would do well to learn from the mistakes of the Pharisees lest we, too, come to oppose the works of God in our generation.

Following are 26 soul-searching questions you may use to see if what troubled the Pharisees troubles you.

1. Are you increasing in pride or humility? In 49 A.D. Paul, a Pharisee, converted to Jesus Christ, went up to Jerusalem to discuss the gospel with the apostles. Of the meeting Paul wrote, "They added nothing to me." Such arrogance began to melt, however, as the Holy Spirit began to work on his character. Six years later he called himself "least of the apostles" and confessed, "Now we see through a glass darkly" (1 Corinthians 13:12). In A.D. 60, he wrote, "I am the least of the saints" (Ephesians 3:8). In A.D. 65, "I am the chief of sinners" (1 Timothy 1:15). Then, near life's end, he wrote, "I do not consider that I have attained it" (Philippians 3:12).

2. Are you hypocritical? Jesus said the Pharisees "do not practice what they preach." He called them hypocrites who bind huge burdens upon others which they refused to lift themselves (Matthew 23:2-4, 15). Saying one thing and doing another is the bane of being religious, isn't it? How easy it is to condemn a woman pregnant out of wedlock, then go home and watch a pornographic film. Or, don't we get angry over someone else's thievery, yet dismiss our behavior when we snitch stamps at the office?

3. Do you have faith in your ideas and traditions about God instead of a relationship with the Living God? Paul observed the Pharisees were "zealous for the traditions of my fathers" (Galatians 1:14). Once, when Jesus ate with the Pharisees, he didn't wash his hands first. And they became so incensed they rejected him (Matthew 15:1-2). Think of it! Their form, ritual, and traditions stood in the way of their knowing Jesus the person.

4. Are you inclined to see what's wrong with everything? Do you have a critical spirit? Jesus healed on the Sabbath. The Pharisees said, "No!" He ate with a harlot. The Pharisees said, "No!" He ate with unwashed hands. "No!" He cast a demon out. "No!" the Pharisees chorused.

In Luke 7:32, Jesus observed that this generation is like school children who pipe and their friends won't dance, who wail and their chums won't cry. "There is no pleasing you!" We simply find something wrong with everything.

John Wesley pointed out that every gift God gives man is quickly sullied by human hands. He said every revival comes with defects. So he'd pray, "Lord, send revival without the defects." But then he told the Lord, "If you won't do it, then send the revival with the defects."

Pharisees only see the smoke, never the fire. They complain about defects, never seeing the revival. Negative, critical persons, they are judgmental.

5. Do you have a martyr syndrome? In Matthew 6:16 Jesus explained how the Pharisees, while fasting, would screw their faces up in misery to call attention to their sacrificial devotion. "Don't do it," Jesus commanded.

Isn't it easy to say, "Oh, woe is me! I'm the only one. Pity me, suffering for Jesus, I am. So persecuted. So misunderstood!"

6. Do you crave recognition? The Pharisees loved to grab the best seats in the synagogue or at a table feast. They sewed bells on their robes so you'd hear them coming, even provided a trumpet fanfare before they made an offering.

Isn't it easy to show off like that? "Look at me! See my zeal for God? Hear my amen? Watch me lift my hands to Jesus in worship! Am I being spiritual or what?!"

7. Do you believe you are closer to God than others? Luke 18:9 says of the Pharisees, "Confident of their own righteousness, they looked down on everybody else."

Isn't it true we judge others for their flaws, ourselves by our virtues, and always get such nice comparisons? And soon we start to believe we're special and God's opinions are the same as ours.

8. Do you have a "That's him!" attitude or a "That's me!" attitude? Luke 18:10 and following is a parable about two men who went to pray in the temple. A sinful tax collector stood in a corner and, confessing his sins, asked for mercy.

He had one eye on God and one eye on himself. The Pharisee, however, stood up front and center, looked to heaven, and bragged to himself, "I thank you, God, that I'm not like other men. I tithe, fast, pray...." He had one eye on himself, one eye on his neighbor, and no eye on God.

Aren't we perfectly capable of hearing a good sermon and thinking, "Boy, he really gave it to *them* today, didn't he?"

9. Are you constantly wallowing in guilt? Do you have feelings that you can never measure up? Are you driven instead of called? Do you feel compelled to work for God? To be clever? To be a super star instead of a super servant? Are you trying to go out and take Billy Graham's place?

Paul, writing of his days as a Pharisee trying to earn salvation, wrote, "O wretched man that I am! Who will deliver me from this body of death?" The Pharisee, motivated by guilt, works to prove he is righteous. The Christian, motivated by gratitude, works in the joy of the Lord.

10. Are you repulsed by emotional extravagance? Once a prostitute knelt at Christ's feet, wetting them with her tears and drying them with her long hair. The Pharisees were utterly scornful.

Later, during Jesus' donkey-bourne triumphal entry into Jerusalem, the Pharisees demanded Jesus squelch the enthusiasms of the adoring crowd. How do I react when in worship others weep, raise adoring hands, or leap for joy? Do I recoil in critical judgment, saying, "I don't like it!"? Or do I ask instead, "What does Jesus think of it?" Is it okay if God blesses someone else in worship?

11. Do you use emotion as a substitute for the Holy Spirit? Paul wrote in Romans 10:2, "I bear them witness, they have a zeal for God." My! My! How the Pharisees could turn it on! Tears at funerals, anger at Christ's Sabbath healings, dancing at festivals. But it was canned religion, calculated to say, "Look! See how much I care!" Beware lest our amens, our raised hands, our tears, be self-generated congratulations instead of true acts of worship.

12. Do you glory in the past? Do I relish so much what God has done that I reject what he is doing? The Pharisees stood before Jesus and haughtily remarked, "We have Abraham as our Father" (Matthew 3:9). A man and movement of God 1,000 years earlier thrilled them more than what God was doing under their noses.

Take Christian music. How George Beverly Shea could sing gospel music in the 1950s! But when we hear contemporary Christian music by Amy Grant, isn't it easy to sniff, "Her music is of the devil!"

13. Are you addicted to self-help pop psychology? Are you basing God's love for you on performance or grace? In Romans 7:7-25 Paul wrote of his days of trying to earn salvation with good behavior. He used "I," "me," and "my" 46 times in eighteen verses, complaining of his utter wretchedness in trying to change. Then in

Romans 8:1-17 he wrote of "the Spirit" fifteen times in seventeen verses, reveling in God's free and intervening help in his life.

A Pharisee tries to fix himself. A Christian trusts God to do it.

Check out your local bookstore. The self-help section is huge! Diet, stress-relief, looks, money, relationships. If the twin results of the fall are fear and pride, you see it focused here. Fear — of health, looks, weight, money matters. Pride — I'll fix it! Just give me a few weeks! I can measure up!

14. Do you bring division or lasting works? Mark 2:16 tells of Christ's meal with the ignorant, harlots, tax gatherers, outcasts, misfits, and lawbreakers. The Pharisees wouldn't join him; they dismissed the entire group as foolish and waved others away.

Still today we can use our influence to tear everything apart that's not perfect, not our taste, not up to our standards, not ... not ... not...!

Yet criticism is the easiest part of any job! But patience, mercy, covenanting, laboring — this is the real work.

It's, "What have you built?" Not, "What have you criticized?"

15. Will you take correction? The Pharisees wouldn't. When Jesus corrected them they were "offended" (Matthew 15:1-2). They were not "coachable." They had arrogant, independent spirits. Me? Will I take correction in how I relate to others? In child rearing? In my comprehension of the Gospel?

16. Do you believe you have been appointed by God to fix everything? Read Mark 2 and 3. Jesus is at work. Healing. Exorcizing. Plucking grain. Discipling twelve men. And the Pharisees are there constantly yammering, "No! No! No! This is not proper!"

Am I like that? Fussier than God? Nothing is ever good enough?

17. Is your prayer life mechanical? Jesus spoke of how our prayers can be public, full of vain repetition, nothing but heaped up empty words. But prayer is not a formula. It is a dialogue between two people who love each other — Father God and a child of faith.

18. Do you believe you are on the cutting edge? John 7:47-48 tells of the crowds flocking to see Jesus. The Pharisees are jealous. When someone asks their opinion, they huff, "None of us have believed in him!" Isn't it too easy to believe we have a lock on truth, that our ministry is the best, that if God was going to do anything he'd surely do it through us?

Just read the church advertisements in the papers: "Home of Old Time Religion." "The State's Most Exciting Church!" "The County's Fastest Growing Church!"

19. Are you bossy? The religious Jews ordered people about. Report this. Stop that. They even ordered Jesus' arrest (John 11:57).

Behold! The god-complex! "Follow me! I'm not lost! I know the best way!" "Just sit and listen! I'll lower some advice to you!"

20. Are you intolerant? Acts 15:5 speaks of a controversy in the early church. The issue was over whether a person must be circumcised before being baptized into Christ. The Pharisees who'd trusted Jesus were saying their way was the only proper means.

Still today, don't we quibble over the form of baptism? Or how renewal comes only through Bill Gothard's Institute, through *Experiencing God* book studies, through the Toronto Blessing, or through Promise Keepers?

"It happened to me like this. It was so right for me. Therefore it must be so right for you!" And suddenly my way is the only way.

21. Do you have pride in comparisons? "Our church musical is the best in the city!" "Our preacher is a doctor!" "Our church is the most prestigious." The Pharisees were into that sort of thing. "Spiritual peacockery," I call it.

22. Are you unmerciful? Sticklers for the law, the Pharisees caught a woman in the act of adultery and gathered to stone her (John 8). In Matthew 23:23 and following, Jesus complained that they "neglected mercy."

A real test of our character, of any church, is how it handles moral failure — the imprisoned, AIDs victims, unwed mothers, liars. An emotionally troubled woman, struggling with alcohol abuse, says, "Most churches you go to when it's all okay. If things are bad you stay home. This church is different. Everybody comes here hurting and it's okay." O Lord, may it ever be!

23. Are you suspicious of new movements? The Pharisees watched Jesus cast out demons and said it was a sham (Matthew 9:34). Their attitude was that if God were going to do something in town, he'd clear it first with them.

24. Are you offended when you are addressed without the use of a proper title? Pharisees loved to be called Rabbi, Master, Father, Teacher (Matthew 23:7). Today it is Reverend, Doctor, Bishop.

Geoffrey Chaucer, in *Canterbury Tales*, wrote of preachers and roosters having much in common. "They love to strut in public and preen. And they're both given to crowing at certain hours each day."

Jesus said, "The greatest among you shall be your servant."

25. Do you over-react when you see carnality? The Pharisees were a sin patrol. Like a smoke alarm constantly sniffing for smoke, they patrolled society for sin — sexual sin, dietary sin, Sabbath sin. And when they found it, they went off like they'd never seen it before! Come on! Get real! Just look inside. It's all there! Aren't we all sinners?

26. Do you glory in anything but Jesus and the cross? Jeremiah 9:23-25 warns, "Thus saith the Lord, 'Let not the wise man boast in his wisdom, or the strong man boast of his strength, or the rich man boast of his riches, but let him who boasts boast about this: that he understands and knows Me, that I am the Lord ...' " 1 Corinthians 1:31 says, "Let him who boasts boast in the Lord!"

Never, "I did it!" Always, "God did it!"

Conclusion

First Corinthians 10:12, "Let every man that thinks he stands take heed of himself lest he fall," invites a serious self-examination. And, ouch! I find so much of the Pharisees in my own character. It seems that Satan has tried to substitute human effort for Christ's spiritual work in my life. The results are unflattering. Self-righteousness for grace, pride instead of humility, cleverness instead of the cross. And if I don't combat it in Jesus, I'll become a wolf instead of a lamb.

In the late 1960s a soldier returned from Vietnam with a war bride. They made their home in rural Virginia. And they went to church.

He was suffering post-battle stress syndrome and drinking heavily. She was Oriental, lonely, and struggling to understand American society.

The town shunned her. She was "different." It was whispered she'd gotten pregnant to trap a husband and escape Saigon. People would not let their children play with hers. No one rang her phone. She grew depressed and finally killed her child and herself.

At her funeral the Lord asked the pastor, "Where are your sheep?" He gave no reply. The Lord asked a second time, "Where are your sheep?" And the pastor said, "I don't have any sheep. I have a pack of wolves!"

What of us? What of us? Will we be Jesus' lambs or self-made wolves? The one is the product of grace. The other of demons and self.

Deliverance: The Forgotten Third Of Jesus' Ministry

Russian novelist Fydor Dostoevsky wrote, "God and the devil are at war in the universe and their battlefield is the human heart." Just after Christ's transfiguration one of these skirmishes is to be seen.

When Jesus was transfigured, the entire mountain shone with the radiance of heaven. Moses was there. So was Elijah. And when Peter found his voice, he said, "Master, it's good that we are here! Let's build!" But Jesus pointed them back down the mountain where they were immediately confronted with a little boy in the awful throes of demonic possession. And it was a messy affair, fraught with convulsions, shrieks, and finally, failure on the disciple's part.

Certainly we'd all prefer the transfigured mountaintop to the complicated valley of human need. Yet Jesus calls us down the mountain into ministries of deliverance.

If one reads the New Testament, he will find Christ spent one-third of his time preaching, one-third healing, and one-third delivering people from the demonic. I call deliverance the forgotten third of Jesus' ministry.

First John 3:8 explains, "The reason the Son of Man appeared was to destroy the devil's work." Christ, you see, never met a demon he didn't dislike. And he met plenty: at his temptation in the wilderness (Luke 4), at his first sermon (Mark 1), while ministering in Gadara (Mark 5), and here, among many others, in a mother's beloved child. Christ always dealt with demons swiftly and ruthlessly. And he gave this ministry to his followers — authority to cast out all demons.

Many Christians are fearful of taking on Satan. Somehow in their minds they've determined we have a Ronald McDonald God and an Arnold Schwartzeneggar devil. But it's actually the reverse. Luke 10:17 explains how those Jesus sent out to minister returned with joy, saying, "Lord, even the demons submit to us in your name!"

So, today from the story of a little girl tormented by demons, let us take a general look at deliverance.

Who?

First of all, who is this presence in the child? The text says the child was "possessed by a spirit." It mentions a "demon," "an unclean spirit." In the Greek "demon" is *daimonia* meaning "devils." The scripture explains demons are "spirits" (Matthew 12:43, 45), Satan's emissaries (Matthew 12:26-27); they are numerous (Mark 5:9), seek embodiment to do evil (Matthew 12:43-44), are unclean, sullen, violent, and malicious (Matthew 8:28, 9:33, 10:1, 12:43), know who Christ is, recognize his authority (Matthew 8:31), and understand their fate is to be tormented (Mark 1:22-24; Matthew 8:29).

One discovers the demonic throughout the scriptures. There is no escaping it. It's there on the first page of scripture at Eve's temptation. It's there in the center of the Bible at Job's affliction. It's there at the start of Christ's ministry when he was tempted in the wilderness. It's there in Paul's life with his illness, "a messenger from Satan." And it is there in the final book of the Bible, Revelation, where Satan makes war on the saints.

The evil behind all this demonic activity is Satan. In Greek his name means "adversary" or "accuser." He's known variously as devil, slanderer, liar, deceiver, murderer, and prince of this world.

What Power?

The second question is: What is the power of this demon in the child? The Bible says it is considerable, using such words as "convulses," "foams," "shatters him," and "tore him."

Scripture explains Satan has three overall powers. He tempts. This is simply an enticement to do evil. (See 1 Corinthians 10:13.)

288

He oppresses. This is a temptation often succumbed to which forms a bad habit. Second Corinthians 10:4 calls it a "stronghold."

Then there is possession which is to be invaded, lived in, and controlled by evil. This can happen to people (Mark 5), animals (Mark 5 and Genesis 3), and even nature, as in lightning, wind, and storms (Job 1-2).

In using his three powers of tempting, oppressing, and possessing, Satan is 100 percent bent on destroying Christ and his works. He follows no rules and is no gentleman.

How?

The third question: How did this demon get into this child? Verse 26 mentions, "Cast it out." Who put it in in the first place? The text simply does not tell us. It is a mystery.

Some paths Satan walks to embody persons include overindulging natural desires. For example, a teen in becoming sexually mature begins to indulge his passion in movies, bawdy humor, and fantasy. Next comes pornography. And the next thing you know he's absolutely infested with the demonic.

Trauma can give opening to Satan. A child of a fine Brazilian missionary couple watched her family get hurt in an ugly church division. She left for college in the USA nursing deep wounds. Afraid to bond with other Christians for fear she'd be hurt afresh, she hopped from church to church, developed a fascination with angels, took in a lot of misinformation, and began to get crazy impulses like driving her car full of fellow Christians head on into a truck.

Satan can also enter a person by invitation. The desire for power leads some to ask for the devil's presence in their lives.

Dabbling in the occult such as seances, tarot cards, Ouija boards, palm reading, and such can make one vulnerable.

Rejecting light also is an avenue. Jesus said in Matthew 13:12 that when he gives us light and we walk in it, we receive more. But if we reject his light, even what we have will be taken away. So always remember when light goes, darkness comes.

A final point of entry Satan uses is rebellion. First Samuel 15:23 warns, "Rebellion is as the sin of witchcraft." Why is this so? Because Satan was the first rebel. And so it is that when we rebel against God, his church, family, etc., we become most like the devil.

What Symptoms?

A fourth question: What are the symptoms of demonic possession? Throughout the Bible we are given hints of what demons in people do to give away their presence: a carnal appetite out of control, unexplainable physical strength (Mark 5; Acts 19), unexplainable intelligence (Acts 16:16), self-destructive tendencies (Mark 5), rage against Jesus (Mark 1:22), pride, rebelliousness, filthiness, and even such physical liabilities as dumbness (Matthew 9:32-33), blindness (Matthew 12:22-23), epilepsy (Matthew 17:14-21), insanity (Mark 5), crippledness (Luke 13:10-17), and disease (Job 1-2).

Now, be cautious here. Just because a person is fat or blind or mentally ill or suicidal does not mean he is infested with demons. One must be discerning of spirits, and look for cumulative evidence. It is when one finds numerous symptoms beginning to add up that one can be more certain. But ultimately it is the Holy Spirit who confirms it.

How To Evict?

The fifth question is crucial: How does one evict demons? In the Bible the disciples often tried but failed. Yet Luke 9:1-2 says Jesus "gave them power and authority to drive out all demons."

Note the power to deliver is not our own. It is given to us.

The other day I watched a traffic cop throw up his hand and stop a line of automobiles. Surely wearing a badge and uniform did not make him strong enough to halt 19,000 pounds of Detroit steel moving toward him at 45 mph. Yet he held his hand up and all traffic came to a halt, not by his power, but by the power of the entire police force, the courts, and the prisons.

The point is, we halt Satan by the power of Jesus. So we must learn to live under his authority, to exercise our given authority to the limit. We are not practicing nominal, defensive Christianity but bold, loving, cosmic take-no-prisoners Christianity!

So how is it we evict Satan? Some basic guidelines: The person must be willing to be delivered (Mark 5). He must honestly confess his demons (1 John 1:9). One must take authority over the demons in Jesus's name (Mark 16:17; Luke 10:19). It is helpful to get the demon to name himself. A name is an essence and knowing it strips a demon of his darkness (Mark 5). The person must renounce the demon. And one must forgive (Matthew 6:15).

Exorcism can be an unsavory ministry. Manifestations of demons leaving can include screaming, weeping, convulsions, shaking, vomiting, nausea, fainting, laughter, retching, and other unsettling behavior.

Can Demons Return?

Jesus spoke of a man who swept his house and put it in order but did not fill it. The evicted demon went and found some buddies also disembodied. They came back to check out the old abode, found it empty, and reentered (Matthew 12:45).

This chilling parable reminds us we must be saved from Satan's power to Christ's power. We must get under authority in a solid church (1 Samuel 15:23; Ephesians 6; Hebrews 10:25), quit sinning (John 5:14), live by the scriptures (Luke 4), praise the Lord, guard the thought life (2 Corinthians 10:5), cultivate right relationships (Proverbs 13:20), and submit to discipline (Hebrews 12:7-11).

Mistakes?

A final question: What are some of the common mistakes we make in starting a ministry of deliverance?

Just to mention a few: seeing demons behind all human misery, seeing exorcism as a means of instant sainthood, getting ruffled and yelling back at demons, draining oneself with too much ministry, panicking when Satan counter-attacks, thinking everybody is ready for this sort of ministry, and believing it is not okay to fail.

Conclusion

In the heat of summer, God sends in a cool front to break the drought. Where cold and warm air collide there is a violent storm full of lightning, thunder, wind, and rain. Just so, in the story to-day one sees the kingdom of Satan collide with God's kingdom. And God's grace prevails as the child is released from his evil tormentors.

If you understand you need this ministry, call out to an elder. We'll interview you at length, and if it is discerned deliverance is needed, we'll set up an appointment with some gifted, fasting, righteous Christians who will pray for you and minister deliverance.

Times of refreshing can be yours in Jesus!

Have You Gone Far Enough?

When I was in divinity school some student had written graffiti on the bathroom wall. And I've never forgotten the humor of it. It went something like this: "And Jesus spake unto Peter saying 'Who do men say that I am?' And Peter answered, 'Thou art, according to Paul Tillich, the very ground of our being. Thou art Emmanuel Kant's deontological categorical imperative. Thou art the man of the Eschaton, the ultimately determinative one!' And Jesus looked at Peter and saith, 'What?' "

Seriously, in the text, Jesus did look at his disciples and ask, "Who do you think I am?" And that question has been asked of every generation down through twenty centuries of human history. And today I ask it of you. "Who is this Jesus Christ?"

Myth

The mildest conclusion one may draw is that Jesus Christ is a myth.

You will recall the heros of your youth — Santa Claus, the Easter Bunny, Puff the Magic Dragon, and Superman. When you grew up you found out they weren't real. And there are those who assign Jesus Christ a place among such mythological creatures. To them, Jesus is no more than a Hercules or a Sinbad. He never really existed. His life is but a cleverly written myth told to inspire, to entertain.

Yet under serious investigation such a conclusion cannot stand. As F. F. Bruce, Professor of Biblical Criticism at the University of Manchester, pointed out, "Some writers may toy with the fancy of a 'Christ-myth,' but they do not do so on the ground of historical evidence. The historicity of Christ is as axiomatic for an unbiased historian as the historicity of Julius Caesar. It is not historians who propagate the 'Christ-myth' theories." The fact is, no serious scholar has ever yet ventured to say that Jesus Christ never lived.

Actual evidence that Christ was a real man is found in 27 different New Testament documents. And non-biblical proof of his existence is to be found in the writings of Polycarpa, Justin, Origin, Tacitus, Lucian, Josephus, Pliny, and the Jewish Talmud.

All of this evidence, and more, has led scholars like Harvard University Professor Clifford Moore to say that Christianity "... was founded on positive, historical, and acceptable facts."

Man

So, what do you think of Jesus Christ? If one cannot say he is but a myth of antiquity, what then can be said of him? Just this: Jesus Christ was a man, an actual human being like you or me.

In the 1970s rock opera *Jesus Christ Superstar* this is the conclusion Mary of Magdala comes to as she sings, "I don't know how to love him." The lyrics, "He's just a man" are repeated over and over again. And many of us may want to rest our convictions here. Jesus Christ was a real man, nothing more, nothing less. He was born, he lived, he died. That's all.

Yet upon a closer investigation of the evidence surrounding the life of Christ, one is most uncomfortable in settling here.

British scholar W. H. Griffith Thomas wrote, "The testimony to the present work of Jesus Christ is no less real today than it has been in the past. In the case of all other great names of world history, the inevitable and invariable experience has been that the particular man is first a power, then only a name, and last of all a mere memory. Of Jesus Christ the exact opposite is true. He died on a cross of shame, his name gradually became more and more powerful, and he is the greatest influence in the world today."

Who is this man who won't fade into history?

Encyclopedia Britannica has devoted more words, approximately 20,000 in all, to Christ than to any other person.

Christ never owned a home. He never put his feet inside a big city. He never wrote a book or held a political office. He never married or had a family or traveled more than 200 miles from the place of his birth. Yet his fame grows instead of diminishing with the years.

Of him Ralph Waldo Emerson said, "Jesus is the most perfect of all men that have yet appeared."

Islam's *Koran* concludes that Jesus is "... the greatest above all in this world and in the world to come."

Jewish writer Shalom Ash says, "Jesus Christ is the outstanding personality of all time."

Historian William Lecky concedes, "The simple record of (Jesus Christ's) ... three short years of active life has done more to regenerate and soften mankind than all the disquisitions of philosophers and moralists."

But perhaps it was Napoleon Bonaparte who summed it up best. "Gentlemen," he said, "I know men, and I can tell you, Jesus Christ was more than a man."

A Great Teacher

More than a myth. More than a man. Who is this Jesus Christ? What can we conclude about him? The next possible conclusion, and perhaps the most widely held, is that Jesus Christ is a great teacher.

This opinion places Jesus in the company of Plato, Aristotle, Socrates, Buddha, Confucius, and Mohammed. He was a real man whose teachings have won him a prominent place in civilization.

This conclusion would certainly be upheld by the findings of a recent Gallup Poll which found 87 percent of Americans affirming the influence of Christ in their lives.

Yet, look but further and you'll discover the great trilemma of this position. And that is that Jesus as a great teacher was either a liar, a lunatic, or God!

Consider: Other great religious leaders said, "I have taught you the truth." But Jesus said, "I am the truth" (John 14:6).

Of all the great religious teachers of history, it is Christ alone who actually claimed to be God (John 20:26-29; John 4:19-26; John 14:8-11).

He asked his followers to believe in him (John 14:1), he said that to see him was to see God (John 14:9), he said all earth would pass away, but never his words (Mark 13:31), he accepted worship from people as if he were God (Matthew 8:2; Matthew 14:33; John 20:27-29), he claimed to forgive sins (Mark 2:7; Matthew 9:5-6), he claimed to be the only way to God (John 14:6), he claimed he would rise from the dead (Luke 18:31-33), and he claimed he would come again to judge all men and reign eternally (John 5:27; Matthew 28:18-20; Matthew 24:30-31).

Now, obviously, a person who said these things about himself is either a liar, a lunatic, or who he says he is.

Was Jesus a liar? Did he know the things he was teaching to be absolute falsehood and yet go on intentionally misleading his followers trying to build his Kingdom in order to serve his own ends? Was Jesus little more than an egotistical and self-serving liar trying to get rich, famous, and powerful? That is one option. Yet his gentle acts of healing, his role as a suffering servant, his refusal to be made a king, his poverty, and his willingness to die for his claims seriously erode such a view.

This leaves us with Jesus the lunatic.

This conclusion states that Christ was suffering from delusions. His imagination had run away with him to the point that he actually believed the lies he was telling about himself. We call this type of personality today a megalomanic. Yet, a renowned psychiatrist from Duke University, Dr. Bill Wilson, said he applied all the different mental illnesses to Jesus and found that none fit. In fact, he concluded, "Jesus Christ is the most whole person who ever lived."

The only other option here is to say that Jesus Christ is who he says he is — God!

C. S. Lewis, a professor at both Oxford and Cambridge Universities, ably summed up the situation for us here:

> *A man who was merely a man and said the sort of things Jesus said would not be a great moral teacher. He would either be a lunatic — on a level with the man who says he is a poached egg — or else he would be the Devil of Hell. You must make your choice. Either this man was,*

and is, the son of God, or else a madman or something
worse. You can shut him up for a fool, you can spit at
him and kill him as a demon; or you can fall at his feet
and call him Lord and God. But let us not come up with
any patronizing nonsense about his being a great hu-
man teacher. He has not left that open to us.

Son Of God

Who is this man Jesus Christ? What can we finally conclude about him? He's not a myth. Indeed, he is a real man. But beyond that one cannot conclude that he is a great moral teacher. For, indeed, he is either a liar, a lunatic, or who he said he is, the Son of God.

A story is told and I believe it is a true one. The year was 1928 and a would-be mechanic was working on his Ford automobile. He could not get it to run. About then a new Ford pulled up, and out stepped a well-dressed gentleman in a Derby hat with a cane. He looked at the engine and confidently suggested, "If you'll adjust this screw here, your car will run." Well, the would-be mechanic stared at the stranger and thought, "He doesn't look like a mechanic!" But then he'd already tried everything he knew to do. So he adjusted that screw, kicked the starter, and, lo and behold, his car sprang to life. In amazement the man turned to the helpful stranger and said, "Just who are you anyway?" And the man stuck out his hand and said, "The name's Ford, my boy. Henry Ford! I made that car! I ought to know what makes it run." And the Gospel of Jesus Christ is that he is the Son of God, born of the virgin Mary, alive some 33 years in Israel teaching, healing, demonstrating God's love, dying for our sins, rising from the dead, and ascending into Heaven. He is God come into this world to tap you on the shoulder and say, "If it's not working, listen to me! I made you! I know what makes life work!"

This is who Jesus Christ claimed to be, the Son of God!

A number of years ago, a famous American general named Lew Wallace and his friend, Robert Ingersoll, an agnostic, agreed that together they would write a book that would convincingly destroy the myth of Christianity and thus deliver multitudes of people from religious superstition. So, for two years Wallace studied in the great libraries of America and Europe trying to uncover evidence which would enable him to write his book. But, while writing the second chapter, Lew Wallace found himself on his knees praying to the Christ he had been seeking to expose as a fraud. The evidence for the claims of Christ was simply so convincing on all levels that he could no longer deny Jesus was who he said he was. And Lew Wallace set his book aside to begin another one, *Ben Hur*, a novel about the life-changing impact of Christ, the Son of God.

Savior

No, Jesus is not a myth. Yes, he is more than a man. And certainly he is more than a great teacher. He is who he says he is, the Son of God! But don't stop there! That would be like acknowledging the law of gravity and yet jumping out of an airplane without a parachute. For agreeing that Jesus is the Son of God without accepting him as your personal Savior is suicide! Yet that is what many of us do. We affirm Jesus is God, but we ignore him. We agree his teachings are true. But we refuse to live by them.

A missionary was called to talk to a small boy who was dying in an African hospital. The man asked the boy if he believed in God. "Yes," came the timid reply. "Do you believe in Jesus Christ?" he inquired. Again came the reply, "Yes." "Well, then, have you ever asked him into your life as your personal Savior?" he inquired. "No," replied the child. The missionary was grieved and he struggled with how he might explain the gospel to the little child so near unto death. Finally he took the boy's hand and said, " 'Jesus Christ is the Savior.' That's five words. One for each finger on your hand. And do you know which word is the most important? The word, 'the' for, you see, the statement, 'Jesus Christ is the Savior' is but history. It's true. But it does you no good. But change the word 'the' to 'my' and that becomes salvation. 'Jesus Christ is *my* Savior.' Will you confess that?" The little boy said he would and the missionary had a prayer for him and left wondering if he'd gotten through to the lad.

The next day there was news of the boy's death. And his parents called for the missionary. "It is strange," they said. "When our son died he was holding tightly to his pointer finger with his hand. We don't understand why, but it seemed to give him comfort." And suddenly it came to the missionary that the gospel had gotten through to the little boy after all. The pointer finger was the "my" in the statement, "Jesus Christ is *my* Savior." For the lad, the Christ of history had become a personal Savior.

Has Jesus become your personal Savior? He is no myth. He's more than a mere man or a great moral teacher. He is the Son of God! That is fact. It's history! But, it's not salvation until you invite him into your own life by a prayer of faith. Have you done this? Will you do so now?

I tell you, one does not have to commit intellectual suicide to do so! The credentials of Christ are impeccable. As George Bancroft states, "Christianity has attracted to itself the profoundest thinkers of the human race, and is in no way hindered by the ever-advancing tide of human knowledge." Novelists Tolstoy, Dostoevsky, and Defoe became Christians. So did poets T. S. Eliot and Emily Dickinson. Musical composers like George Friedrich Handel and J. S. Bach along with artists like Rembrandt knelt at Christ's feet, calling him Savior. But don't receive Jesus as your Savior just because Charlemagne, Shakespeare, and Isaac Newton did. Accept him because Jesus is who he says he is and you believe in him personally.

Lord

But have we gone far enough when we accept Jesus as Savior? Have we accepted Christ for all he is when we believe him as Savior? No. For he is more. He is Lord of all the universe, King forever!

Many Christians treat this last credential of Jesus as entirely optional. According to their line of reasoning, one may receive Jesus as Savior from sin, from death and eternal punishment, but leave off with the Lord of life and master part. This is sort of like buying into Christ for the "fire insurance" he offers, but rejecting him as boss of our earthly lives.

Yet, if Jesus is who he says he is, then nothing of his claims is optional for you and for me! The book of Colossians is interesting to study here. In a brief three-page letter, Paul uses the word "all" 33 times. And what does "all" mean in the Greek? "All" means "all"! It means everything! Completely! And that's how Paul describes Jesus Christ. He is all! "The firstborn of all creation" (1:15). "In him all things were created" (1:16). "He is before all things, and in him all things hold together" (1:17). "For in him all the fulness of God was pleased to dwell" (1:19). "... through him to reconcile to himself all things" (1:20). "... Christ, in whom are hid all the treasures of wisdom and knowledge" (2:3). "... him, who is the head of all rule and authority" (2:10). "... but Christ is all and in all" (3:11). Very impressive credentials, eh? And answer me this! If Jesus Christ is all he says he is, do you think he'll be satisfied with less than all of your life? Do you think you can really get away with giving him second place in your life?

If you read through the Gospels, you will quickly see that the credentials of Jesus Christ do not stop with Savior. He went beyond the cross and the empty tomb to the throne. He ascended into heaven and was given dominion to reign as King forever. And until we make Jesus in our lives right now what he is in the universe forever, and that is Lord and Ruler of all, then we have not gone as far as we can.

I like the way a Christian quarterback once explained Jesus as Lord of his life. He said, "Christ calls the plays. I run them." Are you willing to trust God to call the plays in your life starting right now? Are you willing to obey his Word as regards finances, marriage, worship, child rearing, leisure, giving, prayer, and forgiveness? Are you willing to let Jesus rule your life?

Notice how Paul introduces himself to the church in Romans 1:1. Most of us preachers like to be introduced in our press releases as "Doctor," "dynamic," "in constant demand," or "world traveler." But Paul simply introduces himself saying, "Paul, a servant of Jesus Christ...." Isn't that refreshing? Paul had gone all the way with Jesus Christ. God was his boss. Paul was Christ's servant. Think of it! A servant is a worker. He follows orders. He might be assigned any task here or there. And the Bible says that this Lordship of Christ over our lives is not optional! We must be his servant!

Do you acknowledge the Lordship of Jesus in your life? Is he your King? Are you his servant?

Living under the Lordship of Jesus means all your belongings are entrusted to him. It means you allow him to place you in the home, the job, the church of his choice. It means he can use you to serve in a successful spot or a position where he needs a noble failure or a humble, plodding mediocrity. It means you place all your attitudes, hopes, and expectations upon him.

Have you done this? Is he your all? Is he in your life right now who he already is in the universe, King and Lord forever?

Getting Started Where You Are

The first question in the Bible is found in Genesis, chapter 3. God asks Adam and Eve, "Where are you?" And I'd like to ask that question of you right now. "Where are you in your thinking about Jesus Christ?" Who do you say he is?

Maybe you cannot go all the way in affirming him as Savior and Lord today. Perhaps you can only affirm that he was a real man. What you need to do is approach the next step with study and prayer and reflection. Then when you can honestly and by faith affirm him as the Savior, you can go on to consider him as your personal Savior and then finally, your Lord.

This is what Doubting Thomas did. "I won't believe," he said, "unless I see!" And, beginning there, he made his investigation which led to the highest affirmation of Christ ever uttered by human lips in scripture, "My Lord and my God!" (John 20:28).

Conclusion

He walked here only 33 years ...
Yet we measure time from the year of his birth.
Who is he? A good man? A teacher? God? A Savior?
He never owned a home.
He never put his feet inside a big city.
And he rode on a borrowed donkey.
His followers were common folks like you and me.

301

The only thing he ever wrote was in the sand, yet libraries the world over have volumes written about him.

Who is he?

Who is this man who made such strange claims?

"I am the door."

"I am the light of the world."

"I am the bread of life."

He lived in an obscure mid-eastern country.

He was born in a stable.

His parents were peasants.

Yet who can ever estimate his influence on the human race?

His name? Jesus. Jesus of Nazareth.

Ever wonder who he really is?

Isn't it about time you found out?

Is Your Love Shy?

When I was in college my post office box was right next to a pretty little blonde's. She was a tanned Florida Freshman, if you know what I mean. And her name was Sally.

Now John, a fellow on my hall, was secretly in love with Sally. And he kept trying to get me to switch post office boxes with him. That way he could be close to Sally.

You see, John was painfully shy. Though he longed to know Sally, he couldn't muster the nerve to ask her out. So, he secretly loved her at a distance.

Once he rode a bus four blocks past the place where he wanted to get off just so he could be near her a little longer. (She was in the front of the bus. He was at the rear.) He went to the administrative building and got a copy of her class schedule so he could just happen to be where she was. Another time he signed up for zoology because she would be in the class.

And, yes, I traded post office boxes with John. But it cost him! For three dollars, a coil of rope, a Spanish 101 book, and a nice ball point pen, John got my box next to Sally's.

Well, come the school year's end, John finally summoned up the courage to ask Sally out for a date. She agreed. And over supper John confided in Sally, telling her of his year long love. And you know what? Sally said she'd loved John the whole year too!

Think of all the joy they missed! Think of the romance and comfort and tenderness that will never be because their love was shy.

And aren't we bashful like John was with Sally when it comes to our own love affair with God? We are reluctant to draw near, timid to ask for help. We're shy to ask questions, to find out more about him. Yes, we're bashful lovers of God.

Our text for today tells us that the disciples, too, were shy with Christ. The Lord told them of his impending conflict with the Jewish authorities. He said he'd be killed and later rise from the dead. Such talk confused the disciples. Their minds buzzed with wonderment, but according to our text, "They did not understand the saying, and they were afraid to ask him what he meant."

Why are we afraid to ask? Why do we so bashfully sit back and allow ignorance to cloud our minds?

Pride

Pride, I think, is one reason. We are afraid of showing our ignorance. You know how this is. A school teacher says, "Now I'll explain it and if you have any questions or if you don't understand it, just raise your hand." And after she explains it the class room is full of blank stares, but no one asks any questions for fear of being the only dummy in the class. It's sort of like Abe Lincoln once said, "It's better to keep your mouth shut and be thought a fool, than to open it and remove all doubt."

And people play on our pride, don't they? They profit from our unwillingness to show our ignorance, don't they? How many tactful salesmen come into your home and say, "I'm sure you're an intelligent person; you understand how this vacuum cleaner with its new pulsating suction is more effective than the competitor's brand, so I won't take up your valuable time explaining to you the obvious...." This is true of the art world, as well. How many poets and playwrights nowadays get away with murder because we read their works and pretend to understand them so folks won't think we're tasteless bores?

Do you remember the fable, "The Emperor's New Clothes"? The king was being outfitted for a new wardrobe and an unscrupulous tailor got a hold of him. The tailor was taking the money for expensive clothing but only delivering skimpy garments. Well, at first the king was suspicious, but the tailor flattered him and allayed his royal fears. And of course, none of the king's subjects were about to criticize his apparel. They simply concluded silently that the king was losing his mind. The tailor finished his job and made off with the money leaving the king walking around in his rather skimpy attire while the people didn't dare ask. And then one day it happened. A wee child seeing the king said aloud, "Why, what's the king doing walking around in his underwear?" And can't vanity make a royal fool out of us all!

Do ask! Fire away with your questions. Here in the church feel free to go ahead and say, "I don't understand. Explain it once more." No one will laugh at you for your questing and questioning mind.

Afraid Of The Answer

So, why is it we're afraid to ask? Pride! We're simply afraid of showing our ignorance. And now, passing on, here's a second reason we don't ask. We are afraid of what the answer might be.

Go ahead and ask a doctor about this fear. He'll tell you that few of his patients ever look him in the eye and say, "Give it to me straight, doctor. Do I have cancer? Is it terminal? How long do I have?" Instead, patients edge around the facts, deal in generalities, and engage in subtle delusions. And isn't this how it was in our text? Why didn't the disciples ask Jesus what he meant when he predicted his death? They were afraid. They were afraid of what the answer might be. What would his death mean to them? Was the nature of the Messiah different from what they expected? And someone settled the issue by deftly concluding, "Don't ask."

A pastor once told me he'd been in the ministry 47 years and not once had a church member ever asked, "Pastor, do you think I'm a Christian?" Not once had an elder or deacon queried, "Am I doing my job? Am I setting a good example?" Nor had a convert ever questioned, "Am I doing okay? Do you think I'm growing?" Why? Why are we afraid to ask such important questions? Perhaps we're afraid of the answer.

A family sent their son off to college. And in a roundabout way they discovered that their son had far more money than they could account for. He dressed well, traveled frequently, and lived high.

305

Well, the question was obvious. "Where are you getting all that money, son?" Was he a thief? Was he gambling? Was he selling drugs? And the parents decided to keep quiet. "Don't ask," they concluded for fear of what the answer might be. And do you see the hell of it all? Do you see the shallowness of the relationship, the worry, the lack of love that their don't-ask attitude got them into? And isn't it the same for us here and now? Are you afraid to ask because you're afraid of what the answer might be? Ask! Ask! Some things are too important not to be questioned.

Are you really a Christian? Are you filled with the Spirit? Why is there a cross at the center of our faith? Are you taking your church membership seriously? Why don't you attend group prayer? Am I as an elder doing a biblical job of it?

Brothers and sisters, do ask! Some things are just that important!

I Don't Care!

What have we seen so far? We are afraid to ask because we're proud or afraid of what the answer might be. And there's another reason we refuse to inquire. We just don't care. We're not interested in the questions so we're not interested in the answers.

A *Blondie* cartoon summed it all up when it showed Dagwood awakened from his nap by the doorbell. A salesman standing there again asked, "Aren't you just dying to know what I'm selling this time?" And without a word Dagwood slammed the door. Questions outside our values seldom interest us. They simply pass by us unnoticed.

Don't you know how this is? I once spent the evening out with a young couple who are not Christian. Like most Americans their faith was in things, in materialism and pleasure. And I kept account of the kinds of questions they asked.

"How can I avoid that extra tax?"

"How much does a new Datson 280-Z cost?"

"Have you ever eaten there? Was it good?"

"Did you see that new James Bond movie?"

"Where are you going on your vacation?"

"Want to know where we're planning to build our new house?"

Questions, sure! Scads of them! But questions of the belly, the bank. And not questions of the soul. Gently as I could, I turned the conversation toward Jesus. I asked his thinking on man's nature, on the existence of God, and the church. And he shrugged them off. It wasn't that he was afraid of showing his ignorance. Nor was he afraid of the answers. He just didn't care. All his circuits were jammed with other questions so that he didn't have room for others to get through.

Such sad creatures we can be! To go through life asking questions of food and pleasure and disco and suntans and movies and sports cars is so typical of today. We think questions of hair styles are more important than questions of justice. It's more important to us to find the answer to a television mystery than to find an answer to a troublesome Bible verse. Such glandular people we've become; mindlessly we march though life absorbing food and goods and services and never questioning whence we've come or whither we go.

Is this you we're talking about? Are you only interested in questions of money and sex and recreation? Is your appetite for inquiry into Christianity jaded? Could you care less about questions of salvation, of justice and mercy and ministry and life and death?

Conclusion

Did you hear about the farmer who bought himself a long, red Lincoln Continental? It was his only extravagance and he kicked the cows out to garage it in the barn! The farmer used it for trips into town, for Sunday afternoon drives with his wife, and for family vacations. But he never really knew what all he owned! Let me explain what I mean!

After owning the red Lincoln several years, his oldest boy turned sixteen and commenced to driving himself. The boy behind the wheel now, the farmer was a passenger. And every time they went somewhere the boy would show the father something new his car could do.

Once he put in a tape and his dad said, "What's that?"

The lad taught his father about the car's cruise control, automatic light dimmer, and the seat recliner button. The farmer learned of that hidden map light, the air-conditioner, and even stereo radio.

And though he'd owned the car for several years, it was only after he started asking questions that he began to learn the things it would do. And isn't it just that way with our faith? Christ has bought us more Christianity than we know! He offers so much. And, for our lack of searching and questioning, we know and accept so little. We've become lazy and self-satisfied.

How about you? Isn't it time you started asking questions and looking for biblical answers? To Jeremiah the prophet, God promised, "Call to me and I will answer you, and will tell you great and hidden things which you have not known" (Jeremiah 33:3). And his promise is to you as well. "Ask and it shall be given. Seek and ye shall find. Knock and the door shall be opened unto you" (Matthew 7:7). Don't be bashful! Think of all you might be missing! Yes, and by the way, John and Sally got married and now live in Lima, Ohio. Do you see what questions can start?

No Salt In The City?

Last fall the phone rang in my study. It was a newspaper pollster doing a survey on church and society. His main question was, "What would your city be like without the church?"

I was tempted to be funny in my reply. Like the cartoon that shows a pack of wolves howling at the moon. A wolf on the back row is looking worried and asks another fanged friend, "Do you think we're doing any good?" Sometimes I feel like that when the church seems to be ignored or irrelevant.

Yet anytime one feels he is small and can't have much of an impact, just remember what it's like going to bed with a mosquito in the room!

Actually I told the phone researcher that a city without the church would be like life without salt. Why do I say this?

In the Sermon on the Mount, Jesus said to his disciples, "You are the salt of the earth." That was quite a compliment in Jesus' day, for salt was very rare, yet highly prized.

Greeks called salt "the second soul of meat." A half pound of salt was worth more than a human being. Soldiers were often paid in salt. The word "salary" is derived from "salt." This is where we get our saying, "He's not worth his salt."

So, when Jesus said, "You are the salt of the earth," the compliment must have "wowed" the apostles. They were valuable to God and society. As we say today, they were worth their weight in gold.

But what does it all mean practically speaking?

Flavor

Consider the flavor-enhancing properties of salt. Why, what are french fries without salt's savor? How bland! And as salt adds zest to a meal, so Christians are the spice of life at school, at the office, in the classroom, and down at the local club.

The good Lord never meant for Christians to be dull, lifeless killjoys. Why, Jesus was the life of the party. Not only was he invited to the wedding feast of Cana, he served up some pretty good wine! Jesus explained, "I am come that you might have life, and have it more abundantly" (John 10:10).

Yet how many Christians walk about looking like they've been weaned on a dill pickle? All of this prompted Mark Twain to comment, "I'll take heaven for climate and hell for society."

Young Patrick is a college student and a strong Christian. He recently joined the Sigma Chi fraternity. "In this sign, conquer" is their brotherhood motto. It goes back to Constantine before the Battle of Milvan Bridge. He saw the cross of Christ in the sky and heard a voice saying, "In this sign, conquer." He did and in the early 300s A.D., became the first Christian emperor of Rome. The Sigma Chi's seek to emulate the Christian leadership qualities of Constantine. At least, that was their intention when the fraternity was formed. Yet time, like a careless laundryman, shrinks many of our ideals. And many a fraternity like Patrick's has devolved into a society of drinking, swaggering, and partying hard all day, everyday.

At the lunch table the brothers tell dirty jokes. And for every bad joke, Patrick tells a funnier clean joke. After several months of this, Hank said to Paddy, "I've never met someone like you. You have as much fun or more than we do, yet you're clean and sober!"

De-icer

Not only can salt add flavor, it also owns the property of melting ice. When a snowstorm barrels across our city, road crews busily spread salt on our bridges to melt the ice.

In our day human hearts have grown frosty; long icicles of indifference are suspended like daggers from our lives. We have our cliques, our racial walls, our cold-blooded murders. "I don't care about God. I don't even care about you. All I care about is me!"

And it takes salt, Christian salt, to thaw out a society.

A young lady in our church was looking forward to attending a concert. She and three of her friends had tickets, and the day neared. In casual conversation, she found two other students really wanted to go, but couldn't find a ride. They had room in their car. But these two were of a different race. They ran with a different crowd, lived on the other side of town.

When she suggested to her three chums they take the two with them, she was met with a stout, "No!" Undaunted, the girl pressed on about how the two were human just like themselves, how it was time to build some bridges of kindness in their high school, and how there should be enough of her to love her three friends and two new ones to boot!

Now, that, my friends, is salt!

Thirst

What else can salt do besides add flavor and thaw ice? It can induce thirst.

If you take a date to the movies, just about the time the movie is getting good, you'll feel an elbow in your ribs. "Popcorn!" she'll say. So you scramble out to buy some. But don't be cheap! For while you're out you might as well purchase a drink. For the popcorn is so salty that after four bites, you'll get the elbow again. "A drink," she'll command.

Then there's an old saying, "You can lead a horse to water, but you can't make him drink." True. But you can add plenty of salt to his oats. And he'll find the water trough soon enough.

When my Kathryn and I first married, we lived in a tiny three-room apartment in Atlanta. The complex had about 300 people in it, mostly blue collar workers — divorcees, homosexuals, alcoholics, the unemployed. Looking back, it was a rough place, although it didn't seem like it at the time. There was always a domestic spat, a drug bust going down, or a break-in. The swimming pool was unfit to swim in. Beer cans strewed the lawn. Paint peeled everywhere. And there was no gospel in the neighborhood. Why, come

Sunday morning you could sleep in the middle of the road and not get run over by a single person going to church.

Kathryn and I lived there two years. That's where our first baby was born. We were there without any insurance, so I got a job picking up the trash, mowing grass, cleaning the pool, and painting to make ends meet, to pay the bills of our firstborn.

Come Thanksgiving, just before Kathryn gave birth, we decorated for Christmas. Nobody ever did that there. But it's as if seeing our wreath and colored lights stirred something long asleep in those people. And before many days, the apartment complex twinkled with festive decor.

When spring came, Kathryn asked me to make her a window box for her flowers. I did so, and all summer, banks of lovely flowers spilled over our porch. One by one, I began to see hanging baskets and flower pots added to other apartments.

After graduation we said our goodbyes and moved to work in a church in Virginia. And it was six years before we had a chance to visit our old Atlanta neighborhood. But as soon as we turned the corner and saw it, we burst out laughing! Flower boxes everywhere, newly mowed lawns, a pristine swimming pool, and the resident manager, Ann, told us she'd become a Christian and showed us her 3-D picture of Jesus hanging over her television!

See how salt works quietly? We just live our lives before a watching world and they get thirsty for our savior.

Healing

What does salt do? It flavors, thaws, and promotes thirst. But it also heals. Recall your childhood sore throats, and how Mom made you gargle with salt water? Though it stung, it ultimately brought soothing relief.

Christians are like that in society. If you study history, you'll find Christians going where the hurt is, killing germs, and healing sickness.

Example: the sick. History teaches they were often ignored, abandoned to die in a field, or left to wallow in a bed of pain without sufficient treatment. Christians understood Jesus as a healer of the sick, a man of hospitality. So they began hospitals to show the love of Christ to the sick and dying. And, if you look around, you'll be astounded at how many of our healing centers have their genesis in Christendom — Duke, Bowman-Gray, Presbyterian ...

Example: orphans. Often orphaned girls were reared to be prostitutes. Orphaned boys were horribly disfigured and used as beggars in the street. Christians saw this and came running with salt. Look around you. Elon Homes, Oxford, Thornwell — all Christian havens for the parentless child.

Example: ignorance. A nation that couldn't read, didn't know history, couldn't add. The Bible tells us Jesus could read. And that was in a day when few could. He could also write. And again, Christians were salt. Go down the east coast: Dartmouth, Harvard, Yale, Princeton, William and Mary, Duke, Davidson, Furman, Emory — every one started as Christian ministries to the ignorant. See here how salty Christians see the germs and rush in to bring healing — hospitals, schools, orphanages, counseling centers, day cares, rest homes, housing, fair legislation ...

Last spring drinking got out of hand at the local college. And after a party a young man crashed his car and died. The campus was numb with grief. That's when some Christians began the Greek Christian Fellowship and made it their goal to educate the campus on alcohol abuse, to learn not to let friends drive drunk, and to show their friends how to party drunk on God's Spirit and not on liquor.

Salt! Glorious salt! Flavoring, thawing, inducing thirst, healing!

Preservative

But salt is also a preservative. If you cure a ham with salt, rather than spoil, the ham can last indefinitely.

Stick your head out the door and you can catch a whiff of our society spoiling.

Take New York City. 830,000 people are on welfare (a total bigger than the population of all but ten U.S. cities). 366 cars are stolen each day. 200,000 people a day jump the turnstiles to ride the subway free. There are over two million warrants out for people who failed to show up in court. The public school system has more administrative staff than all of Europe. New York has 500,000 drug addicts. It is the AIDs capital of the world. The illegitimate birth rate in Harlem is eighty percent and rising. 10,000 babies a year are born "toxic." That means the mothers were crack cocaine addicts and it will take $220,000 for each baby in remedial medical attention just to get him or her started in life. There is a stickup every six minutes. There were 93,387 armed robberies last year. Twenty-one cab drivers were murdered.

And what's going on in New York City is but a foreshadowing of where our nation is headed. These problems can be seen in Los Angeles, in Dallas, in Charlotte, and across the whole country. Now is the time for salt. We need the salt of Christian values to preserve marriages, to initiate and sustain friendships, to be an effective parent, to renew racial dialogue, and to preserve values in public schools. If we withdraw, if Christians cocoon themselves, if we keep our salt to ourselves, then our children's world won't be fit to live in!

In the 1930s, as Hitler rose to power as a Nazi dictator, Albert Einstein watched with growing alarm. He expected the newspapers to expose Hitler's corruption, but the media was quickly silenced. So Einstein looked to the universities to stop Hitler. Instead, they went along. In the end, only the church stood squarely in Hitler's path. And Einstein wrote, "What formerly I had no use for, I now praise unreservedly." The salty church of our Lord and Savior Jesus Christ.

George Gallup, the famous pollster, writes that fewer than ten percent of Americans are deeply committed Christians. "These people are a breed apart. They are more tolerant of people of diverse backgrounds. They are more involved in charitable activities. They are more involved in practical Christianity. They are absolutely committed to prayer." And they are "far, far happier than the rest of the population." Then he goes on to say that such devout Christians exert an influence on our society that far outweighs our numbers.

Just like salt. It only takes a pinch to do the whole job! Quite a compliment, eh?

Jesus didn't say we were the sugar of the earth. He called us salt! And of its wonderful properties we share!

But with the compliment comes the warning. "But if salt should lose its saltiness, how shall it be restored? It is good for nothing but to be thrown out and trodden under foot by man."

Heed well Christ's warning, my friends. And be what you are, for the need is great!

Proper 22
Pentecost 20
Ordinary Time 27
Mark 10:2-16

Maximum Marriage

A fifth grade teacher asked the children in her art class to draw pictures of what they want to be when they grow up. Sally drew an astronaut, Sue a doctor, Bruce a missionary. But Karen turned in a blank sheet of paper. "Isn't there something you want to be?" the teacher inquired. The child replied, "I want to be married, but I didn't know how to draw it."

Sad, but isn't that true of our society today? Over 95 percent of us will marry at some point in our life. Yet nearly forty percent of us will divorce.

In 1890 there were nearly 10,000 divorces nationwide. Last year there were over 1,200,000! In Charlotte, North Carolina, last year there were more divorces than there were marriages. Ditto for Fayetteville, North Carolina, and Washington, D.C.

It is as if we've lost the blueprint for building a lasting and satisfying home.

Where? Where can we go to find the blueprint? Can your U.S. Senator supply it? Is it in the pages of *Better Homes and Gardens* magazine? Is it animated on the silver screen from Hollywood? Do you inquire of Ann Landers?

Our text today is the best place to look. It doesn't come from Hollywood, but it does come from God's Holy Word. Jesus' words repeat the oldest biblical teaching on matrimony: "Therefore a man leaves his father and his mother and cleaves to his wife, and they become one flesh" (Genesis 2:24). In fact, this verse is repeated four times in scripture! It is as if God is saying, "Look here! This is vital! Be absolutely certain not to miss it!" So let's give close examination to Jesus's answer to his questioner about marriage and see if we can learn all God is saying!

Leaving

The first discipline mentioned in the text is leaving. Therefore "a man shall leave his father and mother."

Do you realize that in every major world religion marriage begins with a public ceremony of leaving? The man and the woman make a basic public commitment in saying, "Forsaking all others, I choose you!" He burns his little black book. She dreams of no other Prince Charming but him. They leave single life behind and together live in wedlock. Did you hear about the young couple in the jewelry store selecting their wedding bands? The man complained, "But, honey, this wedding band is too wide. I'm afraid it'll cut off my circulation!" She brightened and said, "Sweetheart, that's exactly what it's supposed to do!"

I think the biblical discipline of leaving is rather like climbing aboard a jet airliner. They hand you no parachute. If you fly with them, you commit your whole life. If the plane makes it, so do you. If the plane crashes, so do you. Don't the wedding vows we take before God emphasize this kind of lifelong commitment? "I take thee to be my wedded mate, to have and to hold, from this day forward, for better, for worse, for richer, for poorer, in sickness and in health, to love and to cherish, till death us do part...."

Many older people understand this kind of lifetime commitment. You got married and, for better or worse, you've stuck to it. But the next generation, now middle-aged, they got married until they couldn't stand it any longer and then they got a divorce. And now the younger generation — they get married and stay so until something better comes along! And we are fast becoming a nation that is committed to no one and no thing. We're becoming like yard dogs who are led about by our passions.

But God's Word is very clear: one man for one woman for life!

Here a word needs to be said about another force that threatens the "leaving" dimension of marriage, and that is the former family.

When two marry it is quite natural for the parents to try to interfere. "Does she feed him well?" "Is he buying her enough clothes?" The Bible says, "A man shall leave his father and his mother!"

A young couple had a quarrel and the bride of three months called her parents long distance saying, "Mama, I hate him. We've had a fight. Papa, I want to come home." The father very discreetly said, "I'm sorry, daughter, you have no home here. For better or worse you've left for a new home. Work it out the best you can!" and he hung up the phone. Now I know that was a difficult thing for a parent to do, but it was the right thing. The best advice to a parent is to hold your children very close, love them, and train them up in God's Word. Then let them go! Let them leave! Don't interfere. Don't give them advice unless you are asked. And don't live near them if you can help it. Across town is best!

Cleaving

So, the first discipline of a maximum marriage is leaving. Now the second: Genesis says, "Therefore a man leaves his father and his mother and cleaves to his wife." Cleaving, that's the second discipline of a maximum marriage.

When we hear the word "cleave" today we immediately think of a meat cleaver, a hatchet that cuts things apart. But the Hebrew word used in the text for "cleave" means literally "to be pasted together." It's like licking a stamp and pasting it on a letter. The envelope and the stamp cleave together. They are close. They are inseparable.

Now, dear people, if you try ripping a stamp from a letter you'll know why the scriptures are so against divorce. A stamp tears when it is removed. It leaves pieces of itself behind on the envelope. Divorce is such a tearing experience. In fact, next to death, divorce is one of the greatest traumas that can happen to a person. So you see why Jesus said, "What God has joined together let no one separate."

Cleaving, to be pasted together — "A man shall leave his father and his mother and be joined to his wife." This means that a man and wife are close. They are best friends. They communicate.

They spend time together. They romance and share common interests. Is that how it is in your marriage?

I saw a cartoon recently. The man was sitting in front of the television. His wife was walking through the room and the television announcer was saying, "We interrupt your marriage to bring you the latest football season!" Isn't that how it is with so many of our marriages? Our cleaving is interrupted. The man cleaves more to his hunting dog or to fishing or to his career. And the woman cleaves unto the garden club, the children, and her shopping sprees, and the result is a marriage grown cold.

I know in my own marriage it is easy to get my priorities out of line. I can get so caught up in my work that I neglect my wife. And when I catch myself doing that I repent and cleave again. The verse doesn't say we cleave to our work, but to our wife! If you don't learn anything else from me you will at least see me cleaving unto my wife and not my job.

But what about you? Is your marriage interrupted? Has something come between you? If it has, then admit it, repent, and start over! Good marriages require falling in love and cleaving over and over again, but always with the same person.

But you're saying, "Okay, that sounds good. To cleave. Fine! But how? Can you give me some practical suggestions?" Well, try setting aside one night a week for a date. Get a sitter and go out. Open the door for your wife. Fix your hair for your man. Give your mate a gift when it's not his/her birthday or Christmas. Say, "Honey, I saw this in the store window. It was lovely, it made me think of you, and so I wanted you to have it." Get a couple of rocking chairs, sit down together, watch the sun go down and talk. In short, treat your wife like a queen, men, and you'll get to be the king. The same is true for you, ladies. If you treat your husband like a king, you'll get to be the queen.

In case you didn't recognize it, that's another way of stating the Golden Rule — "Do unto others as you would have them do unto you." Many a marriage begins to break down when each mate begins to treat the others like a slave. The couple stops giving and starts demanding, and the whole marriage hurts.

So cleave! Be pasted together in love for one another. That's the second discipline of Christian matrimony.

Become One

Now for the third part of our text — becoming one. "For this reason a man shall leave his father and his mother, and be joined to his wife, and two shall become one flesh."

Becoming one flesh certainly means sex. And this is no embarrassment to Christians. After all, sex was God's idea in the first place. And God did look on all that he'd made, sex included, and say, "It's good."

So, there's nothing wrong with a married couple frankly discussing their likes and dislikes as regards to the sex act. There is much to be gained in reading a book about sex and learning as much as you can about how things work.

But becoming one flesh certainly means more than sex. Contrary to popular belief, it takes more than sex to make a marriage last. Just because a couple can make it in the bedroom doesn't mean that they can make it with the checkbook or children or in-laws. There are a lot of things a couple must become one in, if a marriage is to work. And thus we are drawn into the fine art of Christian argument and compromise.

That's right, the pastor said argument! Mrs. Billy Graham said, "When two people can live together and never disagree, one of them is not necessary!" Soon after you've said, "I do," you'll find out she likes pink and his favorite color is red. What color will you paint the bedroom? She would like to vacation on the beach. You like the mountains! How will you become one? You want that job in Raleigh. She wants to stay here. How will you settle it? So, you see, any couple who marries is setting the stage for conflict. Thus an ability to become one is very important.

Marriage counselors say that the number one source of marital arguments is money. After that comes lack of communication, emotional immaturity, inability to resolve conflicts, and finally, infidelity. Did you hear about the couple in the small town who had a fight? The neighbors heard the shouting and the dishes breaking and called the police. An officer was dispatched, but by the time he got there all was quiet. "Is everything okay now?" he asked the husband. "Sure," he said, "My wife came crawling to me on her hands and knees." Surprised to hear it, the policeman asked, "What did she say?" "She said, 'You'd better come out from under that bed and fight like a man!' "

Fight like a Christian to become one — that's what this last part of our text is saying. And how does a Christian fight? With love and listening ears and swallowed pride. With a willingness to build a win-win situation, an obligation to soothe, to say, "I've been wrong, forgive me." Not having always to have one's way, but with prayer and so much more!

In the mountains of Georgia there is a waterfall called Anna Ruby Falls. It is a perfect example of what becoming one in marriage is like. Two separate mountain streams lap and gurgle down a mountain and plummet separately, one 150 feet, the other 300 feet, in a dazzling display of watery lace and rainbow colors. At the base of the mountain both falls enter a common pool. Here the two creeks are joined and flow on as a river together. Marriage is like this, too. We become one and flow on. His is hers and hers is his. Neither mate loses his identity. They blend. Talents, strength, faults, faiths, needs — they are joined in marriage and the two become one.

On The Rocks

I think marriage is like a three-sided tent. Leaving is one side. Cleaving and becoming one are the others. And you will note that a tent will not stand unless all three sides are secure. So it is with marriage. How's the leaving side of your wedlock? Have you made a total commitment to matrimony? How's the cleaving? Are you pasted together with nothing between you? No interruptions? And what about your becoming one? Are you fighting like Christians?

Jesus once told a parable. He said that those who heard God's words and did not do them were like a man who built his home on the sand. And when the storm came, it fell in. But Christ said that if a man both hears and does God's word he'd be like the man who built his house on the rock. When the storm came, the household stood.

What about you? Have you heard these words? Will you do them? If you do, Christ is saying that even though the storms of life beat upon you, your home will not break. How can it? It is founded upon the sure foundation of God's Word!

Sermons On The Gospel Readings

For Sundays
After Pentecost
(Last Third)

Cathy A. Ammlung

To Rich,
dearest and best,
a wise, patient, sensitive,
and insightful man,
he is God's greatest gift to me.

Ephesians 4:2

Foreword

One of the enjoyable by-products of serving in a staff ministry is that I get to hear other pastors preach — associate pastors, guests, and sometimes interim associate pastors. It was during one of our interim periods between full-time associates that I had the opportunity to meet and share in ministry with Pastor Cathy Ammlung. She served among us for almost a year in an interim capacity, and I got to experience her preaching regularly during that time.

As most preachers know, sermons in books or on the internet can be very flat, one-dimensional. Preaching is by its very definition an event that combines a text with a context.

However, even a cursory glance at the sermons in this volume will be enough to convince those who practice this art that here is a person with gifts for communicating the Gospel. I have found her sermons to be insightful about human nature and filled with passion for the task. Pastor Ammlung preaches with fresh eyes and shares what she sees with a flair for the creative. Her illustrations touch hearts and draw us into her sermonic world where she paints pictures of God's emerging Kingdom with words and expressions that leave me thinking, "I wish I had said that!"

In short, I admire her preaching style. It is creative, fresh, alive, hopeful, and articulate. She can preach to me any day, which is probably the biggest compliment I can offer her.

Read and enjoy. There is something here that feeds the heart, soul, and mind. And if you experience these sermons as alive on paper, just imagine what the event was like when she delivered them to hungry souls in need of food!

Glenn E. Ludwig, Senior Pastor
First Lutheran Church,
Ellicott City, Maryland

Acknowledgments

Most of the people I want to thank probably haven't the faintest idea that they influenced this book. Nevertheless, they have shaped me as a pastor and as a preacher, and I am forever grateful. Any "off-key" ideas and words are my fault, not theirs.

The Reverend Michael C. D. McDaniel was pastor of Edgebrook Lutheran Church in Chicago when I was a first year confirmation student. He was (and is) a fine preacher, but a challenge for a confirmand to write sermon notes for! I strove for an "excellent" grade from him, and that striving caused me really to listen to the sermon and meditate on the Good News it conveyed.

The Reverend Andy Weyermann was pastor of Holy Cross Lutheran Church, Creve Coeur, Missouri, when I started seminary. The former professor of homiletics at Concordia and Christ Seminary (Sem-inex), he introduced me to the concept of Law and Gospel in preaching. He also used fascinating analogies and illustrations and helped me connect the Word to everyday life.

The Reverend Dr. Richard Thulin was my homiletics professor at Gettysburg. Besides being a fine preacher himself, he possesses the gift of encouragement, helping me find my own voice as a preacher. He also taught me a lot about narrative, especially preaching from personal experience.

The Reverend Glenn Ludwig, senior pastor at First Lutheran, Ellicott City, encouraged me to write this book and offered helpful suggestions, plus a gracious foreword.

I must say thank you to all the congregations who have endured my preaching over the years. I served often as a supply preacher and as an interim, so I was constantly preaching to people I scarcely knew, except that they were sisters and brothers in Christ. Their support, feedback, and witness to me have been most precious gifts. God bless you all.

Proper 23
Pentecost 21
Ordinary Time 28
Mark 10:17-31

The Impossible Option

Before there was Harry Potter, there was Bilbo Baggins, the hobbit. In J. R. R. Tolkien's wise fantasy, this short, hairy-footed resident of the Shire in Middle-Earth was a well-to-do bachelor and country squire. Comfortable and conventional, but just a touch bored with life, he nevertheless was shocked when the mysterious wizard, Gandalf, knocked on his door one spring morning and requested his services as (of all things) a thief. The clever, nimble-fingered hobbit was just the person to help a struggling band of dwarves reclaim their treasure from a greedy dragon. And of course, there would be a cut of the profits for Bilbo, too!

Gandalf proposed more than a business venture, though; he invited Bilbo to an Adventure, capital *A*. And much to his own surprise, the comfortable, conventional Bilbo at last agreed, running out the door after the departing dwarves without so much as a handkerchief. And Adventures he had! He encountered elves and other wondrous characters, including the magnificent, jewel-encrusted dragon. He trekked through mountains, was lost underground, and found a magic ring. He was carried by eagles, escaped from prison in a beer cask, and finagled his way into the dragon's lair. There were battles, songs, a treasure recovered, friendships made, reward received, and a long trip home where he settled back into his comfortable routine.

Except ... not quite. He was changed by his adventures. He was known as the local eccentric. He entertained strange guests, learned ancient languages and stories, and wrote poetry. At last, he passed into the Uttermost West with the elves.

Perhaps it's surprising to mention this story while hearing the Gospel story of the rich man and Jesus. True, *this* man came running *to* Jesus, and not thievery but eternal life was under discussion. But how like Bilbo the man was! Comfortable, well-off, law-abiding, he also sensed that his life didn't quite add up. And when Jesus invited him to sell everything, give the proceeds to the poor, and follow him, the poor fellow was as shocked at this crazy proposal as if Jesus had suggested a stint of thievery for him. Unlike Bilbo, he not only wavered but finally refused the invitation to an Adventure with a capital A.

Because when all the pious religious language is stripped away, that's what Jesus was offering. This was invitation to *Adventure*, not proposal of a business venture. Following Jesus would mean taking roads and making choices that might have never occurred to the man. His priorities and expectations would be turned topsy-turvy. Following Jesus wasn't a matter of examining the bottom-line profitability of doing so; nor did it mean taking charge of his own destiny, even by doing good and doing right. It meant losing his heart (and possibly his life) to this One who beckoned.

If Bilbo found the label of "Thief" off-putting, the rich man certainly found the notion of "Penniless-By-Choice Disciple" equally unpleasant. To give away his vast wealth — not as a tax write-off or personal do-good project, but as the necessary paring away of everything that was non-essential to following the Son of Man ... it was a sort of death. It meant losing control of *his* image, *his* plans, *his* destiny. It meant the death of one identity, and who knew what (if any) new identity this Jesus would raise up from the ashes. The up-front loss and sacrifice involved in following this engaging young rabbi outweighed the prospect of a life-transforming journey with him.

At least the rich man was realistic about what he stood to lose, and honest about his fear of losing it! Often we seem to think that we can follow Jesus with baggage, riches, priorities, self-image, identity, and control neatly packed and easily toted. We sometimes act as if following Jesus is more like an occasional weekend ramble, not a life-long journey with its own logic and demands — and certainly not as a life-altering Adventure.

330

And we compound the problem. At times, we're so eager to draw new people into the life of the Church that we make it sound like discipleship really is a jaunt in a spiritual Winnebago, complete with all the comforts we're used to. We soft-pedal obedience to Jesus, and are uncomfortable mentioning self-discipline and sacrificial giving, living, and loving. Maybe we fear that we'll scare people off if we talk about that kind of radical "stripping down for the journey." Or maybe we really don't believe in it ourselves.

Other times, we get *too* caught up in the oughts and shoulds, the duties and responsibilities of Christian life. We really *do* make following Jesus into drudgery, a series of losses, burdens, and duties with precious little joy or adventure about it. We are so anxious to talk about "taking up one's cross" that we forget all about how Jesus himself looked *beyond* the cross' agony to the joy that was set before him. Maybe we sympathize with not only the rich man but also the disciples, who bluntly remind Jesus that they have given up plenty to follow him — so what will they have to show for it?

And sometimes we're just not in synch with the sweeping nature of Jesus' command or his invitation. Sell *everything* and give *all* the proceeds to the poor? Follow Jesus? How? Are we supposed to drop everything to become a missionary or evangelist? Our minds boggle. "You've got the wrong person, Jesus!" we protest. "I'm no great saint or preacher or anything, I'm just little old me, trying to muddle through the best I can." No easier is it for us to put ourselves in Jesus' picture than it was for Bilbo to imagine himself a bold thief or unlikely hero.

And yet the command and the invitation stand, blunt and uncompromising. All the excuses we trot out to defend our wavering lie limp on the ground. We are left with the disciples' almost forlorn question when Jesus said that wealth (whether measured as possessions, power, or ability) hinders entry into God's kingdom. "Then how can anyone be saved?"

"For God," says Jesus flatly, "nothing is impossible." *Nothing.* He actually sounds as if he means it. Nobody has an excuse; there is nothing in our lives that *inevitably* provides an impenetrable barrier between us and the Kingdom of God. Our Lord himself has seen to that. And so he can look at an earnest, perplexed rich man ... and ask him to do what *seems* to be impossible, because Jesus himself intends to accomplish the really, truly impossible. To put it another way, once you believe that God is serious about saving anyone who'll accept the offer — rich, poor, bad, good, Gentile, Jew — then visualizing yourself divested of wealth and humbly taking your cues at Jesus' feet *ought* to be a piece of cake!

The problem, of course, is twofold. It's terribly easy to talk ourselves into believing that what our Lord commands really *is* impossible, dangerous, foolhardy and otherwise inadvisable. Bilbo nearly did that, and the rich man certainly did. We re-erect a barrier that our Lord had resolved to tumble down.

The second problem is that the road down which Jesus invites us to follow him inevitably leads to a cross — and not just for Jesus, at least figuratively. The rich man was right on target if he feared that following Jesus was a small death, the loss of one identity with no certain prospect of a new one.

It all comes down to trust, of course — trust that the Lord, for whom nothing is impossible, *will* bring any who follow him into the fullness of his Father's Kingdom. And trust that the goods and houses and eternal life he promises to those who leave everything behind to follow him will more than compensate for the losses, the dangers, the risks, the persecutions — and the deaths, both small and great.

Does that sound too up-in-the air? Then imagine the "impossible" options for those who might dare to trust our Lord's promises. A rich man *does* donate all his fortunes to charity and works in a drug addiction program. A woman relinquishes a wealth of resentment and for Jesus' sake forgives her estranged sister. A teenager gives up a chance to play in the championship soccer game to take part in his youth group's Habitat for Humanity project. A family decides to simplify its lifestyle as a response to the Gospel, and to give more time and financial support to the ministry of its church. Small things? Maybe. But they may be the first fruits of a new life that our Lord raises up when the old dies.

Who knows what sort of new life God will shape in us as we begin to take him at his word? Who knows what things that we "give up" in order to travel lightly and gracefully with him will be taken up and hallowed and transformed to the good of many? Who knows what marvels we will see, what lives we will touch, what joys we will experience on this blessed adventure of discipleship? Maybe we'll end up more like Bilbo, resident eccentric, than like some great, heroic saint. But we'll never know — until, graced by God, we lose our hearts to our Savior and set off down the road, hearts quaking but secretly hungering to be upended and stretched and challenged and changed. And then — well, who knows? After all, with God, *nothing* is impossible. Even when he's dealing with us. Amen.

In The Hot Seat

Everybody who thinks you could have done better than James or John, raise your hands. "If *I* worked up the nerve to ask Jesus to do anything I ask him to," most of us probably think, "*I'd* have done a lot better than their lame-brained request. Sitting next to Jesus when he comes into his glory — what nerve! *I'd* have asked for something much more worthy — an end to war, or a cure for cancer, or at least for wisdom. Good grief, what was Jesus thinking when he recruited those two?"

Maybe we should call it the Hot Seat Syndrome. Anyone who's ever watched the game show, *Who Wants To Be A Millionaire*, has groaned, shouted, and rolled eyes at contestants who choke on the dumbest questions. "For Pete's sake!" we mutter, "How did these nitwits ever get through the Fastest Finger questions and into that 'Hot Seat'?"

Of course, many of the contestants have admitted that they said the very same thing, only to find *themselves* choking when the cameras zoomed into their sweaty faces. "It's a lot different when you're in the Hot Seat and not sitting in front of your television," one man said ruefully as he agonized between two answers that were perfectly obvious to everyone else.

We need to remember that the gospel doesn't allow us to be uninvolved spectators to its drama and action. No, fast finger or slow, from the moment of our baptism, we were drawn right into a lifelong Hot Seat, with not Regis Philbin as host, but our Lord Jesus calling us by name to be his disciples. Of course, this gospel isn't a game show; and the Final Answer (worth our life, not a mere million bucks) has already been provided by our gracious Host. But there *are* all kinds of questions he might ask us. They could be summed up by just one: "Do you get it?"

And whatever our response to that question, I seriously doubt most of us would fare much better than did James or John.

Picture the scene. The disciples had seen Jesus heal the sick, expel demons, forgive sins, and teach people about God in an unforgettably intimate, powerful way. They had, through Peter's bold words, confessed Jesus as the chosen and anointed One of God, the One who would bring God's redemption to Israel. Yet Jesus was heading to Jerusalem to die. He'd already told his followers this, and now he'd said it again. Oh, he mentioned something about rising on the third day, but it was almost impossible to get past those hard words: *Handed over. Treated shamefully. Suffer. Die.* Jesus made those words sound both inevitable and necessary. But how could the disciples, then or now, wrap their minds around *that*? How could One who had demonstrated the power, wisdom, and compassion of God experience suffering and death?

We think we know better, of course. The phrase, "Jesus died for our sins," rolls easily from our lips. For one thing, it's been pounded into *our* heads for nearly 2,000 years! But, if we were placed in the Hot Seat and asked, "Do you get it?" we'd probably blow it.

So let's phrase that question a little differently. "How is the suffering and death of Jesus related to his power and authority to heal the sick, cast out demons, forgive sins, and bring the Kingdom of God into our midst?"

With careful thought and a little prompting, we *might* say something like this: Jesus' willingness to suffer and die for us proved that he was *worthy* to have and to wield the power and authority of God. And, as far as it goes, we'd be right.

But that shouldn't be our Final Answer. Our response basically follows the rule that leaders need to "pay their dues." If somebody is willing to suffer for a cause or for the sake of others (and hasn't just required others to do so), it gives that person greater credibility when he or she then wields authority. It gives that person a certain moral authority to take action, make decisions, demand loyalty.

And there's truth in that notion, even when we apply it to Jesus. Saint Paul himself quoted an early Christian hymn: "[he] became obedient unto death, even death on a cross. *Therefore* God has highly exalted him and given him the name above all names ..." (Philippians 2:8). Jesus receives not just moral, but divine authority, because of his death for our sake. Assuming that Jesus' words about dying and rising even registered with his disciples, they might have remembered Isaiah's poem about the Suffering Servant of Israel and made a connection to Jesus' words. That's giving them the benefit of the doubt. But their willingness to drink Jesus' cup of suffering as *their* necessary "dues paying" for the favor they requested does point in this direction.

But the question about the connection between Jesus' suffering and his right to do deeds of heavenly power cuts deeper than this preliminary answer probes, and there's the problem. It's one thing to think of suffering as a sort of necessary dues paying. "Okay, let's just get it over with and get on to the good stuff," we might exclaim. "Get Jesus off his cross and on his throne right quick. Fast forward us through suffering and give us our crown of glory."

It's another thing altogether to see suffering and death — especially the kind of godforsaken death that Mark portrays for Jesus — as the *actual shape of Jesus' power and authority.* His betrayal, suffering, and death weren't merely the regrettably necessary precursors to his divine right to forgive, heal, and rule eternally. Instead, his suffering and death actually demonstrated the *reality* — the shape, nature, and scope — of his reign.

Mull that over slowly. It's important. It's also almost inconceivable. Jesus tried to simplify it when his disciples got bent out of shape because James and John had the Fastest Fingers among them. He addressed their desire to share his authority in ruling and judging nations and peoples. "Are you willing to share my cup of pain and baptism into death? That's fine, as far as it goes, but it has nothing to do with seating arrangements in the Kingdom. And if you want my kind of authority, get ready to wear an apron, not a crown."

Jesus' *ability* — his power and his authority — to forgive sins was shaped strictly by the cross. Giving his life as a ransom for many was the actual way he exerted his authority. Serving rather than being served was the way he wielded divine power. Stooping lower than the lowliest slave, descending to more Godforsaken depths than the worst sinner — this was not the *prelude to* but the *way in which* he drew God's kingdom into our midst. His rising from death ensured that his strange way of exerting authority would last forever, to the final defeat of everything that would oppose it.

Do you get it yet?

The only power we wield is the power to forgive sins, in Jesus' name and by his cross-shaped authority. Forgiving others isn't the prelude to glory or power; it's the nature of it for us. We'll never "get" the nature of the Kingdom except that divine forgiveness has defined it and shaped it for us.

The only sort of power Jesus' followers have to rule or judge others is the power to serve them, in his name and according to his model. We have the power to get out of God's way as our Lord acts in our neighbors' lives. We have the power to put their needs above our own. We have full authority to give our lives in loving service to our neighbor. We have the absolute right to allow Jesus' way of exerting power and authority to shape our lives, our decisions, and our actions.

Is this practical in this world? Nope. Does this play havoc with the normal routines of power, success, authority, and judgment? You bet. Do you think most people will "get it"? God willing, many will. It would be nice if *we* got it, of course!

What it means, though, is that we're always in a Hot Seat of our Lord's devising. Humble service, self-giving love, and forgiving again and again are not one-shot deals. They're not our "dues," quickly paid and as quickly forgotten. Every moment of our lives, Jesus is asking us, "Do you get it? Do you 'get' my Final Answer? Do you 'get' how I do things?"

But we're not alone in that Hot Seat. Jesus' throne of power is an ongoing Hot Seat, shaped until the Last Day by two rough pieces of wood. He is always there shaping his Final Answer for us. His answer is always, "The Kingdom of God is at hand! Repent! Believe the Good News that your sins are forgiven and the Kingdom is yours!" A Roman soldier "got it" in the moment of Jesus' apparent defeat. Seeing the way in which Jesus died, he exclaimed, "Surely this man was the Son of God!"

God grant that we "get it," too, and live our lives in thankful response to Jesus' Final Answer. May it be ours, as well. And that's *my* final answer! Amen.

Will The Real Blind Beggar
Please Stand Up?

It's easy to slap some people down. Little kids, poor people, beggars, the handicapped, foreigners, old people, minorities ... the list goes on. *Sit down and shut up and be grateful for what you have. What do you know? Who asked you? You should be seen and not heard.* Those are things we say — or maybe have had said to us. That's assuming the person in question isn't being ignored into oblivion. We sinful human beings sometimes waver between abusing and ignoring someone who offends, disturbs, or makes us uncomfortable.

Ironically, sometimes it's not much better when we try to act charitably! You've heard the story of the frail old woman standing at the street corner. A gallant young man takes her by the arm and propels her across the street, brushing off her feeble protests. Safely on the other side, she glares at him and says, "Now take me back over there before I miss my bus!"

Poor people complain that their input often isn't sought about welfare reform, new bus routes, or urban renewal projects that directly impinge on their lives. Sometimes people "talk past" a person in a wheelchair or hospital bed, as if that person had neither ears nor brains. Many people — perhaps you — have been patronized, talked down to, or offered inadequate, inappropriate, or downright insulting assistance.

There are scads of people who are regularly abused, ignored, or insulted because *other* people deem them unworthy of respect or recognition. And of course, it's not a new problem. Just look at how the Passover holiday crowds treated the blind beggar, Bartimaeus, at the Jericho gate as Jesus began the last part of his journey to Jerusalem. As soon as Bartimaeus started shouting to Jesus, everybody around him *sternly ordered* him to be quiet! "Sit down, beggar! Shut up! Be happy with the coins we throw you! Don't bother the famous rabbi with your problems!"

You'd think the crowd would have known by now. You'd think they'd have seen Jesus healing the sick and caring for the lowly. You'd think they'd have heard his words. At the very least, you'd think his disciples would have remembered what he'd so recently told them. "The Son of Man comes not to be served, but to serve ..." (Mark 10:45). You'd really think everybody would have known that as soon as he started yelling, Bartimaeus the beggar should have been helped to his feet and brought to Jesus' side!

But "everybody" was blind, deaf — and dumb. When they looked at Bartimaeus at all, they saw only a blind beggar. They saw someone who ought to know his place. When they heard his voice, loud above even the excited crowd that followed Jesus as he spoke, they heard only noise. He was an embarrassment, an interruption, an annoyance to be shut down quickly so that his betters could hear. They listened to and walked with Jesus, but didn't seem to think he could, or should, be interested in the affairs of Bartimaeus. Maybe they thought that Jesus should be as blind and deaf to his cries as they were. Dumb!

We can be equally oblivious, of course, even as we gather for worship. It's a little embarrassing that many churches didn't become handicapped-accessible until government laws forced them to modify stairways and bathrooms. Didn't we think that people with disabilities might want to hear the gospel and receive the gift of forgiveness and salvation, just like the able-bodied?

Wouldn't we squirm uncomfortably if odd-looking people wandered into our worship services or interrupted the sermon or prayers with some question or plea that was overwhelmingly important to them? Our first — and very human — impulse is often to shush them, hustle them off to the side, and make sure they're "under control." It's a struggle to push past our fear and discomfort enough to remember that our Savior stops to hear and respond to their cries.

It's even harder to ask ourselves how we can help bring them to their Savior's side.

We might *never* see, hear, ask, or do rightly on our own. Like the crowd that followed Jesus but shushed Bartimaeus, we can be blinder, deafer, and dumber than the most wretched beggar! And yet in infinite mercy, Jesus enacted a double healing on the Jericho road. In the midst of the loud, excited, yet blind-deaf-dumb crowd that tried to silence Bartimaeus, Jesus stopped dead in his tracks. He stood still, and *listened* to the shrill voice the others wanted to ignore. Even blind beggars may receive a hearing before the throne of divine mercy.

And oddly, *Jesus kept standing still!* He could have pushed through the crowd to Bartimaeus' side. He could have ignored the crowd that had demonstrated its own ignorance. But he didn't. He gave the people in the crowd a command, a task, and a dignity beyond their deserving. He said to them, "Call him here" (v. 49). He invited them to participate in what he was doing. He began to heal *them*, there in his stillness and his simple command. *Call him here. You, who did not or could not see or hear or intercede for this blind beggar, go now to him in the strength of my seeing, my hearing, my will to intercede and heed and heal. And call him here.*

And they did! In simple obedience, they called to Bartimaeus, and they used a lovely phrase that Jesus himself spoke to another poor soul in need of his care: *Take heart.* "Take heart, get up. *He* is calling you" (v. 49). In *their* obedient calling to Bartimaeus, the people in the crowd recognized that they were simply voicing *Jesus'* gracious call. And they spoke with his graciousness on their own lips! What a marvel of healing *this* was, before Bartimaeus even stood up.

Call him here! It's strange to think that the healing *we* need, can come as a command to do the very thing we couldn't do on our own. *Call him here!* Go back to the ones you ignored, silenced, disdained, or insulted. Go back and see them with your Lord's eyes. Hear them with your Savior's ears. Speak to them with your Redeemer's very words. Your healing will come in the moment of your obedience. It may not be dramatic. You may still have qualms and fears. But go. Call your sister or brother. Call your fellow blind beggar. And you may both be healed.

We know how Bartimaeus' story concludes. When the crowd speaks to him, he immediately leaps to his feet, casts his cloak aside, and runs — good grief, how did he manage this without falling or crashing into people! — until he comes before Jesus. And Jesus, modeling to us a deep humility, waits. He does not immediately restore the man's sight. With respect and sensitivity, Jesus asks this poor blind beggar, "What do *you* want me to do for you?" (v. 51). He waits to hear the plea of Bartimaeus. He doesn't assume only one possible response. He allows for the possibility that Bartimaeus might say, "Lord, forgive my bitter envy of those who can see." Or, "Give me a silver coin, that I may not have to beg today." Or something else, something unexpected but welling up from the depth of his need.

To Jesus, Bartimaeus was not a problem to be solved, an embarrassment to be hustled away, or even a poor dumb beggar on whom one could inflict one's charity at will. Bartimaeus was a human being — sinful, surely; theologically inadequate, probably; but a man created in the image of God. And God would show him honor, respect, and compassion. God's Son would *wait* and would *listen.* And out of the waiting and listening would come deep healing. "Go; your faith has made you well." And out of that healing would come discipleship: "Immediately he regained his sight and followed [Jesus] on the way" (v. 52).

That deep healing is there for us when *we* are slapped down, hustled away, ignored, insulted, or abused. When we cry out from our deepest need in those times, our Lord waits and listens. He restores our voice, dignity, and hope. He heals us to follow him. He does this in the deep stillness of prayer; in the familiar words of absolution; and in the gracious giving of himself in the humble gifts of bread and wine.

It's said that the last thing Martin Luther wrote was a short sentence on a scrap of paper that was found after his death. "We are all beggars; that is true." He was right, of course. We're all in need of our Lord's compassion and healing. We're all hurting — and hurtful. We're all blind, deaf, and dumb in various ways. We're all ignorant of our neighbor's need or our Lord's intentions from time to time. We none of us have the grace, humility, compassion, or strength to love God or neighbor as we ought. We all of us can only see and hear and speak and live rightly on the strength of our Savior's unutterable love for us.

And for all of us, as for Bartimaeus, our Lord stands still. He listens. He commands us — or our neighbors — with a word that begins to heal our unseen, unconfessed blindness: *You call him here.* With another word he exalts even the poorest and lowliest of us: *What do you want me to do for you?* And he heals the deepest needs and hurts of our souls, making us fit to follow him on his way of self-giving love: *Go; your faith has made you well.*

Will the real blind beggar please stand up? That's me — and you. Fellow beggars, let's go to him. All we need is in his wounded hands, there for the asking. Take heart; he's calling for us. Amen.

Hanging The Law On Love

Compared to some of the pericopes from Mark's Gospel, this one seems a piece of cake. "Hear, O Israel: the Lord our God, the Lord is one; and you shall love the Lord your God with all your heart, and with all your soul, and with all your mind, and with all your strength ... You shall love your neighbor as yourself" (vv. 29-31).

That's straightforward enough! In fact, we might stumble over only four little words: *Love. God. Neighbor. Self.* Love God *with your whole* self. Love your neighbor *as* yourself. Words like these can lead to some questions that are *not* pieces of cake. How do I actually go about loving God and neighbor in such fashion? Why are these commandments linked in such an absolute way? And why does endorsing all this put one "not far from" — but not "in" — the Kingdom of God?

Let's start with that first word: *love.* There are plenty of times we can't crank out an ounce of charitable feeling towards someone. Especially when that someone is near and dear and has grieved, hurt, or angered us, we feel anything but loving. We don't even *like* that person. And to love persons that we're not close to, or who are actually strangers, just because they're in our vicinity? *Riiight!*

Beyond that, there are times we doubt God's care or are angry with God. Luther himself was almost driven to despair by the command to love a God whose commands and demands were so high and absolute. "Love God?" he's reputed to have cried. "Why, I *loathed* him!"

Other times we experience a spiritual dryness where we don't feel much of anything. Prayers seem mechanical; worship leaves us flat; reading scripture becomes a bore. Like Luther, we may be driven almost to despair by a command to love God with the totality of our being. How can love be *commanded?* Isn't that as realistic as asking a terrified child just "to relax"?

Love is not primarily an emotion or feeling. You don't have to like someone in order to love someone. Loving God means this: through the power of his Spirit, to pray deliberately and work for God's gracious will to be accomplished on earth as in heaven. Loving neighbor as self means this: through the power of God's Spirit, to pray deliberately and work for God's will to be done in the neighbor's life as it is done in your own.

Whatever feelings and emotions crop up when we love, at its core, love is about faithful obedience to God and gracious extension of God's justice and mercy to neighbor. We know a fair portion of God's will: that everyone comes to believe in his fierce and holy love for them, shown in the life, death, and resurrection of his Son Jesus. That all that opposes God's love be destroyed and that new sons and daughters be raised up from that watery burial. That everyone receives daily bread and life's necessities. That the sick are healed, the despairing given hope, the poor and weak have their burdens lifted. That the Good News is shared with them all. That sinners turn from their sin to receive life in God's kingdom — and that they are welcomed into the fellowship of forgiven sinners. To love God means to say, "Yes!" to God's will with every fiber of our being. To love our neighbors means to pray for their good and to allow God to do, through us, even a small portion of his will for them.

Even when we don't *feel* a particular way, we can still, with God's help, begin to pray that God's will be done, and work for it to happen in our neighbors' lives. We're already answering the question, "Why are these commandments linked so absolutely?" But there's more to why our Lord was so emphatic about that point, and backed it up with the authority of heaven itself. It has to do with who God is, how God loves, and what it means that we are created in his image.

Jesus intends for us to look to his life as the pattern *and source* of our own love for God and neighbor. His own love for God is the human expression of the eternal Son's love for the Father. Within God's own self is a communion of absolute love between the Father and Son, shared through the Spirit. That loving God creates and redeems humanity with an equally enduring and passionate love. And Jesus' whole life was a demonstration of divine love for the "other," for the "neighbor," for ... us.

Think of that beloved verse: "For God so loved the world that he gave his only begotten Son, that whoever believes in him should not perish but have everlasting life" (John 3:16). I doubt that God *likes* us when we are rebellious, selfish, destructive, and unfaithful. Nevertheless God *loves* us utterly. Jesus proved that love by actively and deliberately praying and working for our redemption, forgiveness, and reconciliation with God. That wasn't pleasant, easy, or convenient for our Lord. But do we doubt that he did it out of love?

As I said earlier, loving God is deliberately praying and working for what God desires and for what God names good. That's the kind of love for his Father that Jesus himself constantly showed. Now, we are still fallible, sinful human beings. We may still get angry with God, and sometimes we won't feel any exalted emotional response when we worship or pray. We may still doubt or wrestle with God. Even our Lord did that in Gethsemane! And yet in his next breath, he prayed, *your will be done.* Think of his anguished cry from the cross, too: "My God, why have you forsaken me?" And yet with his dying breath he gave a great shout and (if we are to believe Luke as well as Mark) commended his Spirit to his Father. Do we doubt that Jesus' love for God was absolute?

Loving God in faithful obedience, and loving neighbor by praying for and working God's will for them is precisely the pattern of love displayed by the Son of God himself. And we are created in his image and likeness. In Baptism we are grafted into his everlasting life and loving heart. What other kind of love could we possibly be meant to display?

There is an additional point to be made here. Jesus' love for his Father — and for us — is never a mere sterile, logical "Act of Will and Duty." There's never anything grim, calculating, guilt-inducing, or grudging in his love. Instead, words like joyous, compassionate, humble, shepherd, even mother hen are used to describe him. He's completely immersed in his Father's love; how else could he respond? Everything was grounded in his active, obedient praying and working of his Father's will for the good of his sisters and brothers. His joy, compassion, peace, holiness, and sheer loveliness are grounded in the love of his Father. That's what he wants us to experience and how he wants us to act. That's why he shares with us the Holy Spirit of his loving union with his Father: so that we can love rightly and beautifully, with his own love!

The scribe who came to Jesus with his question about the greatest commandment heartily endorsed Jesus' answer. He had a deep understanding of God's Law. Of him, Jesus said, "You are not far from the Kingdom of God" (v. 34). Which begs the question: Why did Jesus say, "You are not far from," rather than, "You are in," the Kingdom of God?

Could it be that Jesus was "teasing" the scribe into seeing that the great, twofold commandment was literally enfleshed before his eyes?

Looking at Jesus, who stood an arm's length away, and hearing his words, the scribe was actually in the presence of God, whose will it was to save and redeem Israel and the world. *Could he see that?* Could that arm's length be overcome by an arm's embrace of this loving and self-giving One?

Looking at those around him, could the scribe actually see them as his neighbors? They included disputatious Sadducees, a poor widow, ostentatious wealthy contributors, and even those who refused Jesus' authority and words. And yet this same Jesus would willingly give his life for them, and open the riches of his Father's Kingdom to all who would turn to him in repentance, faith, and humility.

In spite of all the times we speak of and pray for (and even act on behalf of) "the sick," "the oppressed," "the poor," and so forth, loving our neighbor comes down to actual contact with individuals. It comes down to making concrete decisions that get our hands dirty, our schedules loused up, and our hearts broken. That's Jesus' way of loving; it won him a cross. Can we let his love shape ours, no matter how risky and painful those "close encounters with the sinful kind" may be?

I think it was Charlie Brown who said, "I love humanity! It's people I can't stand!" Yet the costly love that Jesus embodies involves an intimate encounter with God's fierce and holy love. It involves pouring out self for real people, sinners all, with all their real-life quirks, faults, smells, and flesh-and-blood sins.

Would the scribe allow Jesus to "hang" his knowledge of the law on a cross? Would he allow Jesus to "flesh out" God's will in his own life? Will we?

That harried young mother in the doctor's waiting room (or maybe the next pew): perhaps loving her as yourself means offering to watch the toddler while she feeds the baby. That person in line at the bank who's stumbling over the English language and struggling to understand deposits and withdrawals: could loving him mean stepping out of line and helping him get it straight? That next-door neighbor struggling to keep his marriage together, that daughter who pushes your buttons every ten minutes, that husband scared of being laid off — these are the ones who desperately need the strong saving love, the compassion and mercy, the challenge and holiness and presence of Jesus. In those moments, dare to risk being rebuffed or inconvenienced. Dare to look foolish and make mistakes. Dare to love God and that person, even if it wrings your heart with pain to do so. It's what we've been created, redeemed, and commanded to do. Hang your whole life on love, for the truth is, it's God's love, active in you. And his love will never fail. Amen.

When Nothing Is Everything

I was startled by a recent analysis of per capita charitable contributions by state. Massachusetts, with the fourth highest personal income in the country, ranked last in charitable contributions. Mississippi, forty-ninth in income, ranked first *in actual dollars contributed.* Mississippians gave, on average, about forty percent more to charity than did their Yankee cousins! Converted to *percentage of income* contributed to charity, the disparity was even greater.

Another fact emerged: Wealthy people tend to give more to secular charities than to religious institutions. Poorer families give mostly to religious institutions and their social ministries.

What's going on? Are lower income families more generous or more religious? Do rich people see more direct benefit to *their* well-being from museums, colleges, or concerts than from worship, outreach, and fellowship at their churches?

Any of these possibilities might be true for some people at some time. But we shouldn't make caricatures of people based on their income and their apparent choices. Some rich people contribute generously to religious institutions. Look at the parade of wealthy donors in today's Gospel. Mark makes a point of noting the sheer size of their gifts. Some poor people give very little. The widow in our story drops in two tiny coins — a pittance, even for the poor. Who are we to judge the circumstances, motives, and values of anyone who gives (or doesn't) to the church? Only God can see into the heart and know what's there.

And there's the rub. Jesus looks at the wealthy givers and sees them skimming "off the top" of their deep and overflowing pockets. More, he sees them giving in order to *appear* generous and charitable, whereas in fact they might never miss the amount they contribute to the Temple treasury. An unspoken corollary to this observation then arises. Just how much is their devotion to the God whose Temple they give to, also "skimmed off the top" of the deep pocket of their many priorities?

Jesus' comments about the Temple scribes only increase our unease. Surely they, of all people, should be digging deep into the pockets of their souls as well as of their robes! Their lives, as well as their gifts, should display the great commandments to love God with their whole heart, mind, and strength, and their neighbors as themselves. After all, haven't they dedicated their lives to the service of God and his people? Yet Jesus says of them, "They like to walk around in long robes, and be greeted with respect in the marketplaces, and to have the best seats in the synagogues and places of honor at banquets! They devour widows' houses and for the sake of appearance say long prayers. They will receive the greater condemnation" (vv. 38-40).

That's scary. However much we (or God!) may disapprove of wealthy people who give *little* to charity (especially religious charity), it's disconcerting to hear Jesus' condemnation of those *who give much* (in actual coins at least) of their treasures, time, and talents to those very causes. It's as if he is laying into those Massachusetts residents who *are* giving generously, who *are* outstripping their poorer Mississippi cousins! It's as if he's laying into *us*, who struggle with mortgages, tuition, orthodontist's bills, and all the rest. Surely we can't give *everything* to the church! Surely we can't spend all our time as volunteers in a food pantry! We give what we can and we do what we can; what more could God ask of us? Are Jesus' words simply a religious version of "Give 'til it hurts"?

When we hear his approval of the widow who "out of her poverty has put in *everything she had, all she had to live on*" (v. 44), we could conclude that this is exactly what his words mean. Give until it hurts; no, give *past* the point of pain. Give everything. Nothing held back. Period. The widow did what the earnest rich man couldn't conceive of. You remember what Jesus told him: "Go, sell what you own, and give the money to the poor ..." (Mark 10:21). And he went away grieving, because he had many possessions and couldn't part with them, even for the sake of Jesus and the life he offered.

C. S. Lewis wrote that Christian charity is neither Christian nor charity unless our giving "cramps our style" and causes us to sacrifice some *needs* as well as luxuries. And that sort of giving, he added, was simply the *starting point* of Christian charitable giving, not its terminus! In his mind he could hear Jesus' words to that rich man, and his approval of the poor widow. "Sell what you own. She has put in everything she had."

If we have any scruples at all, we squirm. Against such a blunt and absolute standard, we know we fail. Even that lesser standard that Lewis holds up as a starting point is a stumbling-block for many of us. Will we, like the scribes, receive the "greater condemnation"?

Let that question chafe against our soul as we consider something else as well. For most of us, wealth in its many forms is intimately linked with our self-identity and self-worth. Our wealth may not be in coins and stock options. But most of us have other kinds of wealth: a pleasing personality; the respect and friendship of our peers; perhaps some genuine authority at work; various skills, talents, and gifts; leisure time; the benefits of a reasonably just, orderly, and free society. We use them, enjoy them, have them at our disposal. They're valuable to us. They're the "coin of the realm" of our social interactions and our self-image. Without them we feel diminished, threatened, even dehumanized.

We'd fight like mad if someone tried to take them from us. Giving them up willingly is an almost incomprehensible act of foolishness and humiliation. What could the church, or anything else, provide to compensate for their loss?

With that in mind, *now* consider the widow and rich man. Consider Jesus' words about each. Which words would he say of us?

The widow's gift of her whole livelihood was unthinkable and foolish. She didn't give *in order* to get anything, nor did she give *because* she had gotten anything from the Temple. Jesus had already noted what widows were likely to receive at the hands of the Temple's worthies! She gave everything in exchange for nothing!

Or did she? The widow gave all she had — all her wealth, symbolized in two tiny coins — because she considered nothing she had as her own. Everything she had and everything she was, down to the most intimate core of her identity, was from God. She wasn't sacrificing a portion of her livelihood to God; by the grace of God she was entrusting her whole self into God's keeping. Her two tiny coins were the final, foolish, unspeakably humble outward manifestation of that absolute gift. Her gift was so humble that nobody knew its magnitude except her Lord.

She is, in fact, what we are called to be: a tiny, flashing mirror that reflects the final, foolish, unspeakably humble and utterly complete self-giving of God to us in his son Jesus. You might say that he truly gave everything in exchange for "nothing"; for the forgiveness and redemption of flawed, broken, sinful human beings who can no more entrust themselves to God by their own power than they can do brain surgery on themselves.

Luther put it well: "At great cost [Jesus] has saved and redeemed me, a lost and condemned person. He has freed me from sin, death, and the power of the devil — not with silver and gold but with his holy and precious blood and his innocent suffering and death. All this he has done that I may be his own, live under him in his kingdom, and serve him in everlasting righteousness, innocence, and blessedness, just as he is risen from the dead and lives and rules eternally."[1]

Because of our Lord's lavish self-giving of all his "wealth" — life, power, authority, holiness, *everything* — even destitute widows are freed to give themselves recklessly and beautifully into his wounded hands. Their "nothing" is turned, by his sovereign foolishness, into "everything."

Because of Jesus' self-emptying, even pompous scribes and self-satisfied "fat cats" might be freed to pour out their bounty of wealth in self-forgetful gratitude. Hey, it could happen. Zacchaeus and Matthew are a couple of examples.

Awash in the incredible riches of God's outpoured and forgiving love, even we anxious, harried, and (let's admit it) wretchedly self-centered middle-class folk might cease from saying, "*My* wealth. *My* time. *My* personality. *My* skills, talents, interests, and gifts. *My* life." We might dare to say (and mean, and live by), "Not I who live, but Christ alive in me. Not my will but yours be done. Take my silver and my gold, not a mite would I withhold. Take my love; my Lord, I pour at thy feet its treasure store. Take *myself*, and I will be ever, only, all for thee."

Hey, it could happen. Our Lord spent himself on us so that it could happen. Whether we're from Massachusetts or Mississippi, the equation becomes the same when our lives are immersed in him. Everything — however little or great "everything" is — is nothing. It's his, not ours. And nothing becomes everything. He can fill even the emptiest, stingiest heart with the bounties of heaven itself. And he can make the gift of our "nothing" into a mirror reflecting the brilliance of *his* incomparable gift into the dark, cramped, poverty-stricken, wealth-cursed corners of our world.

God grant that it may be so. God grant that our Lord Jesus will say of us, "Out of their poverty they gave everything they had, all they had to live on. And by my grace, their nothing I claim as everything." Amen.

---

1. Martin Luther, *The Small Catechism in Contemporary English* (Augsburg Publishing House, Minneapolis, 1979), p. 13.

Proper 28
Pentecost 26
Mark 13:1-8

Birthing The Kingdom

I for one am heartily glad that the millennium (and its attendant madness) is well behind us. I'm glad that the millennium comes only once in a, well, millennium. The major reason for my relief is that I became sick of "Millennium Fever" and the doom-saying prophecies that (mercifully) did not come to pass.

End of the world prophecies are nothing new, of course. They were around for centuries before our Lord was born. They exist in most major religions and cults. And every time a new disaster — of natural origin or human construction — is inflicted on the world, a fresh spate of doomsday predictors makes the rounds. The cynic in me figures that someday, *someone* is bound to guess right. It was weirdly refreshing to hear one recent prophet of doom apologize for misreading "the signs of the times." He'd actually predicted that, just before the turn of the millennium, Jesus Christ would not only return to earth but would be a guest on this gentleman's talk show! Oops.

Many Christians are fascinated by end time prophecies. They search the books of Daniel, Ezekiel, and especially Revelation for hints and signals that the Lord is coming to end history and usher in the Day of the Lord, a day of darkness not light, and of judgment and wrath for those who oppose the reign of God. The popularity of the *Left Behind* series of books, co-authored by Tim LaHaye, highlights the intensity of this interest.

Probably an equal number of Christians are turned off by discussions of time-lines, dispensations, pre- versus post-tribulationism, the rapture, and assorted other end time esoterica. Their rallying cry is

359

Jesus' comment that not even the Son knows the day or hour, but only the Father. They're a bit repulsed by biblical apocalypse. And so to hear Jesus talk about wars and rumors of wars; to hear Jesus solemnly say "the end is still to come"; to hear *this* Gospel text — well, let's just say that many good people would rather *not* hear any of this!

But of course we must hear Jesus' words and struggle with them. We're his disciples or else we think we'd like to be. And Mark's Gospel puts these hard words of our Lord in the last week of Jesus' life, when everything he says and does is brought to its sharpest, most piercing peak. Jesus wasn't a mere armchair speculator offering his opinion about what is to come. He wasn't spouting theories for examination and argument. Instead, he was preparing his followers for the challenges they'd face after his own death and resurrection.

The forces of sin and evil aren't going to roll over and play dead because Jesus broke their back upon the cross. With their final strength, they protest, defy, and oppose our Lord and the Kingdom he establishes. The disciples may confidently step into the world with the Good News, knowing that Jesus had indeed won the war; but they aren't to be fooled. Battles and dangers loom ahead, as sinful people and broken creation itself fight a rearguard action against Christ's claim upon them.

In Jesus' opening words, heard today, he sketches out several threats. Later he'll deal with some of them at greater length. Some of the dangers are associated with a singular disaster that was looming upon them: the destruction of the Temple in Jerusalem. It happened in 70 A.D. Others are ongoing dangers: persecution of his followers, and the rise of false leaders and prophets within the community of faith itself. And of course there is the turmoil that intensifies as "the end" itself approaches and opposition to God's coming Kingdom reaches its climax.

Two things amaze me. First, Jesus is so matter-of-fact about it all. These terrible things *will* happen. Jesus doesn't apologize for them or pretend that his followers will be immune to their dangers. He doesn't go on about "ain't it awful, how the world is going to hell in a handbasket." He simply reminds his followers to beware.

These things *must* happen; they're to be expected. Don't be caught off guard when they come.

But the other amazing thing is Jesus' calm confidence. He sees in these dreadful things not a world gone haywire, not a disease process that will end in corruption and death, and not a pointless and terrifying descent into chaos before God finally steps in to end it all. Instead he says, "This is but the beginning of *the birth pangs*" (v. 8).

With these simple words, Jesus puts the entire discussion squarely in a new framework. *This must happen; this is the beginning of the birth pangs.* In his commentary on the Gospel of Mark, Donald Juel states it with succinct accuracy: "The necessity is viewed here as due to the decision of God — the same necessity that stands over Jesus' career ... The necessity that governs the future is reason to take heart if God is to be trusted — which is the point of Jesus' instructions and of Mark's Gospel."[1]

The necessity that governs the future is reason to take heart *if* God is to be trusted. What a remarkable truth that is for us anxious post-millennial Christians to savor! If God is who he says he is, if God really is the One whom Jesus revealed, then God is in control no matter what hell seems to be breaking loose.

God knows what terrible dangers loom over his broken world. Wars and rumors of war, terrorist acts, famines, earthquakes, and plagues are the steady headline diet we ingest every day. Any person of good will, Christian or non-Christian, prays for peace and healing, and is dismayed by the intensity of violence, hatred, suspicion, and sheer human suffering seen on every side. How easy it is to become discouraged to the point of despair: our best efforts at peacemaking are constantly overwhelmed and despised. How easy it is to believe that God doesn't care or can't act. How astonishing — and bracing! — it is to hear Jesus tell us: This must happen. Do not be alarmed. These are birth pangs, not just death throes.

Now we must be careful here, because the *last* thing we want to say is that God wills and desires bloodshed, mayhem, and disaster. God isn't a sadist. And yet if we look at the model of Jesus' own passion and death, don't we see Jesus' words acted out before us? Jesus said that he *must* be handed over; *must* be betrayed, mocked, and scourged; *must* suffer death on a cross. He also announced, in almost the same breath, and with astonishing conviction, that he *would* be raised from death on the third day; that he *would* give his life as a ransom for many; that he *would* bring to suffering, broken humanity the life and forgiveness and Kingdom of God, by means of his death and resurrection.

God took what otherwise would be deemed utter disaster, utter evil, utter awful sinfulness — and fashions it into the crucible in which his Son forged our salvation. And, because of that, and on the strength of that great and terrible act, God now takes what is horrible, God-despising, and death-dealing in our lives and communities and world — and fashions *these things and no others* into the birth pangs of his new creation.

Frankly, I'm not sure whether to be appalled, exalted, comforted, or energized — or maybe all of the above! But at the brink of his own passion and death, Jesus speaks of the passion of the world and, more particularly, of his followers. He holds out no easy comfort. How could he, who agonized in a garden and on a cross before entrusting his will and his life into his Father's keeping? Those who follow him can expect no less hostility and tumult.

And yet Jesus himself emerged from a tomb *as from a womb*, which unexpectedly and gloriously ushered an entirely new sort of life into our world. He is the firstborn of a new creation, and the old creation groans in labor pains for our redemption and for its own deliverance from futility (Romans 8:20-23). Because Jesus' own anguish, death, and resurrection have embraced the world in all its brokenness and sin, something entirely new and unexpectedly glorious has happened. Upheaval, persecution, and disaster will not have the last word over his beloved people. What the world, the devil, and even our sinful selves try to make into a tomb *our Lord transforms into a womb.*

Terrible things will happen; they are no less painful because of Jesus' words and work. We can still be torn apart by controversy and wounded by betrayal. Persecution still happens, even in the supposedly civilized twenty-first century. Like a woman gasping in anguish hour after hour, struggling to deliver a breech baby into the world, creation and humanity also cry out in fear and anguish. God's new creation certainly is long a-borning!

And yet, it is coming to birth. We are coming to birth! Because of Jesus, firstborn of the new creation, we are assured that this will not be a stillbirth. Because Jesus has joined us to himself, we can cry out and know we are heard and answered; we can grieve yet not without hope; we can face the worst the world throws at us and not despair. We can endure the painful small insults and rebuffs with forgiveness and fortitude. We can weather the natural disasters with generous and merciful concern for others. We can withstand human brutality with faithful witness, confident hope — and with a passionate commitment to justice, so that others may be spared. We can do these things because God has promised that he will make sense of it all. God will bring life from our deathly experiences. God will turn the world's tombs into the womb of his new creation. We can pray with his suffering Church in all times and places, with longing and joyful confidence, "Even so, Lord, quickly come! Amen!"

---

1. Donald Juel, *Mark: Augsburg Commentary on the New Testament* (Minneapolis: Augsburg Fortress, 1990), p. 176.

Heart Transplant

Imagine the scene: you are in the doctor's office, an array of EKGs, echocardiograms, and other test results splayed around the room. The doctor's face is grim but resolute. "Your heart is so severely damaged that you will surely die without a transplant. I've placed your name on the waiting list; in a few months, we'll schedule the surgery and when it's over, God willing, you'll be healed. No more gasping for breath when you walk across the room. No shooting pains. You'll be your old self again, only better."

Your mind is reeling with the news. There are so many questions you want answered! Patiently the doctor walks you through what is to come, and eventually, the day you dread and hope for arrives. "Get to the hospital. We have a new heart for you." Most of your energy and thoughts are focused on yourself, the surgical and medical team, your family, and just getting through this radical procedure. But late at night — perhaps the night before surgery, maybe a few days afterwards, as you wait for pain medication to kick in or for the anti-rejection drugs to reduce a fever — there in the silent room, late at night you have other questions.

Who was the person whose heart is now yours? Was it a man or a woman? Was he or she white, black, Oriental, something else? Was the person Christian, Jewish, Muslim, Buddhist, Hindu, atheist? What did the person do for a living, what hopes and sorrows did he or she bear? How did the person live, and how did he or she die? What does it mean that you bear a living portion of another person's body there within your chest? What does it mean that you live only because another person died, and allowed a part of his or her own body to be given to a stranger? Does something of that person's history or essence or soul pass into you with the living tissue? How will you be changed — not just by the surgical procedure but by this astonishing and deeply intimate gift that will beat within your chest for the rest of your natural life? What will it be like to live, knowing that each breath you take, each word you speak, each thought and gesture and action is possible only because of this new heart, gift of a stranger, powering your body?

Perhaps, half-embarrassed, you share some of your questions with the doctor or someone else. You're assured that, no, you're not suddenly going to gain the characteristics of a different gender or race; you're not suddenly going to start watching the old movies and sitcoms you'd heard the other person liked. In fact, your body is constantly going to try rejecting the new heart, deeming it alien, dangerous, and "other." Only the anti-rejection drugs you take will allow the new heart to become an integral part of your own body. Perhaps the doctor was right: this heart transplant has allowed you to be your old self again, though wiser, deeper, more grateful.

Imagine the scene: you come to church with your new baby, and you hear disturbing words. "Your baby's heart — not her physical one, but her *real* heart, the seat of her soul and the core of her identity — is as deeply damaged as yours was. Without a heart transplant, she will surely die. But there is great hope," the pastor continues, voice warm with resolution and joy. "Our Lord Jesus has promised to give your child his very own heart, just as he gave to you and me. Let's schedule the baptism for next Sunday, shall we?"

You sit there, reeling with questions. *My beautiful baby?* Die? Deeply damaged as my own heart — what didn't my parents tell me? Heart transplant? What are you talking about? Isn't there something less radical, less dangerous? Our real heart? What's going on?

The pastor patiently answers your questions. "If our physical heart is wounded, clogged, malformed, it affects the whole body, doesn't it? If it fails, the whole body dies. And in the meantime, before the transplant, you're in bondage. You're a slave to pain, to the terrible limitations enforced by the malfunctioning heart. And without a transplant, you die in that bondage.

"Sin is like that; it's like terrible heart disease of the soul. It keeps us in bondage — we keep on hurting ourselves and one another, and we anger and grieve God. Even if we wanted to live healthy, sinless lives, we couldn't — just as when you have a failing heart, even giving up smoking, eating right, and mild exercise only postpone the inevitable. Without a *real* heart transplant, we're doomed to die in bondage to sin."

"But my baby!" you say. "She hasn't lived long enough to sin! Is she born with this?"

The pastor nods gently. "It's like being born with a really terrible heart defect: even though she's being fed the best baby food and is getting all her shots and seems healthy, she could have a condition that is life threatening, right? Well, that's the human condition, there in the depth of what *makes* us human. Following God's laws and commandments ameliorates the worst of the side effects, but it only postpones the inevitable. Only a heart transplant from God can correct it — after all, since we're all in the same boat, who else could do it?"

You think hard for several minutes. "With a regular heart transplant, you're still the same old self, just healthier. You don't change colors or religion or gender because of it. What about this — this baptismal transplant you're talking about?"

"Ah!" the pastor beams. "That's the big surprise. Jesus puts his own heart in us! He died under sin's load and rose again and is forever immune to its deadly effects! His heart is completely in tune with his heavenly Father. God's intentions are engraved on Jesus' heart. His is the heart of God's beloved Son — and when we receive it, we're not only set free from slavery to sin and death, we are counted as members of God's family, too! He knows the justice and mercy of God deep in his heart. When we receive it, we begin to know God that way, too! We don't stay our same old selves when we get a heart transplant in Baptism. We begin to be like Jesus. No, no, let me rephrase that. We're made part of his own Body when his heart is put in us. And he will never, ever reject us as foreign and dangerous. Sin and death will never have the last word over us. We're *his* when we receive his heart, life, and future from God's hand."

"Don't *we* need anti-rejection drugs, though?" you ask, half-kidding. "I mean, this is a lot more radical than real — uh, I mean physical heart transplant surgery!"

"That's why we're given his Body and Blood every single week — almost 1,900 years ago a great saint called Communion the 'medicine of immortality.' Maybe he was more right than he knew! Being here in worship with other transplant recipients, constantly hearing what God has done that we could never do for ourselves and what he wants to do for all his people, and receiving his presence in bread and wine, his promise that we're forgiven all our attempts to 'reject' him — that's what keeps us healthy after this great heart transplant. And we're promised that it will last not in our physical lifetime, but forever. As Jesus said, if the Son makes you free, you're free indeed. Forever!"

Dear friends in Christ, that isn't a hypothetical conversation. It's one our Lord has with us every week, and we hear it very pointedly on Reformation Sunday. Maybe it's the deepest meaning of Reformation: That always, throughout the world, the Church announces that it is comprised solely of people who live with a new heart in them: the heart of Christ. They are alive solely through his grace. Anyone who believes this and is baptized — who received this incredible, intimate gift of God's own life — will live forever as a child of God's house. For if the Son makes us free, we are all free indeed. Amen.

The Making Of A Saint

Today's Gospel is difficult to preach on All Saints' Sunday. The story of the raising of Lazarus is familiar and uplifting, but this section is a little awkward. We enter just in time to witness Jesus' tears and anguish, some graphic words about how the body would smell, an odd little prayer, and — almost as an afterthought — the calling forth of four-day-dead Lazarus, still bound in his shroud, shuffling awkwardly from his tomb before the astonished mourners. No ringing words about Jesus as the resurrection and the life; just a, shall we say, former corpse blinking newly-restored eyes against the light of an ordinary earthly day.

Because that was what the still-present shroud signifies: Lazarus has been *raised* but not *resurrected*. He's been given a new lease on his old life; he hasn't been ushered yet into the life of heaven. What happened to him when Jesus called him from the grave is marvelous but is at most a foretaste or symbol of the rich, endless new life that Jesus promised. Lazarus is raised to live on earth again, with a death still in his future, and with the life of heaven still a promise.

Makes you want to run to the ringing promises of Isaiah: "And he will *destroy* on this mountain the shroud that is cast over all peoples ... he will swallow up death forever" (Isaiah 25:7). That's more like it! Get rid of that shroud! Destroy death forever! That's what we should be hearing on All Saints' Day: a celebration of the Resurrection Life for God's saints, especially for those who have died. We want to hear that their grave-clothes and shrouds are replaced by festal robes and mantles of joy. Why not visualize glorified saints instead of resuscitated corpses?

It's not that we wouldn't like to have our loved ones restored to us, here on earth, in robust good health. We'd long and pray for just that restoration. Wouldn't you ache to embrace a beloved spouse who suddenly died of a heart attack or who wasted away from cancer? What parent wouldn't gladly give a king's ransom to cuddle a SIDS baby or happily endure hours of grunge rock for the chance to have a suicidal teenager back again? Things that had gone unsaid "before" could now be said. Unfinished business could be concluded. Milestones could be reached: an anniversary, the birth of a first grandchild, graduation from college. Perhaps even that forlorn phrase, "If only ..." could be given a proper burial! I'm sure Mary and Martha were just as overjoyed to welcome Lazarus back for all these reasons, for however long God granted them to share those lives again.

In the back of our minds, though, we know that those loved ones would die again, perhaps once again before us. More things might go unsaid, more business would dangle unfinished, more milestones would not be reached, more "if onlys" would be raised up. However wonderful a miracle of resuscitation might be, in the end *it isn't miracle enough.*

So this Gospel reading has a bittersweet tang to it. How much more comforting to turn to other words that fast-forward past death. How much less painful to leave behind all talk of the smell of death and the business of unwinding burial sheets. How much better to talk about saints at rest in the peace of God!

I'm not sure when it finally hit me. This story isn't just about the revival of Lazarus or what happens when one of God's saints dies. It's about what happens *when God makes us his saints*. It's about our own death and rising ... in Baptism.

We, like Lazarus, have contracted a deadly sickness. It's called sin; it festers in the soul and poisons the body. *We*, like Lazarus, have loved ones who call upon God for our deliverance. They're called parents and baptismal sponsors. *We,* like Lazarus, are drawn down into a death: a real one, even though it doesn't look as drastic (or smell as bad!) as Lazarus'. *We,* like Lazarus, emerge at the sound of our Lord's voice to live again.

What Lazarus didn't know; what Martha heard but only dimly understood — and what we believe, teach, confess, and experience is this: that watery death of Baptism is joined to the suffering and death of Jesus himself. The tears and anguish of Jesus hint at this: in Lazarus' death, Jesus sees the preview of his own death and tomb. And *that* makes all the difference. It makes this more than a story about a miraculous resuscitation of one lucky man. It makes it more than a bittersweet meditation on a loved one's death. It even makes Lazarus' raising, and our Baptism, *more* than a mere restoration to ordinary, earthly life, with death still before us and the life of heaven still only a promise.

The only way to explain this properly is to step "outside the story" and look to that other tomb, that other set of grave clothes, that other death. The same Jesus whose voice called Lazarus from death into life, the One in whose presence no dead body could remain dead, because he was the Lord of Life — this same Jesus shared our death. And on the third day *his* grave was opened, *his* burial clothes were laid neatly aside, once and for all, and *he* emerged not merely resuscitated, but *resurrected.* His human body and soul were raised to the rich, endless life the Son of God had from all eternity shared with his Father.

And this Jesus who shared the shame and sorrow of our death bids us share his life. Lazarus was returned to his family and friends, to the ordinary mortal light of his everyday world. But his fortunes were now forever joined to the One who commanded him to come out of the tomb. Even though a death still loomed before him (for one day Lazarus would grow old and die), in the most important way of all, *death now stood behind him.* Whatever he did or didn't know about "what lay beyond" was irrelevant. He knew, in the marrow of his re-enlivened bones, that because of Jesus, death would never, ever have the last word over him. He had heard Jesus' Last Word pronounced over him, and that word was, "Come Out! Live!"

So it is for us! When we emerge from the "tomb" of baptismal waters, blinking (and, if we're infants, probably wailing) in the ordinary light of our everyday world, we do so with our Lord's wounded but glorified arms embracing us. We're reborn not to escape from but to return to a world of doubts, disease, divorce, and death. In this life we'll always struggle with unspoken words, unfinished business, unmet milestones, and countless "what ifs." We do so, though, with Jesus' life filling and strengthening us. Like Lazarus, we live with the worst part of death behind us. Death will never have the last word over any who have been joined to Christ Jesus' death and resurrection.

Ultimately, *that's* what "being a saint" is all about — not perfect, sinless, goody-two shoes existences, but lives bound to the life of Jesus Christ and lived in the messy, sometimes smelly realities of our sinful and broken world. When God goes about making us his saints, he doesn't make us immune from grief. Instead, he binds us to his risen Son and makes us people who grieve but who have a hope that cannot be shaken. When God makes a person one of his saints, he doesn't make life problem-free. Instead, he gives the *rest* of us saints Jesus' command to Lazarus' friends: "You unbind him, and let him go" (v. 44). He gives us, also, the grace and strength to do it!

We need to hear the words of Isaiah and Revelation about the fullness of eternal life that his saints will enjoy. But it's good to be reminded that our entry into sainthood, and our most devastating encounter with death, have already taken place. The only one whose words have final power and authority over us is one who speaks words of command and promise and hope: "Lazarus, come out. People of this place, come out." Come out, and live in the strength of his promise and his life, until all shrouds are destroyed and death is swallowed up forever. Amen.

The Dangerous Truth

I'd rather hear Saint Matthew talk about Christ the King. His story of the Last Judgment is vivid. Concrete acts are laid out. "As you have done to the least of these," Jesus says, "you have done to me." We may disagree or cringe, but we can picture this King claiming kinship with the lowly.

Luke's story is good, too. Jesus hangs between two criminals and promises to one that "today you will be with me in Paradise." We see a dying King offering kingly gifts to the dying who trust in him. We may be puzzled, we may object, but again, we can picture it.

Then there's *this* year's Gospel! Jesus doesn't stand with or make kingly promises to the poor, lowly, suffering, or dying. Instead, he trades words with a Roman governor who probably wishes he were back in bed and not mulling over the death penalty for this strange Jew.

We can't make a picture from Jesus' words. Instead of a vivid description of how Jesus acts as King, we get negatives and generalities: "As it is, my kingdom is *not* from this world ... *You* say that I am a king; for this I was born ... to testify to the truth" (John 18:37). But Jesus gives no details about "the truth." Is it any wonder that Pilate responds, "What *is* truth?" We might add, "What sort of kingship *is* this? What's truth got to do with it?"

Truth and a kingdom not from this world aren't easy to visualize. They don't reduce to sound bites or Kodak moments. There's nothing to grab hold of. For concrete thinkers, such words are frustrating. To see how Jesus claims kingship through his testimony to the truth, here at the end of his earthly life, let's look at what Jesus *says* about truth elsewhere in John's Gospel.

In the beginning, we read: "And the Word became flesh and lived among us, and we have seen his glory: the glory as of a father's only son, full of grace and truth" (John 1:14). Later, Jesus says to Nicodemus: "The one who comes from heaven ... testifies to what he has seen and heard ... Whoever has accepted his testimony has certified this, that *God is true*" (John 3:31-33).

Jesus says this to the Samaritan woman: "The hour is coming, and is now here, when the true worshipers will worship the Father in spirit and truth" (John 4:23). To the Jews who had believed in him, he said, "The one who sent me is true, and I declare to the world what I have heard from him ... If you continue in my word, you are truly my disciples, and you will know the truth, and the truth will make you free" (John 8:26, 32).

On the night before he faced Pilate, Jesus spoke words of assurance to his frightened disciples. "I am the way, and the truth, and the life. No one comes to the Father except through me. If you know me, you will know my Father also. From now on, you do know him and have seen him" (John 14:6-7).

In John's Gospel, *truth* isn't a fact, a scrap of data, or even a system of thought that explains the world. Truth is the life-giving power of God, graciously given to the world through the death and resurrection of Jesus. Truth is the love of God revealed in Jesus' words and deeds. Truth is the disclosure of God's heart to us. Truth is summarized, "God so loved the world that he gave his only-begotten Son, that everyone who believes in him might not perish but have eternal life" (John 3:16).

Jesus' whole identity — his words, his works, his dying and rising, his breathing of the Spirit upon his followers, *everything* — was the embodiment of that simple, confounding truth.

That makes Jesus' kingship unlike any other. *He doesn't act like a regular king!* Most kings make laws and decrees, fight wars, make treaties, order ordinary people around, and act as the kingdom's ultimate judge, jury, and executioner. But according to John's Gospel, what Jesus does is reveal the perfect light, utter love, and endless gracious life of God to people who are blind, bound, and dead in the darkness of sin. And he offers us a way to enjoy all this with him forever. That's it. He doesn't judge, though he has the right. He doesn't throw his weight around. He doesn't offer lists of do's and don'ts. Even his deeds of power are simply "signs" meant to bring people to a new, freeing, saving relationship with his Father. That's *the truth* of what Jesus does and says and is. That's how he "acts out" the kingship over creation that was his from before the world's foundation. There's nothing else and no place else we can look for it.

How strange that must have seemed to Pilate! He was used to hidden agendas, mixed motives, and wheels within wheels. He knew how the world operates. He understood imperial power that dictated what subjects would do at the emperor's pleasure. He could handle truth as a weapon or a tool. He probably couldn't make head or tail out of Jesus or his claims.

It's not much easier for us. It's hard enough to absorb and proclaim those *other* images of Christ the King: the King hidden in the lives of the wretched, or the dying promiser of kingly blessings. How much harder it is to acclaim and adore him as the One who sheds the holy and inextinguishable light of truth in all the dark corners of *our* hearts and our world!

We'd rather die than reveal some parts of ourselves. Some truths are so dangerous that we deny, cover up, or run away from them. We have mixed motives, even while doing something worthwhile. We bring "baggage" and hidden agendas to conversations and relationships. Bear testimony to *God?* We don't even know our real selves!

So can we imagine a king who insists his power consists solely of bearing faithful testimony to the *truth* of God? Can we imagine *anyone* being so transparent to God's heart that his whole identity is summed up as bearing witness to the One who sent him? Can we imagine what might happen when that sort of kingship, that unwavering fidelity to the truth, that kind of utter transparency to God, lays claim to our lives?

Because if we name Jesus as King; if we worship him as the way and truth and life of God dwelling in our midst; if we confess that we belong to the truth because we have listened to his voice, then that's what we're going to get from him.

It's nice to talk about Christ as the King who testifies to the truth and essence of God's heart. It can be alarming to experience him up close and personal. He spoke to the Samaritan woman of worshiping God in spirit and truth — but only after he had brought her heart's secrets into his light: "You have had five husbands, and the one you have now is not your husband. What you have said is true!" (John 4:18). Yet she used that searing encounter as a basis for witnessing to her whole village: "Come and see a man who told me everything I have ever done! He cannot be the Messiah, can he?" (v. 29).

Jesus asked a searching question of a man paralyzed for 38 years: "Do you *want* to be made well?" (John 5:6). When the man gave excuses for why he'd never been healed by the pool's miraculous waters, Jesus healed him — but promptly warned him, "See, you have been made well! Do not sin any more, so that nothing worse happens to you" (v. 14). Touched by Jesus' truth, he then began to testify to Jesus' healing power.

Nicodemus' encounter with Jesus was awkward: To an honest question, Jesus retorted, "Are you a teacher of Israel, and yet you do not understand these things?" (John 3:10). Pierced by that truth, and by the greater truth of God's love revealed in Jesus, Nicodemus later defended him and helped to bury him.

When this King brings the clarity of God's truth to some, they listen and take to heart. They testify to his truth, as he testifies to his Father's truth. They live, forever changed, forever alive in the unsparing yet unspeakably gracious light of God.

Then it was Pilate's turn. Would he listen and take to heart? Or would he cave in to the tired old versions of kingly power and truth-spinning that he'd always known? We know how Pilate responded when confronted by Jesus' kingly claim.

How will *we* respond to Christ our King? Will we listen? Will we take his voice to heart? Will we testify to the searching, liberating truth that is God's inmost heart revealed to us in Jesus? Will we live, forever changed, forever alive in God's unsparing yet unspeakably gracious light?

What is truth — for us? The heart of God, revealed by his Son? Or something else? Who is King of our lives? The One who bears witness to the heart and will of God? Or someone who makes us feel good about ourselves and our little world? Here at the end of the church year, as at the end of Jesus' earthly life, those questions confront us.

God grant that *we* listen to our Lord's voice, and belong to his truth, and dwell in his kingdom forever. Amen.

Anxious Thanks

On Thanksgiving, isn't it odd to hear a Gospel that talks about anxiety and worry and not about, well, *thanks?* At this time of year, we offer thanks for food, shelter, health, favorable weather, peace, and a whole raft of other blessings. Isn't it a bit jarring to hear Jesus tell us, "Do not worry, saying, 'What will we eat?' or 'What will we drink?' or 'What will we wear?' For it is the Gentiles who strive for all these things"? Why is this text rubbing worry into our faces?

Worry — and trouble. "Today's trouble is enough for today" (v. 34). Isn't it *just swell* to hear that today? Isn't that *just* the Bible verse we want served up with the turkey, cranberries, and stuffing? Wouldn't most of us just rather pass on it and save up for a dessert course of "Now Thank We All Our God"?

All this is unsettling. For one thing, our nation has recently endured a calamity unlike any other in its history, with who knows what salvos to follow. Second, people have braced themselves for a long, drawn-out, and very peculiar war against a shadowy and frightening enemy. And third, we know how many people have worried about job layoffs and loss of income and financial security on top of fears about personal and national security and safety. Jesus' words about not worrying, and about letting today's troubles be enough for the day, almost come across as flip and shallow, don't they?

On top of all that, there are people for whom worry and trouble are constant companions, even in times of peace and prosperity, and even on Thanksgiving. You can list them as well as I: the home-less; terminally ill patients; people recently bereaved, divorced, or laid off. Abused children, battered spouses. Parents whose son is on drugs or whose daughter just had an abortion. Adult children with parents lost in a haze of dementia. People with severe mental illness, and their families. The list goes on and on.

And our hearts go out to these people. Maybe we've been on that list ourselves at some point. We know the crushing anxiety and the sense of being overburdened by trouble. We know how painful and pointless the holidays can be — especially a holiday devoted to thankfulness for blessings and to celebrating family ties. And this year, more than most, we resonate with their worries, fears, griefs, and cares.

And so our Lord's words jar us. At best, they spoil the mood of Thanksgiving gratitude. Even to say, "Don't worry about these things," is to make us a little anxious. It's a bit like saying, "Don't think about elephants." You know what happens!

Worse, Jesus' words reveal an uncomfortable truth about grati-tude. We know how close beneath its surface anxiety does lurk. We're thankful for the food we have today (but will there be any tomorrow?). We thank God for our good health (but how do we prepare for bioterrorist attacks?). We give thanks for peace and freedom (but just how vulnerable are we because of that very free-dom?). Unless we're awfully complacent or completely clueless, we're aware of life's fragility. We know how quickly things could be different. So even when we sing, "Now Thank We All Our God," a part of us wonders, "Will we have anything to thank God for tomorrow or the next day?" That part wonders if God can be trusted to love us and care for us — tomorrow.

There have been many articles written about the spiritual cri-sis many Americans are facing in the aftermath of the so-called "9-1-1" terrorist attacks. Many people wonder what America has done wrong, that we should be so hated in some parts of the world. Still others ask, "Why is God letting this happen to us?" and they come up with explanations both simplistic and repellent. And under all *these* questions are others that were hard to voice: Does God still love us? Does he care? Can we trust that he is blessing us even now and will continue to?"

So long as a family, an individual, or a nation hinges gratitude upon "stuff" — even good, necessary-for-life "stuff," even "stuff" that we may rightly call blessings given by almighty God, there's always that underlying fear that maybe tomorrow it won't be there. "Stuff" is notoriously fickle and unstable!

Jesus wants his followers to ground their gratitude — indeed, their lives — in something a lot more solid than "stuff." "Strive first for the Kingdom of God and his righteousness," he urges, "and all these things will be given to you as well" (v. 33). And he's already begun fleshing out what "the kingdom of God and his righteousness" are all about. They exist wherever and whenever God's name is kept holy by his people. They're present when God's will is accomplished to create, sustain, redeem, forgive, heal, reconcile, empower, and love us and all creation. God's kingdom and righteousness are shown when fearful, fallible people share the same forgiveness with one another that they have already received from the One who knows perfectly well what they need for daily existence. They're active when God lifts up those who hunger and thirst, who mourn, who are persecuted and who humbly endure whatever "stuff" a broken world dishes their way. God's kingdom and righteousness are present whenever we place our hope and trust in God above any and all the good "stuff" — the good blessings — with which he has graced us.

God cares even for birds and wild flowers and graces them with loveliness. God doesn't freeze the flower in timeless perfection; the day comes when flowers fade, die, scatter their seeds for another year, and are finally gathered for fuel. Is God's care any less real because the flower isn't eternally fresh?

God graces our lives with the loveliness of his blessings: everything from savory food to joyous family reunions to a land of peace and liberty. And, no, those blessings aren't frozen in place. Like flowers, they have their season. They may wither for a time. So do troubles; they come, they pass, and new ones take their places, as surely as weeds in the flower garden.

And God is still good. God still loves us. His love is as constant as the wildflowers are ephemeral. His will for us never changes. His kingdom still draws near to us, in every whispered prayer, in every bite of bread and sip of wine, in every moment that we draw upon his forgiveness, lavished upon us from a cross. Neither "stuff" nor its lack can keep God from loving us in Christ Jesus. Not death itself can do that. Neither fear, nor anxiety, nor the worst troubles that beset us can actually stop *God* from caring for us; but they certainly can make *us* blind and deaf to that care!

"Do not be anxious...." Even churches may flourish like wildflowers — and sometimes fade. Membership and contribution numbers ebb and flow like the tide. Yet God's Kingdom is still faithfully preached. God's righteousness is sought and received in Word and Sacrament, fellowship and forgiveness. Thanks be to God for his unutterable goodness and favor!

"Today's trouble is enough for today...." Families, communities, and nations grow — and sometimes struggle and splinter. Boom follows bust, or vice versa. Strife and even bloodshed disrupt peaceful communities. And yet God still offers us healing and reconciliation in his Son. He still promises to save us in our times of trial and deliver us from the powers of evil and death. Thanks be to God for offering us treasures that moth and rust do not consume, and which thief nor circumstance of life can steal from us (Matthew 6:20). Pray to God that we have the wits — and trustfulness! — to receive them.

Often on Thanksgiving we sing, "Now Thank We All Our God," and reflect on words overflowing with gratitude for God's bounty:

> *Who, from our mothers' arms, has blessed us on our*
> *way with countless gifts of love, and still is ours today.*
> *O may this bounteous God through all our lives be*
> *near us, with ever thankful hearts and blessed peace*
> *to cheer us!*

The writer of this beloved hymn was a pastor named Martin Rinkhart. During the awful strife of the Thirty Years' War, Pastor Rinkhart buried many members of his parish — including his own wife. Bloodshed, disease, and even famine took a terrible toll of his village. The people were understandably frightened and despondent. Even when the fighting waned, troubles loomed large and anxiety wore people down. They wondered if God still cared. Does this sound familiar?

In the midst of all this, Martin Rinkhart wrote a hymn to remind people of God's continuous, endless, eternal goodness and care. We know the words:

> *Now thank we all our God with heart and hands and voices; who wondrous things has done, in whom his world rejoices ... O may this bounteous God through all our lives be near us with ever thankful hearts and blessed peace to cheer us; and keep us in his grace and guide us when perplexed, and free us from all harm in this world and the next.*

Pastor Rinkhart knew, deep in his bones, the truth of Jesus' words about worry and trouble. More importantly, he knew that in every circumstance, God's blessing, grace, guidance, and protection embraced his embattled people. And so he received all *these* with thanks — and was given a heart to thank God for all God's other blessings, so dear, so precious, so fleeting — whether he enjoyed them now in fact or only in patient hope!

"Strive first for the kingdom of God and his righteousness, and all these things will be given to you as well." They're given not as a quid pro quo or a bribe, but as part of God's mysterious but gracious ordering of his Kingdom. Don't worry. God is good. Happy Thanksgiving.

Lectionary Preaching After Pentecost

The following index will aid the user of this book in matching the correct Sunday with the appropriate text during Pentecost. All texts in this book are from the series for the Gospel Readings, Revised Common Lectionary. (Note that the ELCA division of Lutheranism is now following the Revised Common Lectionary.) The Lutheran designations indicate days comparable to Sundays on which Revised Common Lectionary Propers or Ordinary Time designations are used.

(Fixed dates do not pertain to Lutheran Lectionary)

Fixed Date Lectionaries *Revised Common (including ELCA)* *and Roman Catholic*	**Lutheran Lectionary** *Lutheran*
The Day of Pentecost	The Day of Pentecost
The Holy Trinity	The Holy Trinity
May 29-June 4 — Proper 4, Ordinary Time 9	Pentecost 2
June 5-11 — Proper 5, Ordinary Time 10	Pentecost 3
June 12-18 — Proper 6, Ordinary Time 11	Pentecost 4
June 19-25 — Proper 7, Ordinary Time 12	Pentecost 5
June 26-July 2 — Proper 8, Ordinary Time 13	Pentecost 6
July 3-9 — Proper 9, Ordinary Time 14	Pentecost 7
July 10-16 — Proper 10, Ordinary Time 15	Pentecost 8
July 17-23 — Proper 11, Ordinary Time 16	Pentecost 9
July 24-30 — Proper 12, Ordinary Time 17	Pentecost 10
July 31-Aug. 6 — Proper 13, Ordinary Time 18	Pentecost 11
Aug. 7-13 — Proper 14, Ordinary Time 19	Pentecost 12
Aug. 14-20 — Proper 15, Ordinary Time 20	Pentecost 13
Aug. 21-27 — Proper 16, Ordinary Time 21	Pentecost 14
Aug. 28-Sept. 3 — Proper 17, Ordinary Time 22	Pentecost 15
Sept. 4-10 — Proper 18, Ordinary Time 23	Pentecost 16
Sept. 11-17 — Proper 19, Ordinary Time 24	Pentecost 17
Sept. 18-24 — Proper 20, Ordinary Time 25	Pentecost 18

Sept. 25-Oct. 1 — Proper 21, Ordinary Time 26	Pentecost 19
Oct. 2-8 — Proper 22, Ordinary Time 27	Pentecost 20
Oct. 9-15 — Proper 23, Ordinary Time 28	Pentecost 21
Oct. 16-22 — Proper 24, Ordinary Time 29	Pentecost 22
Oct. 23-29 — Proper 25, Ordinary Time 30	Pentecost 23
Oct. 30-Nov. 5 — Proper 26, Ordinary Time 31	Pentecost 24
Nov. 6-12 — Proper 27, Ordinary Time 32	Pentecost 25
Nov. 13-19 — Proper 28, Ordinary Time 33	Pentecost 26
	Pentecost 27
Nov. 20-26 — Christ The King	Christ The King

Reformation Day (or last Sunday in October) is October 31 (Revised Common, Lutheran)

All Saints' Day (or first Sunday in November) is November 1 (Revised Common, Lutheran, Roman Catholic)

U.S. / Canadian Lectionary Comparison

The following index shows the correlation between the Sundays and special days of the church year as they are titled or labeled in the Revised Common Lectionary published by the Consultation On Common Texts and used in the United States (the reference used for this book) and the Sundays and special days of the church year as they are titled or labeled in the Revised Common Lectionary used in Canada.

Revised Common Lectionary	Canadian Revised Common Lectionary
Advent 1	Advent 1
Advent 2	Advent 2
Advent 3	Advent 3
Advent 4	Advent 4
Christmas Eve	Christmas Eve
Nativity Of The Lord/Christmas Day	The Nativity Of Our Lord
Christmas 1	Christmas 1
January 1 / Holy Name of Jesus	January 1 / The Name Of Jesus
Christmas 2	Christmas 2
Epiphany Of The Lord	The Epiphany Of Our Lord
Baptism Of The Lord / Epiphany 1	The Baptism Of Our Lord / Proper 1
Epiphany 2 / Ordinary Time 2	Epiphany 2 / Proper 2
Epiphany 3 / Ordinary Time 3	Epiphany 3 / Proper 3
Epiphany 4 / Ordinary Time 4	Epiphany 4 / Proper 4
Epiphany 5 / Ordinary Time 5	Epiphany 5 / Proper 5
Epiphany 6 / Ordinary Time 6	Epiphany 6 / Proper 6
Epiphany 7 / Ordinary Time 7	Epiphany 7 / Proper 7
Epiphany 8 / Ordinary Time 8	Epiphany 8 / Proper 8
Transfiguration Of The Lord / Last Sunday After Epiphany	The Transfiguration Of Our Lord / Last Sunday After Epiphany
Ash Wednesday	Ash Wednesday
Lent 1	Lent 1
Lent 2	Lent 2
Lent 3	Lent 3
Lent 4	Lent 4
Lent 5	Lent 5
Passion/Palm Sunday (Lent 6)	Passion/Palm Sunday
Holy/Maundy Thursday	Holy/Maundy Thursday
Good Friday	Good Friday
Resurrection Of The Lord / Easter	The Resurrection Of Our Lord

Easter 2	Easter 2
Easter 3	Easter 3
Easter 4	Easter 4
Easter 5	Easter 5
Easter 6	Easter 6
Ascension Of The Lord	The Ascension Of Our Lord
Easter 7	Easter 7
Day Of Pentecost	The Day Of Pentecost
Trinity Sunday	The Holy Trinity
Proper 4 / Pentecost 2 / O T 9*	Proper 9
Proper 5 / Pent 3 / O T 10	Proper 10
Proper 6 / Pent 4 / O T 11	Proper 11
Proper 7 / Pent 5 / O T 12	Proper 12
Proper 8 / Pent 6 / O T 13	Proper 13
Proper 9 / Pent 7 / O T 14	Proper 14
Proper 10 / Pent 8 / O T 15	Proper 15
Proper 11 / Pent 9 / O T 16	Proper 16
Proper 12 / Pent 10 / O T 17	Proper 17
Proper 13 / Pent 11 / O T 18	Proper 18
Proper 14 / Pent 12 / O T 19	Proper 19
Proper 15 / Pent 13 / O T 20	Proper 20
Proper 16 / Pent 14 / O T 21	Proper 21
Proper 17 / Pent 15 / O T 22	Proper 22
Proper 18 / Pent 16 / O T 23	Proper 23
Proper 19 / Pent 17 / O T 24	Proper 24
Proper 20 / Pent 18 / O T 25	Proper 25
Proper 21 / Pent 19 / O T 26	Proper 26
Proper 22 / Pent 20 / O T 27	Proper 27
Proper 23 / Pent 21 / O T 28	Proper 28
Proper 24 / Pent 22 / O T 29	Proper 29
Proper 25 / Pent 23 / O T 30	Proper 30
Proper 26 / Pent 24 / O T 31	Proper 31
Proper 27 / Pent 25 / O T 32	Proper 32
Proper 28 / Pent 26 / O T 33	Proper 33
Christ The King (Proper 29 / O T 34)	Proper 34 / Christ The King/ Reign Of Christ
Reformation Day (October 31)	Reformation Day (October 31)
All Saints' Day (November 1 or 1st Sunday in November)	All Saints' Day (November 1)
Thanksgiving Day (4th Thursday of November)	Thanksgiving Day (2nd Monday of October)

*O T = Ordinary Time

388

About The Authors

Paul E. Flesner has served for over fifteen years as the pastor of Lutheran Church of the Good Shepherd in Prospect Heights, Illinois. A graduate of Carthage College (B.A.) and Luther Seminary (M.Div.), Flesner currently chairs the Illinois Multi-Synodical Candidacy Committee, which serves the ELCA's three Illinois synods.

Robert A. Noblett is the senior pastor of First Congregational Church (UCC) in Kalamazoo, Michigan. He has also served congregations in Illinois, New York, Massachusetts, and Ohio. A graduate of Ottawa University (Kansas) and Andover Newton Theological School, where he received his D.Min. degree in pastoral care and counseling, Noblett is a frequent contributor to preaching publications.

David G. Rogne, during 39 years of active pastoral service, served as senior minister of the largest United Methodist congregations in southern California. A graduate of the University of California at Berkeley, Rogne received his M.Div. degree from Fuller Theological Seminary and his D.Min. degree from the Claremont School of Theology, where his doctoral project involved first-person preaching. Rogne currently writes, lectures, and preaches on special occasions, and is a resident of South Carolina. He is also the author of *Telling It Like It Was* and *Let me Tell You ...* (CSS).

Stephen M. Crotts was educated at Furman University (B.A.) and Emory University (M.Div.). He recently left the senior pastorate of the 1,500-member Myrtle Grove Evangelical Presbyterian Church in Wilmington, North Carolina, to become the director of the Carolina Study Center, a campus ministry in Chapel Hill, North Carolina. A member of the Fellowship of Christian Athletes, Crotts is a popular speaker and a frequent contributor to Christian magazines. Among his previous CSS publications are *Long Time Coming!* and *The Beautiful Attitudes.*

Cathy A. Ammlung is the pastor of Messiah Evangelical Lutheran Church in Sykesville, Maryland. She earned chemistry degrees from Loyola University of Chicago (B.A.) and Northwestern University (M.S.), and received her theological training from Lutheran Theological Seminary at Gettysburg (M.Div.) and the Aquinas Institute of Theology (M.A. in preaching).